Two Birthdays in Baghdad
Finding the Heart of Iraq

Two Birthdays in Baghdad
Finding the Heart of Iraq

by
Anna Prouse

translated by Elizabeth Griffith

 **COMPASS**

The Compass Press
Washington, DC

Published originally in 2004 titled *Un'italiana in Iraq*
Copyright © 2004 by Touring Editore srl, Milan, Italy

Translated from the Italian by Elizabeth Griffith
Edited by Mellen Candage, Grammarians, Inc.
Cover design by The Artists Garrett
Book design by Laura Johnson Hurst
Printed (alk paper) and bound by Edwards Brothers, Ann Arbor, MI

Library of Congress Cataloging_in_Publication Data
(pending)

Contents

Reflections

Amman. It is from here that almost everyone enters and leaves Iraq.

"Hello, Miss Anna."

It is Hassan, my favorite official. By now we know each other well. Especially after the time I made the metal detector go haywire.

"I've got a hand grenade," I tell him, laughing. The other passengers don't catch my words. Hassan laughs. He laughs this time. But the time when he found a bullet in my rucksack he didn't laugh. Nor did I.

"Sit down," he had ordered in a threatening tone that time.

How odd. Until then, he had always been so polite, yet within moments he had summoned an entire army. Again and again, my rucksack was passed through that hellish metal detector. Everyone was pointing at something. I remember trying to make myself useful.

"Sit down!"

This time it was a chorus of voices. Armed men, angry and agitated. I sat down. I didn't try to argue. Never lose your cool with men in uniform, especially if they have mustaches. Never. It's better to feign calmness. Not too calm, however. You don't want them to think that you are putting up a front. Another error to avoid: never give the impression of superiority. It's a delicate game, and I'm usually good at it.

By now my rucksack was attracting everyone's attention. Even the other queuing passengers were peering at it. I remember the ironic smiles emerging on their lips when they caught sight of a roll of toilet paper sticking out from the front pocket of my rucksack. I was certain that each of them would also have a roll hidden somewhere. Because one thing for sure was that everyone, at least once, had found himself forced to adapt to local customs. Once, however, is more than enough. After that you make sure you're prepared by bringing your own roll of paper.

In vain I tried not to make a fool of myself under the gaze of the astonished policeman. He was probably unaware. In the meantime, the search for the mysterious offending object continued. I was calm, certain that there had been a mistake.

"Go into the changing room and undress," I was ordered.

A woman in a chador appeared from behind the black curtain of a cubicle and beckoned me to enter. My growing irritation was beginning to show. The woman was not impressed. I undressed: I had nothing suspicious to hide. Enraged, I turned toward the policemen.

"Would you like to tell me what you are looking for? Perhaps I can be of use?" I asked icily.

"A bullet. Or perhaps more than one, Miss. That's what we are looking for. Tell us where it is. We've seen it" was the equally icy reply.

Bullets? Oh sure. And perhaps a gun too? And while we're at it, why not a rocket launcher? But then it dawned on me... my lucky bullet. My lucky bullet that should have hit me. My lucky bullet that had somehow managed to miss me. Damn! I'd forgotten all about it. For almost a year I had taken it with me everywhere.

I squeezed it in my hand. My fingers caressed it for the last time. A gesture that I had made time after time, praying that fortune would hold out. Just as it had done on that day. How many times have I felt that cold bullet against the flesh of my fingers? How many times have I relived those tragic moments: the driver lying in a pool of blood at my side, bullets everywhere, a deafening noise, thinking that I was a goner. But of all this these mustached men in uniforms could not know.

"What were you thinking? This is a dangerous object!" Hassan had exclaimed.

"It was dangerous," I replied. I didn't try to convince him. I would never have been able to pull it off. I didn't even try to explain to him how much the bullet meant to me. Those days had passed. And maybe it was time for me to leave it all behind.

"Miss Anna, are you going to Baghdad?" Hassan asked. This time he spoke jovially, happy in the knowledge that he wouldn't have to search me again from head to toe.

"No, I'm going home. I'm going to Italy."

Amman. For those of us who had spent so long isolated in Iraq, Amman was a haven. No, don't think that I'm referring to anything transcendental. I mean a private bathroom, a normal size bed, and, most of all, vast, soft pillows. We all competed to go to Amman. Attending even the most tedious meeting became a bone of contention among us.

"I can channel hop and eat crisps in bed," said Scott.

"To sit outside a tea room without the fear of a sniper taking aim… what a wonderful thought," agreed Gene.

"To know that no missile will rain down on my trailer while I sleep… how comforting," was Alicia's wish, whereas for Bob, the pinnacle of luxury was not having to gulp down yet another portion of greasy chicken Kiev.

Each time I "won" a trip to Amman, I would spend every spare moment I had in bed. No nightclubs or exotic dinners for me. Sleep. This is the magic word for anyone who lives in Baghdad. One precious night of good sleep. You will be so much the better for it when back in Iraq.

"Special embassy price, no?" the hotel's reception asks me every time. I have no idea why they always give me this reduced price. They must really be convinced that I work for the American Embassy. I don't let on. I gave up a long time ago trying to understand how and why some things happen. And the one time that things are going my way, I don't stop to ask questions. All I have to do is avoid giving details about my presumed job in Washington.

Pillows! Bliss! I pile them on top of each other and stretch out on the perfumed sheets. I drift off to sleep, only to be awakened by a mullah's call to prayer.

Here again, after all this time. My friend. Oh, how I have missed your melancholy call! No moment was ever so right. I am sure that the song is for me, perhaps welcoming me back or wishing me luck on my return voyage to normality. Or perhaps the mullah is bidding me farewell. Addio to that mad world…indescribable, nonsensical. I was rarely able to hear these velvet melodies on the streets of Baghdad. Maybe because I wasn't paying attention or maybe it was the thunderous drone of the helicopters, generators, tanks, demonic traffic, trucks.

Silence. How beautiful to hear silence again. My ears are not used to such utter silence. A silence now parted by the mullah's melodic call to prayer. In contrast to the joyous clanging of our Western bells, the Islamic call is a sad one, tremendously soft and moving. Who knows whether one day I will have the pleasure of hearing the mullahs sing in Iraq—praises to Allah drifting out high from the minarets—without the fear that they are perhaps inciting a very different kind of action?

"Move to the left a little… Allah is great…. no, a little more to the right… Allah is great….yes, right there…. wait a moment… SHOOT! Allah is great." This is what I thought every time I heard a mullah sing out as I went past. Perhaps it is precisely for this reason that I refused to heed them. I laughed softly to cheer myself up. Macabre humor. This is one of the first things that I must purge when I am back at home. But it is not the only thing that I must address. One thing I'm certain of is that when I return home I must organize in my mind everything that I have lived through over the last year in that mad portion of the planet that has captured the world's attention. I must ask myself a series of questions, and the biggest question of all will be: why? Why did I stay in such an obviously dangerous country? Why did I not leave when I realized that my life was at risk? Why didn't I pack my bags when I learned that the mission I had been called to undertake would be difficult, if not downright impossible?

Easy. I stayed in Iraq for those faces with dark, penetrating eyes. For those people who waited anxiously for me every day. For the children, for the disabled people, for the ex-prisoners with whom I passed entire days. For my Iraqi colleagues who could barely wait to quench their curiosity by asking questions that they could never ask before. For friends who seemed to reach a zenith of happiness every time they chatted with that Italian woman, who, if only in appearance, was so different from themselves.

I also stayed for my group of colleagues—Americans, Dutch, Irish, Kosovars, and Italians—who worked together day and night to improve Iraq's healthcare services. And did our efforts amount to anything? Yes, they did, even if at times, tiredness and frustration would make me think otherwise.

On several occasions I was tempted by the idea of giving up and leaving it all behind. Even right back on day one, if I'm honest with myself. That unforgettable June 8, 2003, when I first set foot on that great sandy parking area where the unforgiving summer sun beat down relentlessly on a sea of tents. A huge sign on the gate announced Italian Red Cross Field Hospital. I had arrived. Armed police stood on guard on the turrets.

"Run away. You'll never make it here," I said to myself.

These were my first thoughts. If there had been a flight, or if I hadn't been prey to my pride, I would have left immediately. I would have been able to say that I'd seen Iraq, if only for a couple of hours. But it wasn't just for my pride that I stayed for all that time in Iraq. I didn't work for three months at the field hospital and for almost a year at the Iraqi Ministry of Health as an expert for the Coalition Provisional Authority only to placate my pride.

It will be difficult to live without it all. I do not think that it has to do with "survivor guilt," as documented in Vietnam veterans. I will not miss the gunfire, explosions, ambushes, or wailing sirens. I hate these things, though I had to accustom myself to the drone of the helicopters that circled constantly above my barracks—the "giant voice," a long, lugubrious siren that raised the alarm—and to passing many an hour in the bunker. It all became routine, though it is crazy to say it, simply routine.

What didn't become routine was the great sense of uncertainty that followed me every moment of the day. Because in Iraq, life attains a new value. This is a result of all the deaths, including deaths of my friends and colleagues—every disappearance made my world crumble.

"I could have been in that place." How many times did I say this to myself? As their desks lay empty.

One learns to go ahead, to cope, not to despair, not to let the tears show, and to swallow that lump in the back of the throat. But you don't get used to it. You don't forget. You should never forget.

I will miss my friends, my Iraqi second family, who every Friday would invite me for lunch or would bring kebab and hummus to the palace. Yes, the palace. For almost a year I spent a great deal of time in the building that once had been Saddam's presidential palace. And it was right there, under the frescoed ceilings, that my friends would try to explain to me how things work in their country. They made me understand that it was useless to get angry about one too many inshallahs (God willings), that damned "tomorrow." Inshallah, which, like it or not, had now become part of my vocabulary.

I remember Tariq and Ismail, my old roommates at the ministry. Two poets, men from another time whose common sense cheered me up on more than one occasion.

I remember the courage of Badea, the ex-political prisoner, whose accounts of the torture at Abu Ghraib still send shivers down my spine.

I remember Emaddin, the young doctor who chose to leave his country behind and head for England with his wife and children. Who can blame him?

I remember Saba's radiant smile. Saba was assassinated just before Christmas. Her offense was wanting to work with us.

I remember Mohammed, the leader of the Iraqi Association for Disabled Persons, and the beautiful painting that he gave me when I left.

I remember Omar, a Peshmerga combatant who for decades had fought against Saddam's regime, living in a land forgotten by God. Legendary men, ready to die to protect their territory.

I remember, I remember, I remember...

And then there is my American family. Perhaps it was more difficult to be accepted by them, by those men in uniforms who saw me, an Italian woman in civilian clothes, as a threat to the group's safety. It wasn't easy, but I did it. Having to respect orders and the inhumane hours, jogging at dawn, eating dinner at a time when I'd usually be eating a snack, and tackling every day with good spirits. But a dose of light-heartedness and Italian cheerfulness, especially in Iraq, could only ever be welcome.

How am I going to live without this mad world? I'll survive, I'm sure. It will take some effort. Perhaps.

But the time has come when I must say goodbye to that desert land: Addio, Baghdad.

Who would ever have thought that I would fall so deeply in love with it all?

CHAPTER 1

Baghdad, between Myth and Reality

The airplane begins its descent. A slow descent, maybe so that its eager passengers can relish the magnitude of the moments they are about to live.

I see it! At long last, there it is. The Tigris, winding through the vast, dusty, desert land. So much dust. I stretch to gaze down below us. My heart is pounding; my nose is glued to the window.

Everybody is chattering. Please be quiet, I think. It's not out of malevolence but because this is one of those moments when I wish I could focus all of my thoughts and senses on the sights that are unfolding before my eyes. This is one of those moments.

"Grandma's started again on her tales about landing in Baghdad," my grandchildren will moan. Poor things.

But I have clear childhood memories of listening with delight to my grandfather telling stories about his intrepid escape across the mountains

Photo: Baghdad and the Tigris

with all of his family in tow. War stories. Stories of Nazism and Fascism and of concentration camps. I understood—a child's imagination is infinite. A child does not need to experience certain emotions firsthand to grasp them. Will my grandchildren be able to understand? Will they have patience with the old woman who sits back in her armchair and speaks for the hundredth time about that distant June 8, 2003?

If I want to succeed in boring them thoroughly, I can't be distracted by exclamations of surprise and by little comments. Everybody should be able to live these instants in his own way, fully immersed in his own thoughts. Because events like this need to be accompanied by a religious silence.

Silence. If only I knew. This is only the beginning. I have no idea just how much I will come to crave silence over the coming year.

Slowly the plane descends, drawing big loops above what I would learn later were some of Saddam's sumptuous palaces. One of them in particular catches my eye. It stands on a peninsula and is a haven of crystalline lakes surrounded by desert, emptiness.

The Tigris, together with the Euphrates, is legendary. But where is the Euphrates? At school they are always spoken about together, and in my mind, they flowed alongside each other. But that river below me is the Tigris, as it is the Tigris that waters Baghdad. Farther away, toward the fertile Mesopotamian plain, the Euphrates cuts its slow path through the land of the most ancient civilizations.

Spiral after spiral we approach. With my heart in my mouth, I feel the wheels touch the ground. This is the land of Mesopotamia, where an important slice of history has been played out. Ever since I was a child, I have longed to immerse myself in this magical world. I have dreamt about retracing the steps of King Gilgamesh. Today, too many people have forgotten that Iraq was once a mythical land with heroes and deities, a land that has witnessed the birth of great civilizations.

And there it is, the magical verdant plain...well, verdant perhaps not—there are limits even for dreamers like me. In fact there is hardly any greenery at all. But I do not lose heart over such minor details. The allure of this land, between the Tigris and the Euphrates, this whole Mesos Potamos region, is still the same—captivating. The power of imagination!

Barely one foot outside the aircraft and I am hit by suffocating heat and hot buffeting winds. Sweaty, sunburned soldiers come to meet us at the foot of the airplane stairs, smiling.

"Welcome to Baghdad," they greet us in chorus.

We all are wearing Red Cross uniforms, yet each of us has individual touches. Some are in red, others in blue; some are in jackets, others in long-sleeved T-shirts or shirts; some have colored belts. Only the nurses, the famous Miss Red Crosses, are impeccable in their sky-blue trousers and white tunics with the Red Cross emblem on their chests and berets. Even their belts, bags, and suitcases are identical; they seem to belong to a bygone era. I stand out even more than the rest as I am the one sporting a winter uniform. This is not because the seasons have been swapped around, nor because I like to suffer excessively.

"We don't have your size," they told me at Milan's Regional Red Cross Committee. "We'll have to give you the winter uniform."

There was no other choice, which is why I am now the one panting in a huge concrete square, clad in dark-blue synthetic trousers and jacket.

The Spirit of Renewal

Baghdad International Airport (BIAP), June 2003

"Somewhere out there are people who would pay lots to sweat the buckets I'm sweating now," I tell myself.

This cheerful thought does little to relieve my discomfort. But then I glance at the poor American soldiers who, somehow, despite their helmets, flak jackets, camouflage, and weapons, still manage to smile. I am suddenly shocked by how young they seem. Babies. Goodness knows how old they are. Some don't look a day older than eighteen. They are laughing. Perhaps they are laughing at us, a comical motley crew of Italians who have noisily invaded their runway.

Digital cameras are fished out of pockets, and as if they do not already have enough to put up with, the unfortunate soldiers have to come and pose for a group photo. They join in wholeheartedly and do not seem annoyed at our antics at all. By now, the airplane has been unloaded and we all have to proceed to the huge hangar with our luggage. Our group, though, is already scattered. We are totally incapable of keeping together and following directions. Blame the English language that only a few of us can speak.

"Anna! Come and sort this out," orders Gigi, the camp commander. "You are the only one who understands what they're saying."

Gigi Tonero is a formidable man of few words. He is a little gruff and brusque and I take to him immediately. I always seem to get on well with "bear-like" people. Perhaps it is because they avoid getting tangled up in useless conversations and avoid getting bogged down in superfluous words. Gigi and I will become friends, and he will become a great pillar of support during my Iraqi adventures and even after he leaves the country.

Herding thirty people through the labyrinthine Baghdad military airport is not easy. Soldiers, male and female, have made camp everywhere. Camp beds litter the hangar. Some soldiers are reading, sunbathing, working out, or jogging along the runway; they are watching TV, skipping, working at computers, or listening to music. There are others who are trying to sleep. I am anxious about these ones. What would happen if they were suddenly jolted awake? Would they jump up, shooting?

I still have no idea what it is like to be jolted awake. Similarly, until now, I had no idea how friendly Americans were to foreigners. They are friendly even to our undisciplined rabble. But all these weapons, ammunition, men in uniforms… if one bit of me was fascinated by it, the other bit was terrified. It is an utterly alien world to me. I have never seen so many weapons in one place. But then, of course, I have never been in a war before.

It takes us ages to get through passport control. One by one, we undergo a brief interrogation and have many frontal photos taken. Our passports are scrutinized meticulously and scanned. Our information is filed away in individual files. It is an odd feeling.

"So you like these countries, then?" they ask me in surprise when it is my turn.

Naturally, what with all the Iranian, Yemeni, and Libyan visas stamped in my passport, I never manage to pass through checks without comment. To speed up the whole procedure, I am asked to interpret. The poor American official is bewildered by our rapid arm waving and gesturing. Several among our group cannot even answer the simplest questions about who they are. Out of thirty people, only a couple understand English.

"Hello, how are you?" asks a very attractive and friendly female soldier who is in charge of taking our identification photos. Oh, so now my help is no longer required. No prizes for guessing why! She is blonde and blue-eyed and seems to appreciate the interest of our Don Giovanni Italian men.

Worn out, we leave the hangar. Outside, parked under the roasting sun, awaits a dilapidated bus with no doors, a minibus, and a truck for our suitcases and medicines. The nurses, known by their nickname "sisters" even though they aren't all nuns, stake out the minibus, whereas we have the dubious honor of traveling Iraqi style. Inside, the bus is encrusted with sand, the windows are filthy, and the leather seats are so hot that they burn us. We all dive to the side away from the savage sun; this relentless sun will become our worst enemy over the next couple of months. Shaded under canopies that line the road, soldiers watch us as we pass.

"Don't take any photos while we drive through the city," we are asked, politely. However, as we are driven from the airport to the field hospital, I have never heard such a constant whirring and clicking of so many cameras. Not even the huge, threatening signs next to checkpoints, which clearly show that photographs are forbidden, succeed in stemming the flow of our accomplished photography crew.

So many checkpoints, so many soldiers, so many tanks! The road that leads to the airport is a white-hot strip of asphalt cutting through the desert. Never-ending queues plague the traffic heading in our direction. Trucks, tractors, and rusting cars, all waiting their turn for interminable searches before being permitted to enter the airport zone. Weary Iraqis wait patiently for their turn. They are used to waiting; it takes much more than a traffic jam to dishearten an Iraqi. Patience is perhaps one of their greatest virtues. Only those who have a special badge are given access to the airport zone. Like the Coalition Provisional Authority (CPA) Green Zone, the general American quarter, and Camp Victory, the airport zone is off-limits to anyone who does not work here.

A constant stream of different impressions and sensations mingle and overlap in such a homogeneous way that it is impossible to draw any conclusions. I feel as if I am in a film. There is only one difference: this is real.

The dust raised by Humvees—the U.S. Army's most famous combat vehicles, the huge gas-guzzling jeeps seen in war films—swirls around our bus. Unfortunately it gets into the bus and covers us too.

It is surreal. Burned-out truck carcasses are everywhere. Tanks' cannons seem to threaten anyone who passes within their firing range. The odd dusty palm tree struggles to survive in this harsh climate. My eyes are burning. My throat is dry. And those soldiers stand up straight, never wilting, under the midday sun. Soldiers at rest take their vehicles and seek refuge under the shade cast by bridges. They are clearly shattered. Poor boys. I wonder if they knew what they were getting themselves into. For them, Iraq was only an unknown country on a map. Nothing more. They aren't heroes, but victims. Victims of this heat.

But they are heroes for the hordes of children who buzz around them, selling them pistachio nuts, pleading to hold their guns, try on their helmets, and climb up into their tanks, while asking incessantly for chewing gum. Once again, I am suddenly reminded of stories of war and tales of American soldiers who attract children's attention with their chewing gum.

"How we all loved their chewing gum! Only your granddad thought it was repulsive," my mother exclaims, still to this day. In her Nazi-occupied Alsace, the arrival of the Americans could only be greeted with much rejoicing.

The soldiers smile at the pushy Iraqi children who clamber about irreverently. The children are friendly, though, and unlike me, don't seem to be intimidated by their uniforms. Sitting together on the Humvees, drinking Coca-Cola, Mountain Dew, or rany, a local fruit drink, this is the human side of this war. Two cultures, two ways of life, two ways of thinking, two approaches to life that are inexplicably different converge here. Yes, they converge. Rather than clash, here the two worlds converge. And I am a witness.

By now we have arrived in the city. Bombed buildings are surrounded by sand-colored two- or three-story houses. A mosque emerges on the left, shrouded in dust. As is everything else. The sky-blue minaret does not stand out. The sky is thick with dust. Gray Baghdad. A Baghdad that does not have anything in common with the fairy-tale city conjured up in the unforgettable exotic tales and fables narrated by Princess Scheherazade. Ali

Baba and the forty thieves, Aladdin and his magic lamp, and Sinbad the sailor belong here no more.

The bus suddenly makes an unexpected maneuver. It jolts us: it is climbing on the pavement in order to do an improbable turn. And then?

A gate, an armed barricade, a turret, and the sign Italian Red Cross Field Hospital. Carabinieri (Italian military police) in dark blue uniforms come and open the gate. Barbed wire, barriers, and gloomy cement buildings surround this dusty, sweltering parking lot in which we will be camped. I have arrived at the place that is going to transform my life, a place where I will feel a kaleidoscopic spectrum of emotions: intense, extraordinary, chilling, moving emotions. But I cannot know any of this yet.

"I think I've gone too far," I remember thinking. "This is more than I can take."

I look around, dazed in the brightness. About thirty people are here to meet us. There is a handover procedure that takes about half an hour. Then these hot, sweaty souls with distraught and weary faces disappear in a cloud of dust, leaving us on our own. Only a few doctors, the director of the hospital, and a couple of other workers stay to help us get through the first days. And then they leave too.

I feel lost. The nurses make a claim on a tent. I don't know if I can join them. I don't belong to their group, and as absurd as it might sound, there is often friction between different factions of the Red Cross.

"You're surely not going to share with them?" Francesca asks me a little sarcastically when she sees me carrying my rucksack into the tent. I decide to go for it and accept the challenge: to live for a whole month with these ladies whom we deride for their meager aptitude for anything practical, was a once-in-a-lifetime opportunity. Only a couple of them lead what I would consider a normal life back home; most of them, in fact, are nuns.

That the Red Cross nurses don't have a head for practicalities was obviously right from our departure: they got on the wrong coach and got lost and then again in the airport. With patients, though, they really know what they are doing, and so soon they are heading off enthusiastically to the patients' tent. They do not even change or freshen up first. There is no time to lose.

I dash to the toilets to wash my hands. I do not remember the exact words that sputtered out of my mouth when my fingers came into contact with the water. Two burned hands is not a pleasurable sensation and is certainly not a great way to begin. Up from the turret, I hear laughter. Two carabinieri on guard are waiting for me at the barrier. They had not said a word to me about the metal cistern that, lying in direct sunlight, heats the water up to unbearable temperatures—not a word about how washing my hands at this hour might not be the best idea.

"Did the doctor get burned?" they ask me playfully.

"There's no cold water!" I cry, amazed.

"No, you've got to wash either at dawn or after eleven at night, doctor."

Both the carabinieri have smirks plastered across their faces. What a fool I look. I am feeling out of place. I get the feeling that the story about the first-aid volunteer burning herself will soon be making the rounds of the camp.

"Sister, don't wash your hands!" I warn a nurse who is about to do the same thing that I did.

Too late.

"This is hell." Ninetta is quite disconsolate. "You've no idea what's in there," she says, pointing toward the hospital tent. "I've seen lots of things before but this takes the cake."

I decide to venture to the place where it all happens. I am struck by its inexplicably pungent smell. Inside the tent, everything is dark green, all strung together, and the air is suffocating. Doctors run from one section to another. My attention is drawn to one tent in particular. Piercing screams come ringing out. What I see there is indescribable. A child of about six years old is completely covered in burns and is fighting for his life.

"Kerosene! When will they stop using it?" says a doctor in desperation.

He looks at me curiously. He has been here for more than a month. "Don't worry about it. You'll get used to it quickly. If you want, you can give me a hand and you can start getting used to all this." I put on gloves.

My heart is in my mouth. The terrified eyes of the child petrify me. I stroke his face.

"Soak the gauze and place it on him. We have to soften his skin to remove the clothes burned onto him," he explains. "Use these forceps, and the moment you see the clothes lifting away, pull them off... Good luck."

The boy screams. I cannot do anything. His face, his tears, his desperation.

"Don't stop. Be confident. You've got to detach yourself," is the doctor's friendly advice. Easy to say. I could bear it if it weren't for that smell. I've got to get out, right now. I'm gagging. My stomach is heaving. I need some air. I leave the forceps, gauze, and doctor behind me. From the turret, the carabinieri watch me as I rush out of one of the tent's side exits. I don't want to make another scene. I am ashamed of myself. Maybe I'm not ready for all this. It's too late to go back. I return to the boy's bedside. I pretend nothing happened.

"You don't have to do it—only if you want to. By the way, I'm Walter."

We can't shake hands, so we smile at each other.

"He's not going to make it. He is going to die. If not tonight, tomorrow. His kidneys won't be able to cope. We're just trying to lessen the pain." Harsh words contrast with his soft, bright eyes. I feel at ease with Walter. He is not judging me. I am not afraid about making mistakes. I set about work and am there until sunset, when Gigi bursts into the tent.

"Here you are! We've been looking everywhere," he tells me in that brusque way of his. "Leave it. I need you outside."

I follow him. We have to put together a list of medicines to ask Rome for urgently. And if I thought that drawing up the list was the difficult part, then there was trying to send it... I press the same buttons on the fax machine again and again, trying in vain to get a line and send the damn list. Frustrated, I go and sit down on a bench outside the office that is nothing but an iron trailer.

"Come jogging with us, sister."

I look up. Sister? Who is calling me sister?

And there they are, a dozen sweaty carabinieri in shorts and bandannas. This surreal moment is still etched on my mind. Children fighting for their lives, brash young men jogging about, sagging tents struggling to stay up, the sun setting behind barbed wire, a fax that won't send. Slowly, though, as the night descends, everything seems to fall into place.

"Well, we survived today. Another day. Thank goodness I am about to leave, I've come to the end of the road." This is Ferruccio, who was camp commander until our arrival.

"I came here from Italy in a truck. You've got no idea what a nightmare it was. Now you'll see that everything is fine and ready, but in the first couple of weeks it was quite an adventure. We had nothing at all. No water to wash, no toilets, no electricity, no tents. Nada. Do you have any idea what nothing means? Thank God we were a tough group. Good workers who never took a step backwards. The doctors too. They didn't hesitate for a moment about dirtying their hands."

Ferruccio is tired. You see it. Tired but proud.

"And now even women have arrived," he looks at me, smiling. "Women who want cold showers... or maybe a lukewarm shower. We're finished!" Amazing how quickly the rumor has spread.

I listen in the shadows as he recounts his early days in Baghdad right after the war was over. Crossing the borders, thousands of desert kilometers. A convoy, a feeble ordered line of vehicles clearly marked with a huge red cross. Back and forth the escorting carabinieri patrol. In some ways, I am a bit envious.

"Dinner is ready. Don't hold back!" This is Angelo, the cook, worshiped by everyone. Tiny, skinny, and sunburned, he has won everyone's approval with his leeks.

"I suggest that you all enjoy this dinner. Rations are almost finished. Then it's going to be tuna all around," he says saucily. "This lot here brought us only more medicines," he continues, pointing an accusing finger at us. "Nobody thinks about me. But at the end, it's going to be you who suffer. I wash my hands of it," he finishes in a huff.

I join the dinner queue. Inside this tent, adapted as a canteen, there are seven rows of tables to the left and right and everyone crowds around them. It is hot, and the generators are working overtime at this temperature to pump in air. A television grabs the attention of those seated in the first row, who are mostly carabinieri. I feel a bit strange to be surrounded by so many men. There are only about a dozen women and only three young ones: Francesca, a first-aid volunteer; Anna, a doctor; and myself. I take a shine to Anna. Thin, with dark hair and small intellectual glasses, she seems to convey a sense of calm. She caught my attention right from our departure from Italy, when she sat sipping her cappuccino consciously ignoring the sisters flocking about her trying to hurry her along.

The doctor Anna is in the charge of the sisters. I am not quite sure how old she is. She must be slightly younger than I am. She graduated in medicine and is specializing in pediatrics. I have a feeling that she will have a hard time here with all these children. Behind that absent, slightly devious look, I detect an indefinable sense of rebellion. They keep a close eye on her, poor thing. They check what time she goes to bed, what she reads, whether she talks to the carabinieri (men!), if she works enough hours a day. As a first-aid volunteer, I don't have to put up with that sort of pressure. I am a lost cause from the beginning, not being a "sister." So they don't care if I smoke, drink, talk to men, or have any "inappropriate" behavior. The sisters largely ignore me. Well, at least as long as nobody needs me to help out with practical matters: find covers and cushions; call the electrician to fix the air conditioning; get the washing machine to work; get the satellite telephone to call home.

Finally I get in the shower. The water is hot. Not boiling, but always hot. Very hot. I would very much like to have a cold shower, or a lukewarm shower. Just as Ferruccio said. I want to rid my bones of this heat. I dry off and immediately start to sweat again. After a whole day of sun, these iron trailers just keep in the heat.

The camp is immersed in silence. A couple of gunshots. The voices of the carabinieri talking on the turrets. Tanks on patrol. Nothing else. At curfew, beyond the barbed wire, the streets are deserted. This is the scene—as in a film.

"This is the hour of shady deals and armed bandits who terrorize the people," Walter, who is sipping beer with other night birds, tells me. "Anyone out at this time risks his life. When we hear shooting, we know that soon someone will be brought here. And we'll be extracting bullets all night even if the hospital is officially closed. This is all we can do—it's an absurd situation." The carabinieri know it too. They bring them here while we jump out from our hammocks. A month and a half of this, and I am exhausted."

Walter's red eyes say it all. Fatigue, too much sun, and sandstorms: everything is expressed in his tired, melancholic look. "It's been days since I've had a break. The hospital closes during the hottest part of the day. No one can stand outside and queue under the baking sun. But we don't get any rest. The generators blow, the air conditioning packs in, the tents fall down. You'll see for yourself soon. You're going to get the hottest month. I'm not envious of you guys."

I go to sleep. The lights in the tent are on. I attempt to switch them off.

"Leave them on!" I do not remember her name, but she has a very authoritative voice. I do not ask for explanations. Tomorrow...

And there it is; the "tomorrow" that will accompany me everywhere during the coming year. It was the night of June 8 when I first uttered that word. I will use it a lot, but I will hear it even more frequently, and it's always coupled with an *inshallah*. I must admit that it really takes no time at all for me to pick it up.

CHAPTER 2

Disputes at Every Level

Massucco, my bed neighbor, snores; Ninetta holds her own; and Marta, one of the nurses, gives it her best shot. How funny! I have always thought snoring to be a masculine prerogative. But after spending a night with ten other women, I am forced to reconsider. And bulky proportions don't have anything to do with it. Bulkiness is only an issue in the case of Massucco, a tall, statuesque woman with a booming voice. But neither Ninetta, the head nurse, nor Marta is particularly heavy. On the contrary. Anyway, the result spells disaster—I have not slept a wink all night. I cannot, however, blame my insomnia entirely on these three women. Apart from the assortment of noises coming from our tent, the night was also marked by gunshots and the constant drone of the generators.

I had been tempted to use earplugs to cut all the noise out. I toyed with the idea for ages, but in the end I decided it wasn't a good idea. I remember

Photo: Italian field hospital

telling myself that I had to find some solution. I certainly can't afford to be an insomniac for a whole month. With earplugs, though, I wouldn't have been able to hear any signs of danger. The various lessons taught by the major of the carabinieri on what to do and where to go in case of attack, gunfire, or stray bullets are having their effect. I am on edge. I look up at the upper folds of the tent and wonder if it would make good cover. Or at least whether it would cushion the blows.

"You can sleep, rest assured, and sleep well," the major had said, "should anything happen, we'll come and get you."

But as yet, I don't really know the young carabinieri, who are all tanned, in good form, and very respectful. In fact, I had been surprised by their polite ways. Perhaps I should ask them to start using the informal "you" form with me and to stop addressing me as "doctor." These friendly notions aside, however, I still don't know whether I can really trust them when it comes to the crunch. Would they actually come and find me if I didn't wake during an attack? I will have plenty of time to think about it. For now, I would prefer to look after myself.

"You've got to look out for number one," my mother used to say to me. These are wise words and, for once, I decide to heed them.

At dawn, the mayhem begins.

"We can't possibly share a bathroom with the men," laments one of the nuns.

"Anna, the volunteer," she turns to me, "can't you go and see if they'll give us our own bathrooms?"

I must have replied dryly, suggesting that she go to ask the director.

In the mornings, particularly mornings after a sleepless night, I am not at my most amenable. And at dawn, I am even less so. I am still stretched out in my light-blue sleeping bag watching this odd assortment of middle-aged women stand and complain. Finally, I decide to go on their behalf and ask Gigi if he will concede us a trailer with two toilets and one shower.

"No, no, we want two trailers," they clamor.

Their request seems a little far-fetched, if not downright preposterous. There are only six trailers in the whole camp. If two were to be given to the women, the men would be left with four, and what with the carabinieri and the Red Cross men, the male contingent quite heavily outnumbers the female one. Anna, the doctor, is still in bed. She also doesn't seem like much of a morning bird. Massucco is still snoring furiously, perfectly oblivious to the alarm clock.

"Shake that one over there!" cries Ninetta.

Personally, even if she is my "bed neighbor," I wouldn't dream of shaking her up and out of bed. Actually, rather than say bed neighbor, perhaps I should say bed companion: I feel as if I'm sharing a double camp bed with this hilarious character. Poor Massucco, she chose the wrong place to sleep. The air conditioning is blasting an icy wind straight at her. And so to avoid being frozen, she has moved in my direction and has attached herself to my camp bed. She has an eye mask strapped to her face and yellow plugs poking out of her ears, and her rather unfashionable pajamas cloak her formidable body—it's quite a sight. She suddenly jolts awake, yelling, being shaken energetically by the woman whom I have affably nicknamed Fuma-Fuma, or "the Smoker."

Incoming Coalition casualty

Fuma-Fuma—she's another interesting character. She finds the most improbable places to hide from her colleagues in order to have a covert cigarette. In particular, she is hiding from Ninetta. I amuse myself by catching her as she climbs into spaces between trucks and behind tents, or wedges herself in between generators. I just love blackmailing her. She would do anything to secure my silence. I feel as if it's back to school days again with kids sneaking off for a secret drag on a cigarette. What a shame that here the average age is significantly greater. But a self-respecting Red Crosser cannot have such vices, or at least can't let herself be seen indulging them. It is clear that Fuma-Fuma has a passion for cigarettes, and the hoarse voice of a hardened smoker betrays her.

I trip as I leave the tent. From the turret I am greeted with a laugh, reminding me that we are being watched. Damned tower. Why did the nuns have to put themselves right here? With the choice of all these tents, why did they have to choose this bloody one? Two bold young men are up there scanning the horizon. Like it or not, they cannot possibly avoid seeing our every move. Imagine their entertainment earlier on, as they listened to the grumpy conversations of this disconsolate bunch of women waking up on a beautiful morning to find themselves in Baghdad. And this Baghdad is much bloodier than they'd imagined. Perhaps it's better like this. If we had known, we never would have come.

I go into the bathroom. I close the small windows. You never know. I'm sure that you can see everything from that damned tower. And then I realize just how silly I'm being. They must have more important things to do than spy on some nurse or volunteer who's cleaning her teeth. I do close the window, though, just to be on the safe side.

"Anna, we've got to resolve the issue with the International Red Cross."

This is how Gigi greets me in the morning. I had followed the case in the newspapers; finding a solution to this pressing issue is one of the main reasons I have been asked to come over here.

"We've got to do something to calm everyone down," interjects Ferruccio.

"So you're going to meet the Geneva guys and try to sort something out. You are the International Red Cross delegate. You have to fix this," concludes Gigi.

The point of contention is that the International Red Cross has asked the Italian branch to get rid of all armed protection at the field hospital.

I am on edge. I didn't expect such a degree of hostility. I thought we were one big family. When Gigi and I arrive at the International Committee of the Red Cross (ICRC) office, however, we are treated very coldly indeed. Their expressions speak clearly. We are not welcome here.

"It is vital that we differentiate the Red Cross from the military forces," says Jeremy, the deputy head of delegation at the International Committee of the Red Cross in Baghdad, after he invites me into his office. "Having the protection of Italian military police at the hospital contravenes the principles of the Red Cross."

"I didn't realize that we were this famous," I remember saying to Gigi.

"Who do they think they are?" Gigi replied, infuriated. "They're not the ones out there risking their lives day to day. They're sitting here, protected by walls and guards and yet have the audacity to criticize us."

Actually, they do have guards here, too. The difference between our guards and their guards is that you don't see theirs. Theirs don't wave like ours do. Appearances count for everything, even here in Iraq.

"Do you realize that there's no way we could stay in that enormous car park without any protection?" I say to Jeremy. "It would be far too dangerous. We would be at the mercy of every zealot who wanted to do us harm or even just steal our stuff."

"But you are going against the fundamental principles of the Red Cross," replies Jeremy.

I don't get it. I don't think that we are offending the name of the Red Cross. I don't see which of the seven principles—humanity, neutrality, impartiality, independence, voluntary service, unity, and universality—we are disobeying. We give assistance to anyone who appears at our gate, and people come from far away to be treated by us. But we are in Iraq, and in order to carry out our work in peace we need someone to be watching our backs. I can't see anything wrong with that at all.

"You have to move away from there. You'll have to find a permanent structure to operate from," continues the deputy head of delegation.

"That's what we intend to do," I tell him. "But first we've got to find a suitable building. And then it will probably have to be completely restored and renovated. You know better than I do about the condition of hospitals here in Baghdad," I continue.

I feel as if my words are falling upon deaf ears. Our very presence is resented.

"I saw that you've put a Red Cross sign outside the hospital," Martina joins in. On her business card I see that she is the PNS coordinator. I don't have the faintest idea what this means.

"Take it down!" she instructs, "It's an insult seeing it surrounded by armed men."

I bite my tongue. I don't translate this last sentence for Gigi. He certainly would not hold back his feelings. I stand up, saying the appropriate thank-yous. I haven't finished my tea. It would be blatantly hypocritical of me if I were to sit here and make small talk while sipping on chai, the famous sugary Iraqi tea. I would very much like to take the tea, though. Who knows when I will be able to do so again?

Similar meetings are to follow, and they almost all end with a similar conclusion. The International Red Cross will leave Iraq as a result of the attack on October 12 in which twelve people were killed. The Italian branch will stay put.

Red Cross ambulance

I'll admit that my thoughts on the matter can't help but be one-sided, seeing as I am partly involved and work at the Italian field hospital. If I were on the other side of the barrier, I would probably think differently. Who knows? Okay, so I too would prefer not to be surrounded by armed men but still be able to provide assistance. I'm aware of the incongruities of the current situation, yet if this is the only possible alternative, then so be it.

Being an intermediary for humanitarian assistance, the ICRC cannot, by any means, be suspected of ideological favoritism. For the ICRC, the presence of the carabinieri is contradictory to the provision of aid to the local population.

"Presenting yourself with arms to the Iraqi people is only going to incite hatred," the Geneva team maintains. "Sooner or later you will become a terrorist target. It is your responsibility to avoid this." It is hopeless to try to explain to these people that we don't "present ourselves with arms" to anyone—we welcome everybody. Pointless to try to explain that we've never had the slightest indication that someone wants to do us harm.

Wasted breath. To be honest, I do understand their point of view. And I am convinced that they understand mine, particularly those living here in Baghdad. I know that Jeremy appreciates and respects the work of the Italian Red Cross, and he never wastes an opportunity to remind us of this. Indeed, it is not the Italian Red Cross's efforts that are being disputed but rather the ways in which it has decided to carry out its humanitarian work. The solution? As long as we are at the field hospital, there is no solution.

It is a frustrating meeting. My anger increases when we leave their air-conditioned offices and return to our furnace. I feel that their behavior has been wrong and I can't do anything about it. An endless queue has formed outside the gate on this hot June afternoon and things are going to get worse.

"Enough chatting. Let's get water to these waiting people," says Gigi.

We fill up the forklift with bags of fresh water and take them to the sick and wounded and their relatives who huddle under the shade of the tent behind the hospital. It is drinking water that we have produced ourselves. A sophisticated piece of equipment known as a waterline purifies water, making it drinkable after a complex procedure. The water is then bagged up and stored in huge refrigerators. Every morning, trucks load up this precious resource that is so scarce in Baghdad and transport it to schools, orphanages, and hospitals.

While we are handing out water, I watch Alessandro, a young doctor who arrived here with me. He has been given the task of triage, evaluating which patients are urgent cases, which can wait. It is not an easy task, particularly given that, in Iraq, sob stories abound and all tales are recounted with much theatricality. You would think that everyone is on death's door, and determining who really does need prompt treatment and who is exaggerating is an arduous, exhausting task. Alessandro spends his days outside in Baghdad's summer sun examining the people standing in front of the gate and accompanying all the urgent cases into the barbed wired enclosure. He is a young man, full of enthusiasm, and his patience will be put to severe tests over the coming month.

It is entertaining but moving to watch him go about his daily work, shouting; running; grabbing patients; letting some in but blocking others; comforting children; reasoning with desperate mothers; deciphering certificates; posing for photos; wiping away his sweat; running back to the gate to start it all over again... and so on for the whole day. Sometimes the other first-aid volunteers take turns giving him a hand, especially when the confusion is compounded by the arrival of ambulances.

Battered, filthy vehicles. You soon work out that the practice of cleaning ambulances after their use is not widespread here. Considering the fact that most of the patients are in bloodied condition, the idea of dirty ambulances is an even more grisly thought.

After incidents, patients are bundled onto stretchers and driven to the nearest hospital, but if their condition is considered too grave, they are systematically turned away. After being passed from one hospital to the next, they are finally directed to the Italians, who accept everybody, even the most dire cases where the outcome is already clear. Opening the ambulance door on its arrival is a horrific, unforgettable experience.

Brigitte and Graziella run to help unload patients. They are the most energetic of the nurses and are in charge of tending to the worst burn patients. They are attractive, strong, and determined women who have both left husbands and children behind to take on this adventure. They never waver. They go about their jobs in very different ways. Brigitte is so gentle and comforting that she soon becomes the idol of the sick; Graziella, with her drive and doggedness, fast becomes an example for the rest of the group. One tries to ease suffering and sugar the pill; the other strikes awe in everyone whose path she crosses.

In Iraq, both of these approaches are necessary. If you are too gentle, they will brazenly take advantage of you; on the other hand, severity frightens people off. In the burn tent, things work like clockwork thanks to Brigitte's and Graziella's winning team; they are perfect partners. They will be totally worn out by this whole experience. I have no idea how they manage to survive cooped up in that tent where the notion of desperation takes on a whole new meaning. I take my hat off to them. They have all my respect.

A strange character makes his appearance at the field hospital. Escorted by a string of carabinieri, he comes to welcome us new arrivals. He then speaks to Gigi for a long time before they head for the canteen. He throws me an impenetrable look. In time, I'll get to know that crafty, intriguing demeanor of the Italian ambassador. Here it is again: the film! Only here do you see such sights.

Ambassador De Martino looks as if he has walked right off the pages of a John Le Carré or Graham Greene spy story. He sports a white suit and straw hat, carries a white stick, and wears a permanent air of wariness that reminds me of Le Carré's *The Tailor of Panama* or of Jim Wormold, a secret agent in Havana, immersed in the absurdities of the Cold War.

"I need someone to make an inventory of the field hospital," I hear him whispering to Gigi. Ambassador De Martino likes to whisper. This caginess is a legacy of his seven years spent in the former Soviet Union and his five years here in Iraq. His spry eyes dart about constantly and keep watch on everything going on around him.

"An inventory?" repeats a flabbergasted Gigi.

"Eh, yes. The local authorities have asked for it," responds the ambassador. He likes to start his phrases with an "eh"; it's one of his trademarks. "An inventory of everything here. Tents, camp beds, cupboards, computers, telephones. I'm sure you understand."

Gigi does understand. He understands that compiling an inventory of the entire field hospital will be a gargantuan task. Sheer lunacy. Goodness knows who will ever actually use such a list.

"I need someone precise. Someone meticulous," he proclaims. Our eyes meet.

"No! Please, Gigi, no!" I plead.

"I will find someone to help you out," he says, trying to make the task sound more appealing. And so this is why I do not go to bed tonight. I really don't think that it would be a good idea to compile an inventory when the hospital is working flat out with everybody rushing about and moving things. I really don't think that it would be reasonable to request people not to touch things as I frantically count them. I can well imagine the expressions that would adorn my colleagues' faces if I were to ask them not to use a particular chair or monitor for fear of sending my inventory into a tailspin.

"C'mon Salvatore. I would love to get the emergency room inventory finished tonight," I say to the guy whom Gigi assigned to me to give me a hand. "Then tomorrow we can do the accommodation and everything else. It's so bloody boring that I want to get it done as soon as possible."

The concept of getting an arduous task done quickly so you can get on to something else is obviously a foreign one to Salvatore.

"Annina, let me get a coffee first—it's obligatory after dinner. And then I've got to make two telephone calls. And then we'll get going..." is his rather phlegmatic response. I raise my eyes to the ceiling; this young man's blatant lack of interest and listless indolence are getting on my nerves.

"I'll wait for you there," I tell him.

"You pigheaded...," I hear him murmur as I go.

We first-aid volunteers are known as the pigheaded ones. This is the nickname given to us by staff who generally don't take kindly to our manic way of going about things and our excessive zeal, which on occasion go unappreciated. They are probably right. If sometimes they lack a smidgen of enthusiasm when going about their duties, we volunteers make up for it a million times. We make an exaggerated contrast as we charge about, convinced that we can change the world. Taken to the extreme, both of these approaches are wrong.

Anyway, in this instance, we are not talking about a life-saving, world-changing task. For the next two days I must count up the chairs with wheels and the chairs without; I must count up the scissors, the medicine cabinets (those with a single door and those with double ones). Brown stools, black stools, defibrillators, nightlights, life-saving lights, basins... nothing thrilling. Nothing that is going to change the course of history. I am fed up with Gigi. I wonder why he chose me to do this work.

"With all the people sitting twiddling their thumbs," I ask him once the inventory is done and I know him better, "why did you have to pick me?"

"I hoped that you'd get Salvatore going. I hoped he'd pick up a bit of your enthusiasm," was his reply. "And you did try but you ended up killing him," he continues.

Gigi is right. A distraught Salvatore found himself spending a whole night with a frenzied madwoman counting, counting, counting... manically. A madwoman hell-bent on getting everything finished. To tell the truth, I relieved him of his nightmare at midnight.

"But tomorrow you're going to help me measure the tents," I told him in a tone of voice that he didn't exactly warm to.

And as a consequence, I found myself alone measuring tents until, moved greatly by my pitiful ordeal, Gigi came in person to help me. "I see that your friend is shirking," he says, playfully. I shoot him a glowering look and manage to stop myself from jumping at the bait.

By now, evening has fallen. I am exhausted but happy to have finished.

"When you've finished your counting, come and have a beer with us."

It's Walter sitting outside the hospital tent with a couple of other doctors enjoying the night sky in Baghdad. It is almost idyllic. I join them willingly; I am fascinated by the tales of these Iraq veterans. Giovanni takes center stage. A doctor from the Gaslini Institute in Genoa, Giovanni has an innate sense of humor and manages to weave the funniest stories out of even the most tragic of situations. He has us all in fits of laughter until one of the carabinieri appears and asks us to lower the volume.

"I don't want you to be heard by people who shouldn't be out there. Taking aim from over there is a favorite game nowadays in Baghdad," he tells us with a grin.

I stare at the seemingly uninhabited building that the carabiniere is pointing to. It makes me shiver. He is right—anybody could climb up there and shoot. But I don't have time to dwell on this horrible thought; suddenly there is gunfire, a rapid volley of shots.

"Here we go. Get ready guys. They'll be arriving here soon," says Walter. "No sleep again tonight. Annina, will you give us a hand?"

It's only minutes later when five carabinieri arrive. With the help of a couple of Iraqis from the crime scene, they bring in two bloodstained men. One of them has serious injuries; he has been hit by several bullets and has some in his abdomen.

"Call Maculotta! He is the master when it comes to this type of extraction," cries Walter. "And tell him to get a move on. This one here is going to die," he adds.

But before he has even finished his words, the bullet extraction master has appeared. It is going to be a long, incandescent night.

CHAPTER 3

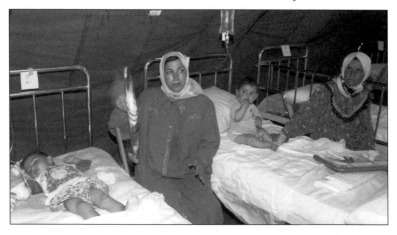

Camp Life

"Get your hands in there and hold his abdomen open," barks the Prof.

"The Prof" is Doctor Maculotta's nickname.

"Otherwise I can't see a damn thing! Quick, girl! Give it everything you've got! More, more! You're not going to hurt him!" he hollers at my timid efforts. "He can't get any worse than this."

Doctor Maculotta knows that this man's life depends on swift intervention. "We've lost him! C'mon, c'mon! We're gonna get him back! Are you just gonna bloody well stand there?"

I feel as if I'm on an ER filming set. It's crazy; if I saw this happen on TV, I'd have to shield my eyes from the screen, but here I am, with both hands and forearms immersed deep inside this poor Iraqi who'd been in the wrong place at the wrong time. Blood is spurting everywhere. His internal organs have been pulled out so that the life-threatening bullets can be extracted. It is horrific.

Photo: Mothers tend their children in the field hospital

But this isn't all. Just as the situation has become critical, the tent suddenly begins to give way. Yes, give way.

"Vito, Vito, where the hell is Vito?" I can hear people frantically shouting. "Go and get him. This whole damn thing is falling down!"

The following scene is beyond the realm of belief. Carabinieri, first-aid volunteers, doctors, and nurses all charge to the edges of the tent and, with a Herculean effort, somehow manage to hold up the whole green colossus as it slowly caves inward.

"The air conditioners!" someone screams from one corner. These lumps of machinery, supported by a structure that is already precarious, suddenly look as if they are going to fall too. Fortunately, the carabinieri rush across to prop them up. I've got my hands up to the elbows in this unfortunate Iraqi but decide it would be better if I swap with a nurse. I would prefer to help out with the unskilled task of keeping an entire tent on its feet. The other "laborers'" faces are contorted with the immense effort.

Suddenly, despite the gravity of the situation, I get a horrible urge to laugh.

"We look like the flying circus!" I hiccup as I try to stifle the giggles that have taken hold of me.

It would be so inappropriate for me to laugh while a man is fighting for his life, even if he is unconscious. But seen from the outside, this scene must be ridiculously funny. If our strength were to waver, we'd all die of suffocation under a mountain of hospital tent.

The generator is refusing to start up again. Despite uttering one obscenity after another, Vito the electrician hasn't been able to get it running again.

"Call in the reinforcements!" yells a carabiniere in front of me, "My arms are going to give way."

He's right. My arms are already trembling under the weight and I don't know how much longer they'll last. In the middle of all this, the Prof has not stopped work for a second. He almost seems oblivious to the bedlam that has descended around him. He's ranting and swearing, but he is the master of bullet extractions and he can do whatever he likes. He enjoys a God-like status here. In the operating theater, Maculotta has a really nasty streak. I hate to say this, as he's a great guy, but he turns into a monster. But then, the moment he takes the surgical gloves off, his face softens and once again he is back to his cheerful, helpful self.

Boy, what fun it is to assist him when he's working. This is a pleasure usually reserved for Ninetta, his favorite victim. She is the one who takes the brunt of his raging outbursts.. She is the one who has to put up with him, day and night, as his surgeon's assistant. Poor woman, she just lets him get on with his tantrums and then lets off steam with us in our tent.

"You'll never guess what the Prof called me today." Then there's great laughter as Ninetta relates her latest lexical discoveries, courtesy of the doctor. Yet beneath all the insults, they do actually get on well. The tension in the operating theater swells to such unbearable proportions that it's not surprising there are often uncontrolled outbursts.

Tonight—this long summer night—it would seem that the devil is tormenting us Italians. But we are giving it our best shot and are just about hanging in there—a scalpel between our teeth, elbow grease in abundance.

Right at this moment, everyone is indispensable, but one more so than the rest. During this never-ending half hour, we've all got our eyes fixed on him. Everybody's hopes are pinned on this man who gravitates to the cantankerous side of life and who has an innate passion for controversy. I am speaking about Vito, an indefatigable worker who is called on to solve the most complex of problems. And almost always in the dark, obviously. Oh yes, because when you call Vito, it normally means that the electric current has crashed.

"Oh kids, keep your hair on," he moans as he tries to find out the source of the problem. "What a mess! This is all your fault, you people! And do you know why?!"

He is interrupted by a torrent of abuse. "Vitoooo! Just fix it! You can moan later," is one of the shouts that makes itself heard above the others.

"Well if you would take a bit more care when you unplug..." The same scene as before with everyone yelling at Vito. But this golden-hearted, grumpy man will not give up.

"Sisters, you've got to understand that..."

"Vito, cut it out! Get the damned thing fixed! Then I'll get you a beer. Maybe that will shut you up." shouts Gigi, who has arrived to take charge of the situation. Muttering and grumbling, Vito gets back to work. Once again, he doesn't disappoint his fans.

"Vito you're a star," shouts a chorus of voices. Everybody is delighted to hear the rumbling of generators as they slowly start working again. Equally slowly, the tents are hoisted back up and finally stop looking so precarious.

"Hey, excuse me! This guy here is dying!"

The thunderous voice of the Prof brings us back down to reality and reminds us that this starry night, which began so promisingly with cold beers all round, has only just begun. The bullet has not yet been found.

"We should give him an X-ray," says Maculotta. "But we don't have enough time. I'm going to have to follow my nose on this one."

We look at each other. Did he say follow his nose? Now that there are no more tents or air conditioners to contend with, I can stand on the sidelines and watch the doctor at work. He is a sturdy, purposeful man whose hands work with such controlled movements. For hours we stand there with bated breath, staring at the patient's bloodied chest cavity and his internal organs. More than once we think it is all over and a shroud of resigned despair descends on the tent.

There are two people, though, who have never once given up and who have decided to fight to the bitter end: the doctor and his patient. It almost seems as if they are somehow speaking, communicating on a wavelength inaccessible to us. And so Adel is saved, or rather, was saved. Alive thanks to the speed of the group's reaction, the fine-tuning between people, the onlookers' silent encouragement, the doctor's tenacity, and Adel's own dogged will to live. Other bullets are also removed from his body.

"Good. Now we'll put everything back in," says the Prof, evidently satisfied.

What I see next leaves me dumbfounded—the organs that were removed for the bullet's extraction are just plopped back into his abdomen.

"But surely there's some sort of order to this!" I exclaim, aghast. They all laugh. Walter pats me on the back. I am beginning to understand why patients who come out of surgery feel as if they've taken a beating.

"Oh, it all sorts itself out," says Maculotta, proud of the umpteenth miracle of the evening.

Now dawn is beginning to break. Empty beer cans are still standing where we left them all those hours ago. I take a shower. This time the water is tepid, just how I like it.

"What a great night that was, hey?" This is Andrea, one of the carabinieri who were trying to keep the tent from falling at the beginning of the evening. I smile at the thought of his shaken look as he tried, in vain, to tear his eyes away from Adel's stomach. "I'm not a big fan of blood," he says when he realizes that I was watching him.

It is strange to think that, for all its pomp and pride, the famous Tuscania regiment does not train its soldiers and paratroopers for this type of mission. I am beginning to get to know these guys by name, the same guys who had filled me with both curiosity and intimidation during my first days. Gradually, I have become to feel more relaxed around them.

In the evening, after dinner, I sit down to drink tea with them. Nicola is the tea connoisseur; he buys all sorts of different teas from his Iraqi friends and tests them on us. In his spare time he is studying Russian, whereas Carmelo is obsessed with Tolstoy and roams the camp in search of shade with an enormous volume of War and Peace tucked under his arm. He is making minimal progress, maybe because shade is so scarce. Everyone here has read Lord of the Rings. I feel rather ashamed that I was put off by its sheer size. I resolve to read it as soon as I get home.

Many of them have families, and to hear them speak about the day when they became a father or about their children's first words is really quite touching. Luca is a marvelous cook, and if we weren't bothered about offending our official cook's ego, I'm sure lots of us would vote him into the canteen.

And speaking of the canteen, by now the reign of tinned tuna is upon us. By the end of August, tuna will have become unbearable. Eventually, the tuna will be replaced by an improbable chicken Kiev, spiced and swimming in an unidentifiable marinade. Chicken Kiev is the staple food on the American canteen's menu. Little do I know that one day I will look back at our tuna with fondness.

I haven't had time to recover from our chaotic night when the sweaty and breathless Italian ambassador De Martino arrives. His white ensemble has clearly met mishap on his way here. I will later find out that eating and drinking without dropping something is not one of his strong points. He always seems to spill something on his tie, jacket, or trousers, leaving large, visible stains.

I savor the memory of eating breakfast with the ambassador in Saddam's presidential palace. It was one of those mornings when everything was going pear-shaped. It was six in the morning and neither of us is particularly alert or nimble at that hour. I still clearly remember my embarrassment when, in front of a hundred people, I managed to knock a full cup of coffee over on him. It was one of those huge paper cups favored by the Americans.

"Don't worry about it," was his reply, never once losing his composure. "If you hadn't done it, it would only have been a matter of time until I did."

For the rest of that day, Ambassador De Martino hurried up and down the presidential palace corridors with a majestic brown stain on his jacket. "I can't help thinking about you," he said as our paths crossed between one appointment and the next. I was so relieved that on that February morning he was wearing a gray suit.

"I've come for the inventory," the ambassador says, turning to Gigi. "Perfect." He seems satisfied with it. Thank goodness. Just the thought of redoing it makes my blood freeze.

"Eh!" And there it is, his trademark interjection. "I need to have it translated into English as well," he continues, looking at me out of the corner of his eye. My stomach sinks.

"Well, this woman's English is perfect," Gigi says, pointing at me. My feelings of foreboding were justified.

"Do me a favor and translate it, will you? It will only take a moment."

I wonder why it is that whenever a job is delegated, it always takes "just a minute"?

"I'll be back in a couple of hours to pick it up. Thank you, signora."

I've only just managed to print out a copy in English for him when he arrives again, breathless, in the trailer that has become my office.

"In Arabic," he says, "you've got to do it in Arabic too."

I must have given him quite a glare.

"No, forget it. It should be sufficient as it is," he decides, hurriedly. I am still left speechless. His bodyguards look at me sympathetically.

"He's always like this," one of them assures me, "don't take it personally."

And then the secret agent-esque ambassador takes his aristocratic airs and his enigmatic ways and vanishes just like that.

His appearances at the field hospital are always fleeting and, I'll confess, are rarely pleasant, particularly for me.

"Excuse me, signora. I'm asking you because I know that I'm not wasting my breath with you," he says one day. A pitiful consolation. I don't enjoy his visits, except one day in August when he will suddenly turn up, even more hot and bothered than normal. He will burst into my tent. He never usually ventures into our accommodation. But there will be no stopping his almost childish enthusiasm.

"Doctor!" he will call me. I will look at him with amazement. I've gone from being a signora to a doctor? Something must be going on.

"Doctor Prouse, I've been sent to ask you if you'll accept a job at the Coalition Provisional Authority working in the capacity of Italy's humanitarian expert. The Americans are really in your favor!"

But the day when he addresses me as doctor is still months to come, and at the moment I am still simply signora. These are eventful months; frustration and joy make unlikely partners in a sweet, heartbreaking dance.

These rollercoaster months can best be summed up by the term Medevac: medical evacuation. Under this program, seemingly antithetical emotions come together. Opposites attract, and no place is this more true than here at the field hospital.

Anna Medevac. This is what everyone calls me: patients, doctors, carabinieri, people waiting at the gate, journalists. It all started the day a local newspaper published an article with photos of me and Gigi together.

Splashed across the front page in block capitals are the words "Italian Red Cross: Ask for Anna. She's the one who makes it happen." Following the headline is a long article about our work.

"Anna, it's all gone crazy outside!" shouts Andrea, a carabiniere, bursting into my trailer. "Mamma mia! It's boiling in here," he adds with his hilarious Florentine accent.

"Yes, Vito took my air conditioner," I reply dryly. "He says the sick need it more than me. But if I were to die here…"

Andrea interrupts my controversial outburst before I really get going.

"Come with me down to the gate. Come and see it for yourself. They're all shouting for you!"

I look at Andrea quizzically. Thanks to his deadly sense of humor, I'm never sure if he's for real.

"No, Anna, I'm not having a laugh," he says, knowing full well what I'm thinking. "You've got no idea! It's almost out of hand. They're going to burst through the gate. And they're all shouting your name!"

What? Is my dream about becoming Queen of Iraq finally coming true? Am I finally going to emulate the great Gertrude Bell, the desert queen? No. Unfortunately, my dreams of glamour and Gertrude will have to wait awhile longer. Andrea was right: I have never seen such a mob flocked behind the barbed wire fence.

"What on earth did you tell this journalist?" demands Gigi furiously, waving the newspaper under my nose.

"Nothing! I just told him that the Italian Red Cross organizes Medevacs on a monthly basis and that we'd just sent five children to Italy," I tell him, getting hold of the paper.

"What a nice couple we are in this picture," I say, examining the paper, having momentarily forgotten about the throng of people. "Oh dear, there might be a little problem with this," I say, with closer inspection. "This could easily be a 'Wanted: Dead or Alive' poster."

"We've already got the bloody problem. Look! The journalist obviously blew your words right out of proportion. Journalists are always the same wherever the hell you go," rages Gigi. "And so now all these people think that they can just hop on a plane and go to Italy."

By now the hordes of people have recognized the pair of us from our photos and are pushing forward at the railings with renewed eagerness. We decide to call an interpreter. There is no way we can send them all home, but likewise there's no way we can see to them all, at least not today. So Alessandro, the triage doctor, helps us arrange and negotiate appointments based on the gravity of each case.

"Salah, you've got to translate for me," I say to our interpreter. "But before we can speak, we need to try to quiet everyone down. The carabinieri will give us a hand."

"My friends," a carabiniere addresses the people in English and then continues in Italian, "get in line and be quiet a moment please."

"My friend" is the term they use whenever they address someone here, even if what they want to say is not that pleasant.

"Salah, tell them that what's written in this article isn't true. Or at least not for everybody. Only a tiny number of people can actually go to Italy," I say.

I really don't want all these parents, children, and relatives to be under false impressions. I really don't want to see their despair when they get turned away again. They have already suffered enough. They really don't need further disillusions and disappointments. But nobody listens to me. Nobody wants to hear. They all want to believe that they will be among the tiny few who are chosen to go. No doubt, actually certainly, I would be the same if I were in their shoes.

From now until I leave the camp, my task will be the most thankless one ever. I have to gather together all the necessary documents for those few who will leave for Italy, and I have to inform all the others (the overwhelming majority) that their cases have been rejected. Every day, I have to face tears, pleas, and desperation. It is unbelievable. How can I tell a father that his son is in such a bad state that even a foreign hospital would not be able to help? How can I tell a mother that there is no hope for the newborn child she is holding in her arms, and that it is best for it to die here in Iraq? I am not prepared emotionally for such a heart-wrenching task. Leaving my trailer in tears and crying myself to sleep becomes a regular occurrence. I feel utterly helpless.

For every hundred rejections, though, there is one person who gets to live his dream. It is difficult to translate a person's joy into words when she learns she is one of the chosen few heading to Italy. Tears of happiness… embraces… kisses. Suddenly, all the frustrations seem to fade. Unfortunately, this joy is short-lived. I watch the airplane take off for Italy and then head back to the field hospital to start all over again with the mass of desperate people thronging at the gates, wanting so badly to be among the next group. Among this crowd there will also be people who have already been rejected but who come back and keep trying, again and again.

I am worn out by the whole experience. Physically and also mentally. I am always aware of the futility of sending a couple of children abroad for treatment, while leaving behind the vast majority to suffer or die in the dreadful conditions that prevail in Iraq. Instead we need to be reorganizing the entire health system. Rather than rejoice in the five children saved, we need to look beyond these individual cases and try to save the hundreds, thousands, tens of thousands of children right here in Iraq. Only then will there be any hope for the future of this country and its people.

I don't want to dismiss the Medevac program and say that it's useless. Although it doesn't help improve Iraq's health system, it does save lives. And it also helps put our consciences at ease. I'll admit that it helped my troubled mind. In this country, in these conditions, it is not always easy to be optimistic. I cannot count how many times I've asked myself if

I'm doing the right thing and if it's really worth all the effort. Yes is the answer.

Even if I managed to get only a few dozens of Iraqis onto those planes, leaving behind many hundreds more. Even if, at times, I lost sight of what I was doing, crumbling from exhaustion and emotional agony. When the mercury is nearing 140 degrees Fahrenheit inside the rubber tents and the generators are crashing and the tents are radiating an unspeakable heat and everything seems to be going for the worse, it is not always easy to welcome each new day with a smile.

"Signora, I need a photocopy of her passport in order to process a visa."

This is Tommaso, who handles visas for the Italian embassy.

"But she doesn't have a passport," is my desperate reply.

"All right, then, get me a copy of her identity card" he retaliates. "And don't forget the translation."

It's not that I've forgotten. I've also not forgotten the umpteen spelling variations for one single name. It's enough to make anyone go crazy. A common name such as Mohammed changes on the whim of the translator or whoever's processing the identity card. First it's Muhammad, then it becomes Mohamad, and then Mohamed, then Mohanned. And goodness only knows what you'd end up with if the name were more unusual.

Another headache is the identity of the companion. Every patient has the right to be accompanied by one person, who is, we hope, female, as women seem to create fewer problems. And this is where the headache begins. To begin with, in Iraqi society women are not expected to hold a dominant role, so when they go abroad and leave their husbands and children behind, the members of the so-called stronger sex do not easily give their approval. And then there is the problem of the identity cards.

"How do I know that this is really you in this photo?" I ask the older sister of one of my fortunate children. She doesn't answer me. Her beautiful dark eyes speak clearly. I have to take her word for it and shoulder every responsibility should things be erroneous.

And thus I learn that in Iraq only married women have the right to a new identity card. Unmarried women only have the one card issued at their birth. And for all the goodwill in the world, it is not easy for me to ascertain that this photo of a tiny newborn baby corresponds with the twenty-year-old before me, looking at me beseechingly. I trust her. I always trust them and then have to face Tommaso's justified irritation when he has to solve the problem of the names that don't match up and handle photos that bear no resemblance at all. These are shocking situations and are typical of this part of the world.

"Anna, I can't cope. Look at this!"

It is doctor Anna who is shouting in despair, showing me another of those children. A lump at the back of the throat, eyes glistening with tears at the sight of the badly deformed girl on the cot.

"I'm beginning to hate them. How can they do this to their children? They know that marriage between cousins…" She stops herself here and has to leave of the room; she needs to go and give vent to her anger.

I am familiar with such moments. I glance down at the creature on the cot. I can barely bring myself to look. I can't describe her. My eyes meet hers and it's almost as if she's pleading for help. She understands. She is not going to survive in that body. I wish she didn't understand and she didn't know that there is no hope for her. Her loving father tries to comfort her. Maybe he should have thought earlier. Now it's too late; the damage is done and it's irreversible. Yet even the father, a middle-aged man, is also a victim.

"I have five children," he tells me. "Two of them are fine, but the other three…" I can see in his eyes what he's going to say. He continues, "She is the youngest. Her two brothers are dead."

Silence.

"This is Allah's will," he tells me.

What if Allah needed to be helped out a little?

"And soon this one is going to die too. And she knows it," he concludes.

I would like to ask him how many more children he wants to bring into this world before he stops. But I don't. He is a victim of a custom that is very much entrenched in

Working facility

Iraq. This is a country where inter-family marriage is quite common, where marrying a relative is perfectly acceptable. The key word is clan. The importance of belonging to one clan rather then another is almost inconceivable for a Western mind. And this man, who will not stop producing children even when faced with such horror, is the best representative.

"But I feel safe like this," a young woman married to her cousin once tried to explain to me. "I know that no one in this family will do me harm."

A debatable opinion.

"Should I marry a stranger instead? Marry someone from work who assures me that I can trust him?"

There are few opportunities in Iraq for women to meet men outside of their own family. There are still fewer opportunities for a woman to date a man and get to know him. Working women have slightly better chances, but only within the working day. Rarely can they meet men outside working hours; that would be considered inappropriate. Consequently, a woman chooses a blood relative who is a regular guest at her family's home. This explains why deformities, coupled with burns from kerosene, constitute a gaping wound in the Iraqi people's health.

CHAPTER 4

Saddam's Sons

"Happy birthday, Barbie Anna!"

A chorus of voices greets me as I make my triumphant entry in the hospital. Every morning, before succumbing to the list of things to do that is given to me at roll call, I go to say hello to the patients. By now, this has become a well-known ritual and everyone calls me Barbie.

"It's because of your blonde curls," an Iraqi nurse explains to me as she touches my hair. "We're all in love with your golden locks. Nobody in Iraq has hair like yours."

By now I am resigned to letting everyone touch my hair. At the beginning, I always tried to dodge their pawing hands, but then I gave up and now almost enjoy their attentions. It's their way of showing me their heartfelt affection. I also was not particularly thrilled about being compared to a doll. But then I realized it is the greatest compliment they can pay me, and so now I accept the hair stroking with good grace.

Photo: Cultural transfer

Presents, presents, and more presents. I am flooded with presents. Everybody gives me something. It is occasions like this that Iraqis' blatant passion for all things kitsch really shines through. Now my desk is exquisitely adorned with little pink and gold figurines.

"Oh dear, I feel as if I'm in a horror museum," exclaims Gigi when he enters my trailer. "Look on the bright side," he continues. "At least if you decide to get married you won't need to worry about buying any wedding mementos for the guests."

He breaks off suddenly, as if he has just seen something frightful. He stares at me, scrutinizing me from head to toe. Then he bursts into one of his charming fits of laughter. "Well somebody certainly knows how to accessorize! You look like a flipping Christmas tree!"

Gigi is right. I should be embarrassed. But I have a dilemma, a grave diplomatic dilemma. Not wanting to favor one gift over another, and not wanting to offend anyone, I decide to put on all the various birthday trinkets. So now I have a ring on every finger, a couple of crosses around my neck, blue rosary beads tucked into a pocket, all sorts of bracelets up my arms, and an improbable sequin-studded headscarf around my head.

"You're not seriously thinking about going out like that?" continues Gigi in jest.

"I don't want to upset anyone by not wearing their gift," I retort. I want it to be clear that my innovative look has been carefully considered and is based upon serious reasoning and rationality.

"Yes, but you're hardly going to be taken seriously dressed like that. Have you actually had a look at yourself?"

No. I'd prefer not to. There aren't any mirrors here in camp and that is fine by me.

"Feeling beautiful is much more important than being beautiful," I respond. "Isn't that what they say? If I feel beautiful, everybody will see me in a beautiful light."

Theories aside, though, all this jingling and jangling is starting to be quite annoying, and so despite my earlier intentions, I take it all off. Ring after ring, chain after chain, bracelet after bracelet, it all comes off.

"Ah, that's more like it," Gigi says, content with my return to normality.

"I've come to a compromise," I tell him. "After all, life is a series of compromises, isn't it?"

"If this is the effect that birthdays have on you, then this is the first and last birthday I want to spend with you. You're so full of clichés and ready-made phrases. At least now you've got rid of all that tacky stuff. The figurines on your desk still have to go, though. But let's not go crazy now; step by step, I don't want too many surprises in one day."

Gigi and I have a lot of regard for each other; we have a great laugh together and tease each other mercilessly. Circumstance permitting, Franco and Giovanni, who are better known as Mimì and Cocò, are always willing spectators at our sparring matches. They stay on the sidelines. They pass their days cooped up in a camper trying to fix the radio or get the Internet going. They spend hours listening to strange noises and then delight or despair depending on the whistle they hear. They are like husband and wife. Having known each other for ages they know exactly how to wind each other up. One likes to go to bed early; the other likes to read until late. One rises at dawn; the other enjoys sleeping late. One does his laundry in the morning; the other does it in the evening. One is the first to the canteen; the other eats when everyone is done. One is nuts about weather forecasts; the other hides the barometer.

They are perpetually giving each other grief. It is great fun to go and visit them in their trailer or dine with them. Even though they have completely different tastes in everything, they always seem to end up doing things together. Complaining of course. Making constant digs at each other. Franco and Giovanni are inseparable, and like Gigi and myself, they like to have a laugh.

"Oh, boys, our Prouse has come to a compromise," Gigi tells our two friends who have dropped by to find out what's going on. It's a rare occasion, but every so often, these two leave their cramped hole of a trailer that is stationed at the opposite side of camp and brave the outside world. What socialites!

"A compromise? C'mon then, let's hear it…" Franco jumps right in. "What the hell is all this stuff?" he says, looking at all my trinkets and knick-knacks in disgust.

"Exactly," says Gigi, "Even if these things don't quite fit in yet, from today our dear Anna has vowed to become a compromising woman." They sit down around me feigning an exaggerated interest.

Insensitive idiots! Then I explain my tormenting dilemma and its solution to them.

"Convenient. Most convenient. I can just see you putting all this stuff on every time you go in and out of the hospital. By the third time, your patience will have run out and you'll be throwing the bangles to the wind and your compromises to the devil," predicts Franco. "And then, Annina, since when did you and compromise walk arm in arm? Getting older may be traumatic… but do us a favor and live with it!"

Live with it? What good advice. But not good enough to help me get through this wearing day. I turn to another means of survival. "Gigi, I'm going to take this afternoon off." I'm feeling inspired and have had an idea.

"Just listen to her. She started off by being all timid, and now listen to her making bold propositions, wheeling and dealing. You'd better watch out or I'll be sending you home," he says, trying to sound threatening.

"Oh right, and on what airplane? If there were planes I'd be gone in a flash."

" I'd be sending you on foot! So, a half-day off, eh? You're mad. It must be the heat."

" I've got to find someone who knows how to make sangria…" I must have said the magic word.

"Sangria? Did someone say sangria?" Gigi bolts as if struck by lightning; as do the other two.

If I'm going to include everyone, then I'll need enough for about sixty people. We'll need at least thirty bottles of wine. Far too much. We'll never find that much wine here in Baghdad. I'll have to go out on a wine hunt. The thing is, I don't want to get shot just for a birthday party.

By now, I'm thinking aloud. "I'll need someone to accompany me. I reckon with a dozen bottles of wine, and some fruit and juice, we should be able to make enough sangria for everyone. Now, about the exact quantities and ingredients—there must be some carabiniere who knows. I'll go and ask around."

I get up and go, leaving my three astonished friends sitting behind in a trailer with no air conditioning.

"Well, for a good sangria we can let her take a half-day off. Great idea."

I hear this remark and spin round, "I heard you, Gigi. Go on, admit it, you'd be lost without me!" I then turn and leave hurriedly before they have time to hurl an insult at me. Or worse still, hurl one of my precious figurines.

Identifying the camp's sangria wizard does not take long. Soon Matteo has given me a list of the necessary ingredients and has offered to give me a hand in making it.

"And while we're on the subject of ingredients, I hope your recipe isn't set in stone," I say, covering my back should it go wrong. "Shopping in Baghdad is not one of the easiest things to do."

I return to the trailer triumphantly and find Gigi with the keys to a jeep in his hand.

"I'm going to take a half-day off too. I'll accompany you on your mission."

Mimì and Cocò watch us enviously. In all this time, they have never once stepped beyond the barbed wire fence. But when we invite them to join us, their answer is clear: "Are you crazy? They shoot out there!"

Getting about the streets of postwar Iraq is truly a fascinating and surreal experience. After four o'clock in the afternoon, the streets empty and Baghdad becomes a ghost town. Everything is ready for the curfew, the time of day that everyone awaits in fear.

I am the one who leaves the camp most frequently. I sometimes go to the offices of the International Red Cross or to the offices of the United Nations, which are housed at Canal Hotel. Sometimes I am out looking for a suitable hospital building that one day we could move to. Other times I am going to the CPA or the American headquarters, or I am off to meet journalists at the Palestine Hotel, which is where all the press are based. I also make trips to the airport to pick up the medicines that arrive in cargo. All in all, I venture out of the camp almost every day. I am good at finding my way around. You have to learn to avoid getting lost in the narrow streets and alleyways as they often turn out to be dead ends. Even though present-day Baghdad is nothing in comparison to what I'll have to deal with in coming months, it's nevertheless a place where you don't want to linger.

It does not take us long to find the little shop that I had learned about some time ago, courtesy of a CNN journalist whom I had asked where I could get wine in the city. I had thought about this well in advance. Having lived in Islamic countries, I have begun to see alcohol as a distant mirage.

We spend all afternoon peeling apples, squeezing citrus fruit, and uncorking bottles. Luckily I've got Matteo on the case; otherwise, who knows what I would have concocted!

"What are you doing, Anna?" A nun asks me.

"I'm making a drink to die for, sister," I reply.

"As long as there's no alcohol in it!" is her response.

I decide to tell everyone who doesn't know better that sangria is a drink made up purely of fruit, juice, and other ingredients. I have to rely on my willing accomplices, notably the carabinieri. As a result, all night there are nuns draining huge cups of this exotic, novel drink.

To this day I am still wondering if they did actually believe my stories.

Golden Arches reach Iraq

I am not convinced. I reckon they were happy to kid themselves they were sipping a "politically correct" drink, that is, one that does not contravene their often restricting customs. Not all the nuns join in this summer revelry. No loss—we have more to drink for ourselves!

These poor nuns, extremely committed to their work, are the inevitable targets of pranks, and probably a little more sense of humor on their part would not go amiss.

I am eating dinner at the canteen when suddenly Alessandro, a carabiniere, leans across to me and whispers loudly:

"Perhaps you could move about a bit more when you're in the shower. Things are getting a bit monotonous. You're not really very sensual. I'm sure you could spice things up a bit!"

He speaks in a stage whisper blatantly designed so that the nuns sitting behind us can hear every word. I also use a stage whisper: "I've been tired," is my poor excuse. "I can't wait for this evening when I can dive into bed. You'll just have to be patient with me. But I promise to try to put on a better show!"

Andrea, the carabiniere with the incomparable sense of humor, joins in our risqué "hushed" discussion. We are trying to keep straight faces and it is killing us. We decide to spread a rumor about closed-circuit television cameras being hidden in the showers. To be honest, I'm not entirely convinced there aren't. Here in Baghdad there is an unnerving trend of film material not being that far from reality.

"I bet you are behind this story of the CCTV," says Gigi to me, the day after the risqué conversation with my two accomplices.

"Wow, you're such a bright spark!" I respond, highly satisfied with our prank.

"Another nice move from our resident comedians. Just where do you get all these ideas? Thank goodness we've got you all to make us laugh. If not, this place would drive us all mad." Gigi most definitely enjoyed listening to my saucy conversation with the carabinieri the night before. And imagine how much the story was inflated as it got passed around!

"But now I need to somehow quash the rumors… otherwise the nuns might just kill me! Anyway, they have done a thorough search of the showers," Gigi informs me.

That evening, as I had a shower myself, I will admit that I also checked for cameras. After all, the story of the CCTV isn't really that far-fetched. You never know.

Living in a field hospital like ours, in a corner of the world like this one, where culture and customs are so very different from what we know, there are so many curious and often incomprehensible events happening on a daily basis that a whole book would be needed to record them.

"You've certainly got a tough general there!" remarks an Iraqi man waiting at the gate while I am distributing water to the queue of people. He does not have any teeth and has a really warming smile. How odd. I get the feeling that rather than wanting to get into the camp, this man is more interested in watching these strange people from a distant land go about their work.

A tough general? What? I look at him in bewilderment. I have no idea what he is talking about.

"Every afternoon at the same time, he makes the poor boys run round the camp. What with this terrible heat, it really is a harsh punishment. Every day he does it! Either the men are really undisciplined and in need of punishment or the general really is a slave driver!"

Now I understand. I will have to try to explain to him what is going on. It is not easy for an Iraqi to understand that it is not a punishment at all—the men actually want to run. It is not easy to explain to this toothless old man, who certainly has bigger problems on his plate other than keeping fit, that we do not have a raging general here like the ones you see on TV. I am at a loss as to how to explain to him that what he is watching on this baking summer afternoon is something that is part of Western culture.

"We call this daily run jogging," I explain, with the help of an interpreter. "For us, jogging is a very popular activity."

He looks at me incredulously. "But why?"

This time it is difficult for me to believe. Are there really people from our planet who do not know what jogging is all about?

"We do it to stay in shape and to relax," I tell him, as if it were an obvious concept. He shakes his head.

"Well it's true then. You're all crazy!"

A year after this conversation, I will come across a group of bandanna-sporting Iraqis jogging through the streets of Baghdad. I will realize just how much our culture has taken root in Iraq. Unnecessary physical exertion is a million miles apart from an Iraqi's natural pace of life; to see them work out for no practical reason will come as a real shock to me:

"Could it be that we're actually ruining them?" I will ask myself.

I'll admit on frequent occasions the listless ease with which Iraqis go about things has brought me close to a mental breakdown. I'll often come across a group of Iraqis in the corridors of the Ministry of Health where we Westerners always dash about. The Iraqis, though, will be meandering along from one meeting to the next. They'll be walking casually, side by side, which means that for all my frenzied attempts, there is absolutely no way I can skirt around them. Maddening!

But then, after one year of rushing about out of breath, I will suddenly ask myself if maybe they have got it right. We run about, but why? Okay, so you make up five seconds by hurrying down the corridor, but then what? Why do we do everything in a hurry? Is it because time for us is something slippery, something that we need to seize, grapple with, and keep hold of? They perceive time in a much broader way and, I'll say this again, it seems as if they are the ones who've got it right. I am beginning to adapt to their way… just now before I leave for Italy.

"What's happening?"

The way we are looking at each other speaks volumes. We are so utterly frightened that we cannot even move, let alone engineer an escape plan. With hindsight, it is just as well. For now, though, we are all thinking the same thing:

"They've come for us!"

Night has just fallen and suddenly, without any warning at all, bullets start to rain out of the sky. Yes! Bullets! Myriad bullets are freefalling around us. By now we are all used to the dry sound of distant gunfire that starts when the heat begins to wane and darkness settles on the camp. But this time the noise is deafening. This gunfire is extremely close.

Tracers leave their red trail against the night's black canvas. The sound of the bullets on the paving… A tremor of fear shudders up my spine. We have no idea what to do or what is going on.

"They want to kill us all!" I hear someone shout.

I don't recognize the voice, but I know for sure that it is the same thought that is paralyzing all our minds. Machine gun bursts and pistol shots. It feels as if the whole of Baghdad is out there firing weapons. At least we have the carabinieri to tell us what to do. Personally, I would have tried to scale the wall, capped by hellish barbed wire, to get out of this prison-type camp with no means of escape. Certainly not one of my better ideas. Once out of camp, I would have started running. To where? I don't know.

"Running can never go wrong," I can remember thinking.

Some staff run for shelter in the tents, as if the rubber could protect them from the bullets. The carabinieri soon fish them out and send them to a pre-determined place. In a couple of minutes, we are all together in this assigned "safe place," crouched down under trucks and motor vehicles. This is really the only place that offers any sort of shelter. We do not know what we are waiting for. Most of us are already imagining being torn apart by the enraged crowd that is thronging at the gate. What have we done? We do not know. Will they tell us before they kill us? My phone rings. It's Nawar, our Iraqi anesthetist.

"Anna, don't worry! We're celebrating!" he tells me reassuringly.

Or at least that's what I want to believe I heard. Then again, Nawar never gets worked up. Chubby and unflappable, he is a tireless young doctor who has yet to learn that sleeping is not optional. Nawar celebrating? I'm not sure if I heard him straight.

Silence.

"Don't worry, Miss Anna!" he repeats.

Okay, I was with him until now. But how can I not worry when machine guns are firing and tracers flying?

"I should be calm? What? While I'm under a truck?!" I scream into the phone, trying to make myself heard over the gunfire.

"No, don't worry. We're celebrating," insists Nawar.

Enough of this talk of celebration. "Well, will you explain what the hell you are celebrating, Nawar?" I am in a state. Slowly though, it's beginning to sink in. I'm getting pictures in my mind of the images often shown on TV. Images of men firing into the air, broad grins stamped across their faces. Proud, gleeful expressions. Proud to pick up a weapon and fire it wildly. A sign of virility. Small satisfactions in life…

"They've got Uday and Qusay!"

This time I detect a flash of emotion in Nawar's tone of voice; this is a man who is usually so reserved and restrained.

"What? Who? Speak up Nawar!"

"Saddam's sons! They've been caught!"

This time I hear him fine. I pass on the information to the others who are desperately trying to find out what is happening.

"You're telling me that they're quite *happy* out there and have no intention of coming in here after us?" asks one of the nuns in utter confusion. She needs to be reassured. She didn't like the thought of falling into the hands of some incensed Iraqis.

It lasts for a couple of hours. Then, gradually, the gunfire subsides and becomes more distant until it dies away into this dark night of late July. We do not venture out of our shelter until the last shot is fired. We are all breathing heavily.

"Let's hope they've finished their cartridges," says Romano, the health director. "It's just as well they have all been disarmed," he continues sarcastically. "All those efforts to round up the rifles, machine guns, missiles, and goodness knows what else? Not entirely successful, then. Congratulations!"

He wants to know how it is possible that almost everyone in Iraq still has a firearm in his possession. The weapons must have been hidden away, only to be whipped out on the first whiff of a celebration. Like this celebration—the capture of Saddam's sons.

I will witness "celebratory fire," a favorite Iraqi pastime, on other occasions. Other occasions to dodge the falling bullets, all fired with the seeming conviction that these deadly projectiles will not fall at all but will remain suspended in midair.

I remember the capture of Saddam; that historic December 14, 2003. I am out on the streets of Baghdad when I receive a phone call.

"We've got him! Get back here now! It's dangerous out there!" warns a voice from elsewhere.

The words have not even sunk in when already I see people running wildly out of their houses waving guns. To say I am frightened would be an understatement. This is an unforgettable fear. I do not think I have ever driven as fast in all my life. Anyone who gets between my Land Cruiser and the gates of the so-called green zone will be flattened. As I near what the soldiers refer to as Assassins Gate, I sink my head into my chest in a ridiculous attempt to make myself as small as possible—yeah, right, this will stop me from being hit by a bullet.

The very words Assassins Gate make me shiver. On January 17, this is where a kamikaze driving a truck laden with explosives will cause a horrific bloodbath. Twenty-four people will lose their lives and one hundred twenty will be injured, making it one of the bloodiest attacks while I am here.

The walls of our barracks will shake with the blast on that cursed winter morning. I will run out to the gate searching for our interpreters missing from roll call. I will remember the desperation, the shredded bodies, the burnt-out carcasses of vehicles, the ambulances, the thick smoke, the blood, and… the rage.

But back to "celebratory fire." After the capture of Saddam's sons and of Saddam himself, the wildest celebrations I experienced were for a football match. People are passionate about football here! When the Iraqi Olympic team beat Saudi Arabia and qualified for the Athens games, the people went wild. Never has there been such frenzied partying. Iraqi-style partying, of course—firing bullets into the air, from rooftops, cars, roads, bridges.

It is May 2004. Having been here for almost a year, I feel like an Iraq veteran. I am out walking with some colleagues within the perimeters of the Green Zone when a tracer flies past our noses. There is no need to speak. We start to run as the sound of bullets ricocheting off the ground around us gets stronger. We take refuge behind the thick walls of the offices and only then find out the reason for all this commotion.

"If only they would warn us about such happenings," exclaims Dave, one of my doctor colleagues. "Who would ever think of a football match? Anna, aren't you a friend of Mark who works for the Ministry of Youth and Sport?"

I only manage to nod my head. I am far too out of breath to speak. My legs are still trembling. Thank goodness I go to the gym regularly. Otherwise there's no way I could cope with such physical exertion.

"Right, well, ask Mark to send us a calendar of all the football matches so we can stay indoors on those days!" Dave concludes.

"Are we sure there aren't any other hobbies we should be watching out for? Boxing matches maybe?" This is Ken speaking. He is a colonel in the U.S. Air Force and is also panting heavily after our manic dash to safety. "I say this because yesterday I saw Iraq's boxing team in Mark's office. I can't imagine they'll ever win anything, but…"

That evening I find a bullet in my trailer. I find it in my left running shoe, to be precise. There's a hole in the metal roof sheeting. This is another memory to take home.

Uday and Qusay were not captured as Nawar told me on the phone; they had been killed. I know that the whole world went into debate over the United States' decision to show the mangled corpses on TV. In Baghdad we never have time for such debates. Often we do not even hear the information.

The Iraqis are over the moon about Uday and Qusay's deaths, and compared to their reactions to Saddam's capture, they are much more fervid in their celebrations. I have thought a lot about why the festivities for Saddam's capture seemed so muted in comparison. They only lasted a couple of hours; soon gunfire ceased, groups disbanded, and everyone went back to their daily grind. I have come to one explanation: Saddam's capture occurred at a time when the people were painfully disillusioned and life-weary. Average Iraqis, the majority of the population, simply did not have the energy to hope and fight. They lived in a sort of coma, letting events wash over them. They had lived with fatalism for almost three decades, and it is this fatalism and resignation that I've consistently fought against for well over a year.

By July, people have rekindled their will to live. Thus, the deaths of the ace of hearts and the ace of clubs, as featured on the most-wanted list of the ex-Iraqi regime, are greeted with unprecedented jubilation. Sometimes I think it was the bloodiness of Uday's and Qusay's end that provoked such exultation. You cannot say the same thing for Saddam Hussein. In fact, most of the Iraqis I have spoken to say they would have preferred to see him dead.

"You should have killed him," one of my Iraqi friends tell me, "just as God's justice dealt with Uday and Qusay, you should have let God do the same with him!"

An interesting concept of justice.

"If God wanted his two sons to die, why would he have wanted to save Saddam? The worst of all!"

This friend of mine cannot comprehend my satisfaction that Saddam did not go the same way as his two sons.

"I know my people," he tells me. "They lived so long in terror under this man and are frightened that he'll make his return. For most of us, Saddam exerted almost supernatural powers… he was almost a God! But of course you won't understand this, especially seeing as you are against the death penalty!"

He is disgusted with me. He cannot possibly see why you would want to keep alive a tyrant like Saddam and wants him to be killed. On the other hand, after all, there are only a handful of people against the death penalty. In a society based upon such violent values, this is hardly surprising. I do not blame them. No doubt I would think exactly the same if I were born here and if a tyrant had murdered my family.

But I was not born here. I think the evenings I spent discussing whether Saddam should be killed or not were among the most constructive I have spent in Iraq. I enjoy provoking my friends by taking my reasoning to its extreme. I enjoy watching their rage escalate knowing that they cannot pick up a Kalashnikov and shoot this crazy Italian woman with her insane theories. The "not being armed" bit is very important and is an essential prerequisite for any discussion, just in case my practical lessons on democracy do not go the way I intended.

I manage to elucidate to my Iraqi friends the concept of democracy, which really is an alien notion here in Iraq. Our discussions about democracy are low-key and take place between four domestic walls or when seated on a swing in a garden. If, during our journey through war-torn Iraq, we do not stop to give practical examples of democracy—in a quiet, subtle way, far from the world's attention—seeds of democracy cannot be sown. Seeds that, in time, may grow.

CHAPTER 5

AL RASHEED

IT IS MORE THAN A HOTEL

.O BOX 8070 BAGHDAD IRAQ
EL.   8851000 / 8861000
ELEX.   213204
AX.   8850359

Turning Point

Although Iraq has never been an entirely safe place, the real turning point—the real cataclysm—has a name, a date, and a time: United Nations, August 19, 2003, local time 4:40 p.m. A kamikaze driver rams a truck laden with explosives into the Canal Hotel's courtyard. The Canal Hotel has been the United Nation's headquarters in Baghdad since 1991, and it housed more than three hundred people.

When I hear news of the tragedy, I do not waste any time on fruitless words. "I've got to go there," is all I say. I am stricken at the thought that someone I know may be among the victims. I know lots of people who work there.

As I approach the highway, I see a cloud of black smoke.

"Salah, please translate what's going on!" The jeep's radio is switched on and a local channel is broadcasting the news. I want to know the death toll.

Photo: More than a hotel, but less than a sanctuary

"Three dead and dozens injured," is the interpreter's reply after a brief silence. "They don't know who did it. No one has claimed responsibility yet."

But as we near the Canal Hotel, I realize that the radio's death toll of three cannot possibly be right. Helicopters flap overhead, land, load up the wounded, and take off again, raising clouds of dust. As if the air was not already thick with dust. Ambulances flash and wail their way wildly down the road leading from that cursed place. We still have a kilometer to go to the hotel, but already we see the first debris from the blast. Fragments of the hotel's blue shutters, thrown here by the forceful explosion, now litter the road, as do car roofs, broken glass, and sheets of burnt black paper. I will never forget how I felt in that moment, the dawning horror of those first moments.

This is the most serious attack on the United Nations in history. We do not know it yet, but this monstrous offense marks the beginning of a new era, plunging Iraq into a new strategy of terror. But even if we still know nothing of this new era, our instincts tell us this is a turning point. The very symbol of reconstruction work in Iraq has been targeted, and we can no longer feel safe. This is a clear and explicit signal that terrifies all of us who are here to help.

"If they did this to the United Nations, they could do the same to us, no?" I remember saying to Romano.

He does not answer. We both know that safety is no longer guaranteed. Perhaps it never was, but at least we lived under its illusion.

As we draw up to the Canal Hotel, the scenes get more horrific. I have been here many times, but now there is nothing left but a heap of rubble. I shudder. There is a crater that is tens of meters wide and flames that will not be extinguished. The entire eastern wing has collapsed; all that remains are lumps of concrete. I do not know where I am going. I am about to cry. I cannot open my mouth. I feel paralyzed. My heart tightens and I am overcome by an emotion that I did not know I possessed until today, an unprecedented sadness, a misery verging on utter despair. This is an act of unheard-of violence and I struggle to come up with an explanation. I will stop trying to seek reasoning in this country. I will learn to go ahead without asking why. Is this a good thing? I don't know. But it is a coping strategy and keeps me from giving up.

Now I know the full meaning of the word violence. I did not need to know. Or maybe I did. Not knowing would definitely have been easier. But if you decide, as I have, to live in this part of the world, I do not think you can ignore a concept that is so deeply rooted. You cannot detach yourself from the hatred that seems to permeate everything. Everything seeps violence: a bloody, merciless, indiscriminate violence. Its victims are very often innocent people who just happened to be in the wrong place at the wrong time. Your first encounter with violence like this is more devastating than you can possibly imagine. Although in my pre-August 19 days, I had lived many intense emotions, I did not realize the sheer force of one of them: the horror of such violence. There is no doubt that this is the fiercest emotion I have felt here in Iraq, if not in my whole life. The fiercest and also most protracted emotion. From today on, my life will be a continuous flirt with this pitiless, cold, ruthless notion. It will become part of my daily life, and I will get used to it. But even if the claws of the incapacitating feeling that is gripping me now, here, in front of the Canal Hotel loosen in time, I will still feel them and cannot be rid of them. I only manage to resist their lure, warding off the precipice of despair. From this evil August day on, violence will be my faithful and indefatigable companion.

"Oliver. Oliver Bousquet. Where is Oliver?" I frantically ask around.

Nobody can tell me anything. I have worked quite a lot with this young Frenchman, but now his mobile phone does not respond. They will not let me see the list of the dead.

"They are orders from above," I am told.

Meanwhile, the death toll has risen to ten, then to seventeen, then to twenty during the night, then again to forty-six. One hundred seven are wounded and have been taken to the capital's various hospitals. Serious cases have been sent to American hospitals, the rest to Iraqi ones. The name Sergio Vieira de Mello, the UN special envoy, is on everyone's lips.

After easily smashing its way through the barrier, the truck laden with explosives and concrete exploded right under his window.

"De Mello is dead under the rubble," I hear people saying.

"He bled to death!"

These words are throbbing in my head. He had been in his office on the second floor. The explosion blew him to the ground floor and left him trapped under a slab of concrete.

"I went up to the second floor," recounts Ghassan Salamè, his senior political advisor. "I saw him down on the ground, immobilized. I shouted down to him and then ran down and told him we were going to dig him out," he continues. But it was too late. His corpse was taken to the mortuary.

After every attack, the dead are always taken to Doctor Bakr. I know this distinguished middle-aged man well, and he has run the country's biggest mortuary for thirteen years. He studied in England and returned to Iraq to help his people.

"I was the one who had to identify Uday," he tells me, in that hushed voice of his. I need not say that Dr. Bakr's "kingdom" is often overcrowded. What with the bombings and the shootings, there is always plenty of work for him. Dr. Bakr does not just have to contend with the dead; for every dead Iraqi, there are at least fifty anguished, screaming relatives thronging at the gate.

"I am stuck in traffic," I tell Franco over my radio.

It is July and I am trying to get to the Ministry of Health. I have to meet Jim Haveman, the senior advisor, who will shortly become my new boss. The road is blocked by hundreds of people, women in chadors and frantic men beating themselves on their chests with their fists.

"I'm going to stop and see what's happening," I say.

"Are you crazy?" Romano tries to stop me.

But my curiosity is too great and so I leap down from the jeep. I do not yet know that I am actually outside the main entrance of Baghdad's mortuary. When I see a body going past me, however, I realize that I'm somewhere out of the ordinary, at least for me. For an Iraqi, there is barely anything that is out of the ordinary!

The man's body is hoisted up and into a wooden coffin tied onto the top of a broken down car. But to get him up there... what a feat! Sometimes the body slips out of their hands and they have to catch it as it drops. What relief when the body finally thuds into the coffin. Made it! And all the time, as a backdrop, is anguished wailing and bizarre shows of grief.

"When the head of a tribe dies, sometimes we get up to three hundred people here," Dr. Bakr tells me.

"Everybody is howling and screaming. They make an unbelievable amount of noise, but it is their custom. They hold up the traffic too. The other day there were at least thirty cars out here just for one man! Every now and then I even have to march out there as a traffic warden!"

Poor doctor. He certainly has a thankless profession. He enjoys chatting as he takes me on a tour of his kingdom. He shows me the doctors at work; he points out decomposing corpses, heads sawn in two, and limbs so deformed that, by comparison, mine reflect the beauty of the Sistine Chapel. I do my best to stick out the tour to its end. I let his contagious enthusiasm carry me along.

"This one has been here for months and still nobody has claimed him."

The doctor opens the cold store. He does not want me to miss such a gem.

"Sorry, Dr. Bakr!" is the only thing I manage to mumble as I gag, staggering to the exit.

"Now we have repaired the air conditioning," he continues when he catches up with me. "It was broken all summer."

I dare not imagine.

"As well as bodies of people who died from suspicious or unknown causes, I also get live ones," he continues, completely unperturbed.

In the meantime, he has led me back in. He really does not want me to give up! I suppose there are not many people interested in his work, so when he finds one who is, he does not let go easily. I have to cover my nose with a hem of my blouse to try to lessen the terrible stench.

"What do you mean alive? Why would they be in a mortuary?"

"Often it's people embroiled in trials. With sexually abused women, for example, I have to decide if they are telling the truth. It is the same with torture victims. I have to work out how much psychological and physical damage has been inflicted. The police send me these cases because they need an expert opinion before they can proceed. I also get people who don't know how old they are and come here for an estimate! And then there are paternity disputes, cases of infertility and impotence… everyone comes to me!"

By now we have got to the laboratories. I can make out jars and pots that contain human organs or sections of organs.

"Here we go again," I tell myself as we enter.

A female doctor, absorbed in her work, is dipping a piece of liver into different colored liquids.

"This is where we do the toxicological examinations," she explains to me in perfect English.

"There are many deaths caused by poisoning here in Iraq. Our task is to establish whether the victim died from natural causes or not."

Bomb attacks, shootings, poisonings, stabbings, strangulations, hangings, burnings—all sorts of criminal acts. Surely this is all?

"So far more than seventy-five mass graves have been discovered in Iraq."

He smiles beneath his bushy gray mustache and looks at me. I close my eyes. I do not want to imagine it. And this time, Dr. Bakr has pity on me.

Why did they choose the headquarters of the United Nations to carry out their first atrocious bomb attack? Why did they choose to begin their policy of destabilization right here? Who can say?

"It was almost predictable!" I say to my Iraqi interpreter as I look around. "The security checks of people coming and going from the building were minimal."

Although I have scarce knowledge of preventive security, even I was surprised by how easy it was to get into the building.

"They were too confident." I am talking to myself as I push through the smoke, trying to find a familiar face. Salah follows me.

"Neutral! They think that being neutral makes you immune to such horror. But this is a battle for power. Why don't they understand this?" I am angry with these people who had refused every form of protection. De Mello had asked for increased protection even though it was a request that contravenes the principles of the organization.

"Unlike the Americans, we are well thought of by the Iraqis," Thomas had told me one day.

Thomas works for the Oil for Food program, the controversial agreement that in 1997 replaced the embargoes on Iraqi exports, set by the United Nations as sanctions for the Kuwait invasion. The embargoes had crippled Iraq, depriving it of medicines and essential items, and had provoked conflicting reactions in the West. The Oil for Food program enabled Iraq to export limited quantities of petroleum in exchange for food and medicine.

"Are you sure?" I say, trying to provoke a debate. "From what I know and what I've been told by lots of Iraqis, confidence in the United Nations fell because of the way you administered the sanctions."

Thomas begins to look flustered.

"I'm not the one who said that," I clarify. "I don't know enough about it to have my own opinion. I am just relating to you things that I have been told on more than one occasion."

We go on to have an enjoyable and animated conversation. I'm still none the wiser though.

The United Nations will leave Iraq after another serious attack two months later, this time on the International Red Cross. It is one of the most tumultuous days Baghdad has ever experienced, a really memorable October 27, the first day of the holy month of Ramadan.

After the massacre at the headquarters of the United Nations, it was clear that the Iraqi insurgents had no regard for anyone. The UN was, nevertheless, a political target. The Red Cross was not. If being engaged in Iraq purely in a humanitarian sphere does not guarantee your safety, it clearly means that the guerrillas are attempting to turn Iraq into a battlefield. Within two hours, they staged five separate attacks: one at the office of the International Red Cross and four at police stations. In the same afternoon, a bomb also exploded in the center of Baghdad.

When the attack happens on the International Red Cross, I am unable to go there and assist in the aftermath. I am too busy trying to find new accommodation and pick up the pieces of my life. Finding my own room completely destroyed by a rocket is something I'll never forget.

Twenty-four hours earlier, at dawn on October 26, Paul Wolfowitz, the U.S. deputy secretary of defense, is staying at Hotel Al Rasheed. Suddenly, twenty-nine antitank rockets are fired at the hotel. My room, on the ninth floor, is hit head on. I have slept in this hotel every night for two months. This is the first time I am out of the city.

Two weeks later, after the attack on their offices, the International Red Cross decides to close down its offices in Baghdad and Bassora as a result of the highly dangerous, unstable situation. This is the reasoning given by Geneva. My initial thought is a question: wasn't it from the battlefield that our humanitarian organization was born? I am shocked by the decision to withdraw. But I do not want to make hasty judgments, given the critical nature of the moment, which once again I must endure.

I am in Iraqi Kurdistan, a mountainous area to the north. I feel as if I have slipped into another world that, despite its atrocious suffering, has still managed to retain its vitality and its infectious enthusiasm. This buzzing vitality is extraordinary given that Kurdistan is a land where mass graves, burnt-down villages, and the use of chemical weapons and land mines on a civilian population barely belong to the past.

"Anna, we don't know much about how the doctors and nurses are getting on up there," Jim Haveman, senior advisor at the Ministry of Health, tells me one day. By now I've been working for him for about two months, and the way that he has complete faith in my judgment is a great compliment but also terrifies me completely.

"One step wrong, one error, and I'm finished," I say to Jon as we climb on board the helicopter that is to take us north. Jon Bowersox is a friend. Right from the first day I set foot in the headquarters of the CPA, I was immediately attracted to this hyperactive, resourceful doctor. He travels in tandem with Elias Nimmer, a U.S. colonel of Lebanese origin, who tries to counterbalance his colleague's excessive energies. And now that I have been admitted to the team, he has to deal with mine too.

"You two are impossible!" Nimmer complains when he can barely keep his eyes open. He's completely exhausted. "We've been on the go since five o'clock this morning. Now it's the dead of night and we're still going!"

He hates running about and tries any way he can to slow the pace down.

"I'm Lebanese and I don't like having to pant! Give me a break, dammit! And slow down! You're driving like maniacs. You'll crash us!"

We are known as the "dynamic trio." We are the ones poking our noses in everywhere, checking hospitals, distributing wages, listening to people's complaints, organizing the health section of the New Iraqi Army. We are famous for disappearing into thin air and then reappearing later on as if nothing happened—shattered, sweaty, but satisfied. As far as everyone else is concerned, our missions are shrouded in mystery.

"They're on a mission. Don't ask me where, but out on a mission," say our office colleagues when somebody tries to locate us.

"You vanish for days at a time," says Colonel Gerber one day. He is the director of operations and responsible for our safety.

"A Lebanese, an American, and an Italian—those poor Iraqis! I sometimes wonder what you three get up to all over the country. Well, I trust you. Otherwise I wouldn't let you go. And okay, I'll admit it, your meticulous reports are extremely useful."

Nothing escapes the colonel's attention and he certainly cannot be fooled easily.

"Anna, I know you visit places you shouldn't. I know you don't respect the safety rules. The rules apply to everyone who works for the CPA. There are no exceptions!"

I try to jump in. I want to explain to him that if I were to follow the rules, I would not be able go to any part of Iraq.

"Let me finish!" he demands, with his wonderful tone of authority.

"I know your reasons for doing it are valid and this is the only reason that I will pretend I don't know. But don't get caught! If you do, I'll definitely have to stem your activities. I will tie an anchor to you. You have been warned!

The colonel knows it is not easy for me to take him seriously. It is not that I do not respect him. It's not that at all. There is no one I respect more. But I do not cower in front of his tough-guy approach nor concede to his stern words. I know behind all that the façade and ice blue eyes lies a heart of gold.

Crossing the mountainous north on board a Black Hawk, with your legs dangling down into nothingness, creates a giddy rush of life. We follow the course of the Tigris, flying above villages that do not even have electricity, waving down at children below who are chasing after the helicopter. We seem to have slipped back into another time. This is one of the few relaxing moments I have had in this country. The air is crisp. I take deep breaths. What a wonderful feeling. I feel utterly rejuvenated. It is a moment that is destined to be short-lived. The following morning, I receive a telephone call. Then silence. Then helplessness, breathlessness.

"Elias is in the hospital. He is paralyzed. A rocket landed in his room this morning," I pass the news on to Jon.

I do not understand. I cannot explain. I cannot breathe.

"We have to get back there immediately!"

Jon sits down. Elias is his roommate.

"Gerber says that both of us would be dead if we had been there. It's a miracle that Elias is alive."

We are both stricken by a sense of guilt. Rather than thank the heavens for not being hit in our sleep by a rocket, Jon and I reproach ourselves for not being there for our colleagues at a time like this. As if our presence would have changed anything at all. As if we could have saved Elias from the tragedy.

"Elias…"

Before I can finish my sentence, I burst into tears. My unflappable friend. A compassionate human being. A man who saw in me his own daughter, the daughter he left behind to come here.

"She's the same age as you and has your personality," he would tell me affectionately.

This time the beauty of the mountains is not enough to stem my flood of thoughts. Instead, the brilliant greens and blue only seem to accentuate the vast melancholy cutting deep through me.

Gerber refuses to give me any details over the phone.

"Once again you've been lucky, kid," is all he will say to me.

He always calls me kid. Maybe it's because I am the youngest, or because I am the only woman, or perhaps because they are mainly military, whereas I am one of the few civilians, and he feels obliged to protect me. Or, as he says, protect me from myself, from my impetuosity.

"Be careful on your return," he concludes our conversation.

At about the same time, a helicopter is shot down as it returns to Baghdad. It is not ours.

On the runway, Riccardo, one of the ambassador's bodyguards, is waiting to accompany me.

"I'm here to give you some moral support. You've no idea what is waiting for you." He does not mince his words. "You might want to have a friend by you."

Riccardo is right. The next couple of hours are destined to be trying. My immediate concern is Elias. I do not care about going to Al Rasheed to salvage whatever is left of my belongings. It does not matter now. I want to go and see my friend.

"He is in the operating theater," I am told, at 28th Combat Support Hospital, the American military hospital.

"He will be in the theater for a couple of hours. Come back later."

"I'll be here," Gerber tells me. "You go and pick up your stuff, or at least what remains…" his sentence comes to an abrupt halt. "I will call you when he comes out. I promise."

The ninth floor of the hotel is completely destroyed. Water drips down from the ceiling. The floor is flooded.

"The antifire sprinkler system is working," Riccardo points out.

"At least something bloody works in this country!"

The corridor is pitch black. I walk gingerly, not wanting to trip. A sad harbinger of what I am about to see.

"Here it is. This is my room," I say to the Gurkha guard who is escorting us. The way he looks at me is telling: there's not much to steal from this room.

I am not in the mood to joke around with this Nepalese soldier who has to guard the floor to prevent looting. The hotel has been evacuated, which makes it an easy target for would-be thieves. My room has been completely gutted. This is it, all I have. It would be useless to try to describe the scene of burnt beds, televisions thrown to the ground, broken glass, splintered walls. The rocket came in through the enormous window and then buried itself in the left corner of the room. I need to sit down but I do not know where.

For the first time in my life, I can begin to imagine what it must be like to see your home destroyed by an earthquake. To have everything one day and nothing the next. And this is not even my house! There is nothing left. The place where I slept for so many nights, the only place where I ever felt safe, has been blown to pieces. I feel as if my privacy has been violated. I can feel the tears slipping silently down my cheeks. They should be tears of happiness. I know that. Tears of gratitude for not having been here. But they are not. These tears are of despair.

After the rockets: Nimmer's room...

"You should gather together what is left," Riccardo tells me. "I'll help you if you want. Or I could leave you alone if you prefer."

I pick up the tattered remains of a book ripped apart by shrapnel. It was on the bedside table.

...my room

"There's nothing left," I say to Riccardo.

I cannot bring myself to sift through the rubble in search of any surviving pieces of my life.

I have got to get out of this hell. Quickly. I will come back another day. On my way to the staircase, I stop outside Elias's room. Jon is kneeling on the floor. He looks utterly helpless. I would like to say some comforting words of reassurance. But I cannot. My eyes fall on the bloodied bedsheet. It is Elias's blood.

"I would be dead," whispers Jon. "He had the presence of mind to throw himself on the floor and drag himself under the mattress when he heard the first rockets. I would have stood up and tried to run away. And now I would be dead."

He gets back to his feet and kicks out at the burnt remains of his room. Then he stops and turns to me and gives me a huge hug.

"If it weren't for you, I'd be dead," he tells me. "You convinced me to come with you to the north. I owe you my life."

CHAPTER 6

Group Spirit

"I should have listened to you. You were my guardian angel!"

Colonel Elias Nimmer's words greet me as I step inside the intensive care ward.

Speaking is an arduous task for him. He was in the operating theater for hours. Nobody knows yet whether he will get back his feeling in his lower limbs. He knows that he could stay paralyzed. He is distraught.

"I wish I'd died," he whispers. "If I cannot walk, I don't want to live."

Winces of pain contort his gentle face. His mouth is dry but he cannot drink yet. I wet his lips.

"Don't say that, Elias. Not even as a joke," I tell him. "Think of your wife and your daughter."

"Please hug me, Anna, I need to feel some human warmth."

I start to cry when I kiss my Lebanese friend's forehead.

Photo: The Wolfpack at the dustbowl

71

"And to think that God had sent me signs," he heaves with great difficulty. He feels the urge to talk and express his version of events. I sit down on the edge of his bed.

"He did everything he could to warn me. But to no avail. I am so bloody stubborn."

Elias is losing heart.

"First he sent you to try to convince me to go away with you. And then…" He has to break off. He can barely speak. I wet his lips.

"Leave it, Elias, you can tell me another time," I tell him.

He does not listen. Instead, he struggles to pull himself up a little but the pain is too much and he falls back with a groan.

"Then I woke up at five in the morning and thought about going jogging. Me! Jogging! What an outlandish thought. I almost convinced myself. I want to lose weight and a half-hour morning jog with the others would do me no harm. But then I thought again and got back into bed. It was as if a voice was saying to me 'Go and run, go and run.'"

If Elias had gone out jogging, he would not have been injured. Indeed, it was the morning jog that saved both Shawn and Scott. If they had been in their rooms, well… Cursed ninth floor.

"We were coming back from our jog. We saw the rockets hit the hotel. We watched them pound into the rooms. There were too many to count." It is Scott who speaks. He is still wearing his jogging clothes. He does not have anything else to put on.

"We stopped dead. Petrified. The great brown building began to tremble. For a moment, we thought it would collapse."

From the descriptions I hear, I still wonder how there were no more victims. Only one fatality and eighteen injured. A miracle. If the twenty-nine rockets had been launched a little earlier, the death toll would most certainly have been higher. The Americans' obsession with their implausible early morning run—at a time when us mere mortals are still tucked up in bed—has been rewarded. I will stop criticizing them.

"Before I went to bed, I took off my dog tags, just as I always do," Elias continues. "In the early morning, though, I heard a voice urging that I put them back on. And so I did. I should have known. Someone was trying to tell me that something was about to happen and that the dog tags were about to be of crucial importance."

It is hard to believe my ears. A huge commotion reigns in this ward of the military hospital, and the noise is deafening. The rest of the group is standing back a bit. This is a moment of intimacy between Elias and me. Why it is me with him, I do not know. I do not think that I deserve it. I should have insisted more. I should have dragged him away. Usually I am such a stubborn mule—why on earth I accepted his "no" as an answer I do not know. How could I have let this happen? I will never forgive myself.

"Anna, you've got a sixth sense. It's not the first time I've noticed it. You always listen to the voice," he continues. "If you aren't happy about doing something, then you refuse to do it. You don't need explanations or justifications. You're able to listen to your heart. Remember these words of mine. Now I must let you go. But Jon is still here."

He falters. He looks around for his friend. Jon comes nearer.

"Keep an eye on her, Jon," he says, before collapsing back onto the pillow. These are the last words I will hear Elias say until we meet again in Washington, months later. Words in person—we will often speak on the telephone.

This same evening, Elias will be flown to Germany with Medevac and will undergo further operations before being sent back home. It will take time, but he will regain feeling and movement in his lower legs. The surgeon here in Baghdad performed nothing short of a miracle. And not only the surgeon—if the shrapnel had got lodged just one millimeter closer to his spine, Elias would be wheelchair-bound for ever. He has hearing difficulties. The pressure of the blast was so great, it ruptured his eardrums. Fairly minor when you consider his miraculous escape from death.

"I'm leaving," Jon tells me. "I'm going with Elias. I want to accompany him to Germany. And then I'm not coming back."

I cannot believe what he is telling me. In one stroke I will lose my two friends. I do something now that I will immediately regret: I plead with Jon to stay here with me. I beg him not to leave me alone here. And then I take everything back.

"Forget it," I say. "Pretend I never said that. I can't ask such a thing. It wouldn't be right. If you don't want to be here then you're right to leave. This isn't a country you should stay in as a favor for a friend."

I back off. I do not want to influence his decision. I would hate to regret one day having asked him such a thing. My conscience would never let me sleep. In Iraq, everybody must be responsible for his own decisions and actions. All night I wait with bated breath. I want to phone Jon and ask him his verdict, but I do not. Tomorrow morning at half-past five, I am over the moon to see his familiar slouching gait at roll call. When he answers with his dubious "Yes, sir," it fills me with joy.

Our long sessions with the death squad have begun. Death squad is our nickname for the psychiatrists assigned with implementing post-traumatic stress disorder, or PTSD, therapy. Damned abbreviations! Oh and how the Americans love them! In order to save the extra two seconds it would take to say a whole word or phrase in full, they shorten and abbreviate absolutely everything. It is abbreviations that are responsible for me arriving at the airport, thinking that I was being taken to some hedonistic venue. As it turns out, Biap is the Baghdad International Airport, not a nightclub! It takes me months to work out that Difac, the place where everyone arranges to meet, actually stands for dining facility. People who work for Stratcom do not build websites but instead work on strategic communication. Right on my first day, I realized I would have to work hard to learn the jargon in vogue!

"Anna, run to the dustbowl, where the wolfpacks assemble, and jump on an MP!"

I stare blankly at Major Jim Hanlon, the enormous man before me giving me these indecipherable instructions. Is it some sort of code? He is not actually speaking at all, but rather yelling these instructions at me.

This will make things easier! At the same time, I am struggling to get into my flak jacket. The first time you try to put one on, it seems ever so complicated. In time, I will be able to put one on without thinking, even in the dark. Looking back, I will laugh at this situation: my sheer bafflement about where I should be going, the jacket's straps tangled in my hair!

I leave the room and start running. The problem is that I have no idea at all where I am running to. I dare not ask. Although I will later learn that Jim Hanlon is a truly great person, at the moment, I am afraid of him. I try to work it out logically. He said dustbowl. In Italian this would be palla di polvere—a bowl of dust. So, I have to run to the bowl of dust where packs of wolves, or branchi di lupi, roam, and there I should jump on an MP. Zero. This means absolutely nothing to me. Is he speaking some strange language? I understand the individual words, but when they are all strung together I do not have a clue. Nothing!

It was about now, on this bizarre first day of work at the CPA, that I meet the tall, skinny doctor who is to become my best friend in this so very different world. Jon smiles when I stop him frantically in the corridor asking him to help me.

"There's a huge guy in there yelling something about wolves, dust... He told me I've got to run there..."

I am in a complete state. The fasteners on my flak jacket are sticking out everywhere. I feel completely out of place. I want to look cool and collected; I do not want to look like a dupe. I am a civilian woman, an Italian woman, thrown in among a bunch of American military. I am worried they will not accept me.

"Follow me," says Jon.

He takes me to the dustbowl, an enormous, dusty car park. How was I supposed to know that every morning after the 7:30 a.m. roll call, everybody is supposed to meet over here? At the dustbowl, the 2nd Armored Calvary Regiment is waiting to escort us, just like a wolfpack, to the Ministry of Health. Ah! I see... dustbowls, wolfpacks, the cavalry. I am quite an imaginative person myself, but this takes the cake!

"Anna, the PTSD people are here to see us," says Colonel Gerber. On see-ing my expression, he adds hurriedly, "Don't make that face. They are here to help us."

"Look who's talking," I retort. I know that he, like many others, is not in favor of these therapy sessions that have been laid on by orders from above. By now, I know the death squad quite well. I was sent to them after the shoot-out and the death of my driver. And even this will not be the last time I will have the pleasure of forming a circle with them. Anyone who has undergone a traumatic event is sent to the PTSD group. Whenever they make their ghostly appearance, I cannot help but raise my eyes to the sky. It looks as if their number increases every time I get to meet them.

"I have no wish whatsoever to speak to them," I whisper to Jon. "I want to resolve everything by myself. In my own way. I've also got loads of work to do. I have no time to waste on this pointless chitchat."

How presumptuous of me. I have to admit that last time, speaking about the event and divulging my fears, did take a huge weight off my shoulders. Perhaps throwing yourself headlong into work hoping to elude your fears is not always the best strategy. And this is generally the path people tend to take here. Maybe this is one of the reasons why so many are sent back home with psychological disturbances. For the first session, the shrinks want to see us all together. The whole Ministry of Health.

"You are the ones most affected." The doctor with the arduous task of heading this collective therapy session has got a pleasing air about her. She is quite likeable.

"Who would like to begin?" she asks us.

Nobody speaks.

"Tell me what you were doing when the rockets hit your rooms," she continues.

Thank goodness Charles is with us, an Englishman with very polite manners.

"I was having a cup of tea," he tells us.

We are all bemused. Is there an Englishman who does not drink tea during such events?

"And what did you do?" asks the doctor.

"Ah…"

Charles Dobson pauses as he thinks things through. He is a serene, composed man who spends his holidays reading Shakespeare and writing poetry with friends in the English countryside. Calmly, he reconstructs the events: "Oh yes, I was on the phone to my wife," he says, enlightened.

We stare at him.

"It was dawn and you were on the phone to your wife? It would have been the middle of the night her time. Poor woman!" interjects Shawn, my Mormon colleague. Until today, I have seen Mormons only in films. I will have many a conversation with golden boy Shawn Stevens. Then, after the death of his friend Saba, his perfectly tailored world crumbles around him. He will become a different person. An angry man losing control over everything. His perfect world, which admittedly does exist in some rare places, is certainly not found here in Baghdad. It is best not to have too many illusions. Better to keep your feet on the ground. Then, when you fall, it is easier to climb back to your feet.

"Yes, my wife is a nurse and had just finished her night shift," Charles continues.

How we laughed that day thinking about their conversation.

"My wife told me I can't show up at home if I've lost any more weight. But I am eating! It must be the stress that is making me lose weight. Oh dear, I'm risking divorce!"

There is no doubt that Charles is impressively skinny. What with his helmet that comes down almost to his chin, he is quite a sight. He reminds me of a turtle, pushing his head out of his shell every so often, only to then return to his sanctuary.

"Imagine your wife's fear," comments the doctor.

"Fear?" asks Charles. "No, no! I didn't tell her that rockets were falling on my head! Do you think I'm a fool?"

"Okay, well what did you tell her?" we ask him, intrigued by this Englishman's unnerved tale.

"I said I had to run and catch the bus."

Run for the bus? We are all speechless.

"I didn't give her time to hear the hullabaloo, I just hung up. I needed to get out of there as fast as I could, but I certainly couldn't tell her the real reason for my rush."

The room erupts with laughter. We are all imagining this wonderful scene of Charles speaking to his wife in cold, faraway England: "Honey, I've got to go. The bus has just arrived. I'll phone you later."

Tears roll down our cheeks. We just cannot hold back the laughter. Maybe these therapy sessions are not such a bad idea after all. We all needed to let go for a moment. Unfortunately, the gaiety does not last long though, and the sullen atmosphere soon returns. Sitting in our circle, we all stare dully again at the floor.

Charles has done his best. Hats off to him for trying. But our expressions have reverted to what they were and do not bode well. I would like to cooperate with the doctor, but not having a story like Dobson's, I would not know what to say. Inside, we are all furious but do not want to admit to it. There will be a couple more sessions before we finally give vent to our anger. It is Scott who lifts the lid off the pressure cooker:

"Do you want to know the truth?" he levels at the poor psychiatrists, who by now are used to our endless silences. He is not speaking, but snarling. We all look up. We have never seen Scott look like this before. He is usually so cheerful, a real prankster, but now he rises to his feet.

"Enough. I've had enough of pretending!"

It is as if a fit of madness has come over him.

"Do you want to know how I feel?" he continues, getting more and more incensed. "I am angry. No, I'm not sad, not depressed, not demoralized, not frightened… none of this shit. I am plain angry."

If our analyst friends wanted some sort of reaction from us, then this is it. They could not have hoped for better. Scott has triggered something and there will be no going back. I know what he is about to say. We all know. We are not clairvoyant, but we know because we all feel exactly the same. Livid. Betrayed. The only difference is that we were afraid to speak about it whereas he could no longer hold it inside him. Even the times when we talked about it, without any of the psychiatrists present, no one ever had the courage to express the real reason for their rage. The cause of so much anguish and desperation.

Scott is now dishing out all his wrath and indignation. He makes it clear who he thinks is responsible for the attack. No, not the terrorists, the insurgents, the bombers, the attackers, or whatever else you want to call them. No. Someone else, way up in the hierarchy of power.

The psychiatrists are shaken. We are all glaring, clenched fists, at the floor. Our jaws tighten. I clench my teeth—my way of dealing with what has been plaguing me for some time.

"I am here to serve my country and president. I am prepared to die, but not to be a futile sacrifice!"

I share his rage, even if love for country and president do not rate that highly in my own scale of values. This is one of the things that separates me from my American colleagues, who, from my point of view, have a tendency to be obsessed by these two values. But this does not mean that I also do not feel betrayed.

"All these months, working night and day and nobody bothers to protect us or guarantee us minimum security."

The psychiatrists look at me anxiously. They did not expect me, the calm Italian woman, to bolster her colleague's argument.

"I am not ready to die. Not for anything or anybody. At least not here in Iraq. But I have always gone about my duties in a professional way and I expect everyone else to, too. Where the hell were the people who should have been looking after our

Comic relief for stress

lives? Were they asleep? Or had they decided there were reasons enough for us to be sacrificed?"

I stop here. I do not know what I might say if I were to go on. On that cursed Saturday, we all knew that with the opening of the July 14 Bridge, sooner or later we would become targets. They had already tried to hit us once before but had not been able to get close enough. Yet then, with free access to the bridge, hurling a few rockets at us became child's play.

On Saturday, October 25, we greeted the news of the bridge's reopening ceremony with anxiety. The bridge spans the river Tigris and had been closed since the fall of Saddam's regime. Its reopening was of enormous symbolic importance and had great political implications. It demonstrated to the world that the situation in Iraq was vastly improving, to the extent that this road could be opened and the curfew could be lifted.

The July 14 Bridge is one of the busiest and most important thoroughfare roads in Baghdad. It gives access to the northwestern zones of the city. What a shame that it is barely a mile from Hotel Al Rasheed, which houses most of the civilians and military staff employed by the CPA. Like it or not, we represent the symbol of occupation, and thus halting our efforts is analogous to blocking reconstruction. A tempting target.

The July 14 Bridge has nothing to do with the French Revolution, but instead marks the Baathist regime coming into power. I always wondered why they did not change its name. They managed, with great effort, to pull down the enormous heads of Saddam that adorned the presidential palace, yet they did not change the name. It is clear then, that this played no part in the de-Baathification process.

"We were the laughingstock of the soldiers," Scott starts up again. "They even asked me what the hell we had done wrong. Everybody knew that with free access to the bridge it would only be a matter of time before we got hit."

"The soldiers laid bets on it at the checkpoints. Some reckoned it would be the first day; others went for the second, and yet others held out for the third. Nobody put money on the fourth." This time it is Chuck who is speaking. "They didn't waste any time. For people whose life motto is tomorrow, inshallah, their timing was extraordinary.

In fact, the rockets were launched at dawn on the second day. Any earlier would have been impossible.

It took us time to regain our faith. As far as I am concerned, I never regained mine. It opened my eyes. The process of disenchantment was long and wearisome. It is not easy to accept that you stand alone and are considered to be expendable. For weeks I pursued meaningless motivations, none of which were sufficient to keep me here. I know the others also had their own phantoms to battle with.

Cannon fodder. We are just fodder for their cannons, just like those poor soldiers who patrol the streets, is my recurring thought. Far from being elite people chosen to reconstruct a country. Far from being workers thought of with pride who should be protected.

"How am I going to reconstruct a health system if two times out of every three I'm being shot at or having rockets fired at me?" I ask Jon in one of our long conversations.

Out of everyone, Jon, the doctor, is the one who struggles most to get over the shock. It was not easy for him to pack up Elias's personal belongings and send them to his family. The wound does not want to close. Weight slips off him before our eyes and he throws himself more than ever into his work. He seems to have lost all sense of danger perception, falling into a vicious circle that will suck me in too. We are losing our grip on rationality. Tiredness can play cruel jokes. And apart from insomnia, it is hard to get any sleep in a barrack shared with seventy other people. There is a constant movement, snoring, alarm clocks going off at all hours—everyone has his own shifts and timetables.

Four long and hard months. No privacy, not a moment of peace and quiet to yourself. Perpetually being surrounded by people could drive anyone mad. Yet how much I learned! What ability to adapt! I take my hat off to it. On the camp bed next to mine sleeps the Danish ambassador, and every morning at dawn, generals, colonels, and civilians all queue up in single file to use the two showers assigned to us. Nobody complains when the hot water starts to run out or when, in the middle of winter, the heating almost never works. What an effort it is to crawl out from under the covers when it is so cold, put something on, and then stand and queue for the showers. And all the time, an armed Gurkha warrior keeps watch.

I am always the last, which means the hot water has thoroughly run out. I can always tell from the gasps coming out from the cubicle. Finally I decide to have my shower when I get back, in the dead of night, even if it means waking up half the shed and tripping over the others. I end up getting to know all the other evacuees' little quirks and peculiarities. Their favorite brands of toothpaste, their morning rituals, the color of their pajamas. Slowly, we begin to form a little community, a group of people who, despite their differences, have shared a harsh, yet extraordinary experience. We form a sort of family, helping each other through the most difficult moments.

"No, I'm staying where I am. I feel safer there," I remember saying to the person responsible for accommodation. He had suggested that I move to a trailer, a type of iron camper with four beds and a bathroom. Sheer luxury, by comparison. He cannot believe his ears. He insists. I do not concede. I will wait until all my friends have moved.

"Anyone who doesn't want to be here can leave," curses Colonel Gerber one day. "I am fed up with seeing you all come to work with your long faces. You look like zombies. Nobody is forcing you to stay. If you want to leave, then just ask and I'll send you home. But if you decide to stay, then I want to see some smiles. Think about those Iraqis out there. They have plenty of reasons to give up. But you don't."

The colonel is right, and I admit that his telling us off has the desired effect. In and among the series of traumatic events, I somehow managed to lose sight of the Iraqi people. They are why I am here. Thanks to them, I rekindled my lost enthusiasm. It was their friendship, their support, and their words of comfort. How much they helped me! And so, if I managed to survive that cursed month of September, I owe it to them. At times I wonder if they gave me more than I could ever give back.

"Anna, I should tell you to leave our country and go back to your family. If it weren't for the fact I care for you from the heart. And that I would miss you too much." This is Ismail speaking, one of my interpreters at the Iraqi Ministry of Health.

"How I wish that you could be relaxed here, travel about without fear, get to know my family, and be a guest at my house. This is not the place for a girl like you."

Despite my best efforts to reassure my friend Ismail that I understand, I do not succeed in releasing him from his feeling of guilt that he and his country have little hospitality to offer me.

"I am a rather particular guest. If you remember, my presence here was… set?" I tell him. "Also, I don't recall receiving an official invitation from you," I say, and smile at him a little deviously.

"Well, I didn't know you then, did I?" Ismail replies. "And how could I have known you? I wasn't even allowed to set one foot outside my country. But now you are my friend, I will give you an invitation. Here it is."

The concept of hospitality is deeply entrenched in the Iraqi people. On several occasions, I have noticed their awkward embarrassment about me seeing their country in these conditions.

"It would be like you inviting a friend over and your house being a mess," he tells me.

A mess… He is always so polite.

Every time I enter their office, both Ismail and Tariq stand up as a sign of respect. These are men of a bygone era, especially here in Iraq. Ismail Habib, tall and thin, is the silent one; Tariq Mubarak, with his round and friendly face, is the chatterbox. Two poets. Two distinguished, educated men, born in the pre-Saddam era. They have survived more than thirty-five years of the Baathist regime and now play an important role in the reconstruction of their country.

It does not take long before Tariq opens up. His black-and-white photographs that trace his seventy years of life in Iraq are more powerful than any narrative. There are photos of a young Tariq with his family; after his school-leaving certificate; during his four years at the British Teachers College; in England for three months of training; with his wife and five children; in India for six months; in Lebanon for work. These men share a common interest in different cultures and foreign countries.

"I've also traveled a lot," Ismail interrupts.

I detect a slight tone of contention in his words. Once again, Tariq has attracted the attention and Ismail resents it. But Ismail is a man of few words, at least until he gets to know his audience. Only then does this wary and refined man, born in the 1930s, begin to speak, letting his feelings run free. His appraising eyes dart about constantly. Nothing seems to pass him by. Nothing escapes his notice even when he is delving deep into his past.

"I studied English literature at night school in Baghdad. I was the oldest of four siblings and during the day I had to work. My family was not rich," narrates Ismail.

"I also came from a large family," breaks in Tariq.

His need to speak about himself and his troubled country is so great that he fails to notice the flicker of impatience in his friend's eyes.

"My parents divorced when I was only six. I had a brother and two sisters. They were young and stayed with my mother. I, though, was to stay with my father, who would later remarry and have four more children. My stepmother hated me. I cried every night. My mother also remarried and had two more children. I saw her on Fridays. Only on Fridays."

A sad childhood. A story of solitude. It reminds me of a Dickens tale.

"But there was a positive aspect," Tariq adds. "Being a schoolteacher, my father fully supported my education, and I owe him my passion for English literature and poetry."

Ismail lets Tariq talk. With a calm, intense expression, he watches his irrepressible friend. He waits for a break in Tariq's monologue before continuing with his own story. What is he thinking about? Where is his mind drifting? Who knows? I would love to open a chink in the contours of his intricate mind. How many secrets. How many spoken words. Is he with us? Where are his thoughts?

"Austria is my favorite country," he says brusquely, as if we all should be keeping up with his mind's excursions. "Clean. Austria is clean. That's why I like Austria. And the people are friendly. And the girls are pretty."

Silence. Pretty girls? Ismail has touched upon a delicate, unusual subject. Especially here in Iraq. There is nothing wrong with saying that Austrian girls are pretty, but…

"I was young and single," he continues. "I was in Vienna for three months. Then I had to come back to Iraq. My mother was dying of cancer. Before the outbreak of the war with Iran, I managed to see a lot of Central and Eastern Europe, such as Germany and Turkey and Jordan. And then it all stopped. No more permission to leave Iraq."

He does not speak about his life during Saddam's reign. All my efforts to get him talking are futile. Tariq is also mute on the topic. He is strangely silent and cautiously evades any questions that have anything to do with the dictator. "Life was virtually impossible," is all he has to say.

This is the result of three decades of terror. People who have lived through such horror will need more time before they feel free to express opinions or make judgments.

"The Iraqis have no idea what democracy means," says Ismail.

Interesting. This shy, skeptical, wary man goes further than one may expect.

"In the name of this grand ideal, every rule is violated, crushing any obstacle that would block its route to power. One day Iraq will be democratic. But it can only happen step by step. First we need to learn to respect human rights. No, sorry, first of all we need to add this magical word to our vocabularies…"

Ismail is obviously moved. Something is stirring within him. It must be the idea of a democratic Iraq.

"It will be people like myself and Tariq who will make the difference. People who have traveled, studied, worked with foreigners, and read widely. We can teach others. We can show them how to live in total respect of human rights!"

All of a sudden, the spark of enthusiasm dancing in his eyes goes out. "But the others don't want to listen."

Ismail looks around him disheartened, looking for someone who can help him out of this bout of depression. "I am unhappy," he adds sorrowfully, just to make things easier.

"You're unhappy?" Tariq breaks in. "How can you be unhappy? We have the opportunity to play a crucial role in the history of our country. And you're unhappy? You've just said it yourself—we are the ones who can make a difference! And then, surely you're happy to have written your final war poem? By the way, Anna, have you read it? It's beautiful."

I sincerely hope this is the very last time Ismail has to write war poetry. He deserves an end to war. All Iraqis do.

CHAPTER 7

Coalition Provisional Authority

Moving from the tents of a field hospital to Saddam's palace is a considerable jump. I am anxious. I am worried that I will not live up to expectations. I do not have the faintest idea what they have employed me to do. Americans do not waste time with useless words. Once you have agreed to work for them, it takes off immediately; things only become clear when you start. Two Nissan Pajeros come and pick me up to take me to my new place of work. A young man with a shaved head hands me a flak jacket.

"From today on, you have to wear this every time you go out. You'll get a helmet too," he informs me. "We're your escort. Two jeeps, four gunmen. These are the rules."

"They don't joke around," whispers Gigi. "Good luck, Annina. Take care! This really starts being a dangerous place."

Photo: The Green Zone

Gigi is emotional. He has lost lots of weight during recent months and is happy to be going back home. The atmosphere has changed during these last days of August. We are all tense, knowing that the field hospital must transfer as soon as possible to a fixed building. Contracts with the Ministry of Health have been finalized. Now we are only waiting for the move to take place. Gigi, who will return to Baghdad in autumn, is to dismantle the field hospital.

"How sad," he says, when I go and visit him with my new American colleagues. "Taking it all down is making me miserable. I almost regret having agreed to do it. I know it has to be done. I know we have to focus our energies on other projects. A field hospital can only ever be temporary, but this doesn't stop it all from being so sad! You know full well how many different emotions were played out here."

The Italian Red Cross was one of the first humanitarian organizations to come to Baghdad immediately after the war. It was also the first organization to take part in the Adopt a Hospital initiative proposed by the Ministry of Health.

"It is not easy to say goodbye to all these people who gave my life real meaning for so many months," Gigi goes on, as if I don't know what he is talking about. But he needs to let it out. "Special friendships were born here. Friendships with patients, but also with Iraqis who worked here with us. Friendships based upon few words, yet strong nevertheless. Yesterday evening we organized a farewell party. What a pity you weren't there too, Anna. We all cried like babies. My bag is now bursting with gifts. You know what I'm talking about, don't you?"

I smile. I am sad. This is the last time I will have the pleasure of speaking to my friend here in Iraq. Indeed, tomorrow he will head a convoy of thirty-five trucks out of the country. Destination: Italy. A group will remain behind, assigned to renovating a wing of the Medical City Surgical Hospital and getting it up and operating. The adoption wing, to be precise. It is a wonderful initiative.

"We like the idea of being able to offer our support by working side by side with the Iraqis," Gigi continues. "Too often, the Italian Red Cross arrives in a country, does what it has to do, and then leaves before things have really got up and running. This time, we've got the opportunity to pass our know-how on to Iraqi doctors and nurses."

The striking thing about Iraqi doctors is their hell-bent intent on learning, seemingly desperate to redeem themselves and demonstrate to the world that they are capable of making up for lost time. They are well organized and willing. All they need is updating on the medical techniques in practice today. They are decades behind. It is hardly surprising, given that they could not get permission to leave the country or to consult books or the Internet. Their desire to catch up is extraordinary, and it will not take long for them to update their skills. All they need are people willing to teach them how to get things on track. People who have faith in their capabilities. The Italian Red Cross believes in the immense potential of the Iraqi medical staff; this is shown by its decision to offer expertise in what is undoubtedly its field of expertise: burn treatment.

Italian hospitals are famous for their technical advances in the treatment of burns. At the field hospital, more than thirty serious cases were treated daily. This truly extraordinary number inspired Italy to put together a highly specialized team of doctors and paramedics aimed at establishing a long-term program to tackle these terrible cases. For the program to be successful, professional training for doctors and nurses is vital. Training courses must be provided both on-site and in Italian hospitals. The greatest obstacle in Iraq is the total absence of an expert nursing body. Nurses play a fundamental and crucial role in the treatment of burn patients, and indeed in the treatment of patients in general. It will take time before Iraqi nurses attain the standards in health care seen in the rest of the world.

Entessar knows plenty about this. Entessar Ebrahim Essa has been manager of the Nursing Department in the Ministry of Health since 2001. She is thirty-five and has a clear goal: taking care of others. After graduating from high school, she decided to enroll at Baghdad College of Nursing. There she completed a four-year course to prepare her for one of the country's most demanding professions. Iraq is certainly not a country where young women seem to have a natural instinct for nursing. Eighty percent of nurses are male.

"It's not a matter of instinct," Entessar explains to me. "As a rule, most families will not consent to let their daughters become nurses. Close contact with a man is deemed inappropriate for a woman, even if the motive is strictly professional. Women who do decide to take a job where circumstances require them to nurse and touch men are no longer respected by society. This is one of the main reasons there are so few female nurses in Iraq."

But Entessar did not care. Nor did her family.

"I was lucky," she explains. "My parents never pressured me to change my mind. They wanted me to do whatever I thought best. This is a relatively unusual attitude in my country."

In Iraq, the general disapproval toward the nursing profession is a real social problem. Its roots run deep and are hard to remove. The previous government had tried in vain to change people's attitudes by increasing salaries for female nurses.

"Although we earned more than our male counterparts, opinions remained unchanged. Nurses were seen as untrustworthy, frivolous, and irresponsible. A couple more dinars did not make any difference."

State salaries were extremely low: three thousand dinars a month, which is the equivalent of two dollars. Nobody could survive on such ridiculously low pay.

"But now things are changing," Entessar continues.

"As manager, I earn four hundred dollars a month, and together with my colleagues and medical staff I am putting the finishing touches on a ten-year nursing reform plan."

Entessar is not married. She will not tell me why, but it is quite likely that the career she embarked on did not allow her to lead a normal family life. Her commitment to the nursing cause is incredible. This middle-aged woman does not regret having opted for a tough, anti-conformist lifestyle with its exhausting and often frustrating workload.

"My main aim now is to modernize the profession's teaching programs," she tells me. "After years of futile efforts, I can finally see a glimmer of hope."

Iraq does not have a standard procedure for training its nursing body, and the health sector often employs poorly qualified staff to save money. Many nurses begin the preparatory nursing program having completed only the six years of compulsory schooling.

"This means they start working in hospitals when they're only fifteen," Entessar tells me. "How is a girl of that age supposed to command respect from a bunch of disparaging men?" A rhetorical question.

Now the curriculum and teaching methods of the various nursing practices are being completely revised. Decades overdue.

"It's a colossal task," says Entessar. "Iraq urgently needs a professional nursing body. So many of its health and sanitation problems would be solved if only it had."

Entessar is fighting a tough battle. She wants nurses to be respected, admired, and fairly and adequately remunerated; she wants them to have the freedom to make decisions in their patients' best interests.

"Anna, do you know what has changed around here over the last couple of months?" she asks. "We know now that if we put in the work, we will succeed!"

"You deserve it," Gigi says, before I climb into the jeep with my new work colleagues. "If I never managed to thank you for everything you did here, then this is a fitting reward for you. My little chickadee! Who would ever have thought it? What am I going to do without you?"

I look at him with concern. What? Has Gigi succumbed to sweet talk?

"You know it yourself," he explains. "It's the stupid things that constantly tumble out of your mouth that I am going to miss."

I feel let down. I hoped I would be remembered for more than raising morale. I know it is not important, but...

"Anna, you don't need me to spell it out to you. I've also passed it on to Rome. If it weren't for you, we would all still be at the airport trying to work out what to do."

It was Gigi who accompanied me a couple of days ago to my interview at the CPA. He was more nervous about it than I was. The very idea of the Ministry of Health's senior advisor asking for his little Annina to go and work for him filled Gigi with pride. I must admit everything that happened was thanks to the faith he banked in me, giving me carte blanche on any decision I felt right. I had an interview with the personnel director, Bob Goodwin. He is a little older than thirty and embodies the perfect young American career man. When he speaks it is as if his words get trapped in his nose.

One day I'll tell him, "Bob, could you please speak clearly. You're muttering!"

We had already met up a couple of times to discuss the details of the contract between the Red Cross and the Ministry of Health. My interview lasted all of two minutes. I got the impression that it was merely a formality. Jim Haveman had already made his decision and had no doubts. He met me, liked me, and wanted me in his team. He is of Dutch origin and this is how this white-haired, seventy-year-old man makes all his decisions. And now he directs the Ministry of Health.

"We are at the ministry every day of the week from 8:00 a.m. to 2:00 p.m. Then we go back to the palace and work there until late. If you don't like hard work, then forget it. Although, you don't come across as being work-shy," he adds, without ever changing either his expression or tone of voice. Jim is a tough man. He is a hard worker and expects others to work equally hard. He rarely smiles. He likes to barricade himself behind a frown and scrutinize whoever is in front of him. He is a man of few words and always gets straight to the point. He does not hesitate in cutting anyone off, mid-flow, if he perceives them to be prattling. His e-mails are devoid of any full stops, capital letters, verbs, or adjectives; deciphering them is a real nightmare. I like his succinct manner. And he likes mine.

"You don't speak much. You don't ask questions. You resolve problems without creating others," he tells me one day. This is one of the rare occasions when he pays me a compliment. "Even if every so often you make me worried. You get shot at and don't falter. They give you a bed surrounded by seventy others and it's as though you wouldn't want anything more. Your friend gets killed and you clam up in one of your bloody silences. Speak, child. Sometimes I'd like to know what's happening in that little head of yours."

I can remember smiling at this remark.

"There, you see? You give me that look. An enigma. You are a mystery for me. Perhaps that's why I liked you right from the first moment."

It is true. Mr. Haveman—this is what I am to call him for the seven months we work together—saw me at work; then, at the ambassador's dinner he asked me to work for him. Just like that. I remember the scene well. It was one of those rare occasions, if not the only occasion, that I went out for dinner. De Martino's cuisine is famous and his crème caramele is renowned all over Baghdad. And that's not to mention the wine. What a shame the food appears a good hour after everyone has started to drink, perhaps as a way of ensuring that guests do not stampede the buffet and devour it in minutes! It is a torrid day in late August and the sweltering guests have begun to drink on an empty stomach, myself included. Jim Haveman approaches. No smile. A grim stare. I never know what mood he is in. He gets straight to the point.

"I've heard you're leaving," he says. I nod.

"Will you come and work for me?"

I look at him in wonder. He repeats the words, irked at having to ask the same question twice. As if his proposal were the most natural thing in the world. I nod again. I am still not sure if I have understood correctly.

"Good. Now we only need to work out how to proceed," he continues. "If you were American there wouldn't be any problem. But seeing as you're Italian… I'll speak to the ambassador and let you know. Ah, I need you to start immediately. For at least six months. Certainly no less."

I am standing in the middle of the hall. A white grand piano, a comical toy dog, a great fireplace, sofas, throngs of people, a glass of wine in my hand, and a floating, spinning head.

"Anna, I'm speechless!" comments Romano Tripodi, the enterprising health director, who has overheard our conversation.

"I am so happy for you! Wow, you've made quite an impression."

I am still not sure if I understand. "You heard it too?" I ask him. "Did he really ask me to go to work for him? Or is it just the wine? No, it's impossible, it's got to be the wine!"

But it was true. The following day I go for a pro forma interview and, in short, I make an official request to the Italian Ministry of Foreign Affairs to go to work as a healthcare advisor at the Coalition Provisional Authority. This is how I end up working for Jim Haveman, the senior advisor at the Ministry of Health, who has the arduous task of leading a team of advisors in the reconstruction of Iraq's health system. Haveman works shoulder to shoulder with the Iraqi minister of health, makes crucial decisions, and is entrusted with deciding on the right moment to hand complete control of the ministry over to the Iraqis. His team is composed of thirty people: doctors, pharmaceutical specialists, bodyguards, logistics people, experts in public relations, military assistants, engineers, and architects. Undoubtedly, efforts to reconstruct Iraq's healthcare system have recently caught the world's attention, but work started taking place much earlier. Every single hospital building, warehouse, pharmacy, even the ministry itself, was completely ransacked. Those who did not witness the looting cannot even begin to imagine the unbridled madness that ran rife through the streets.

Many people are convinced that one of the gravest errors took place on those dramatic April days. Rather than stop the looters, the Coalition Forces' troops simply stood by and watched as the tragedy unfolded. They did not lift a single finger to try to prevent the worst from happening. Orders from above, rumor has it. And this is precisely why the Iraqi people felt abandoned. Even those who had welcomed the arrival of the troops.

"I've still not gotten over the shock of seeing my third floor completely ransacked," says Rassmia. "My nursery, which I had sunk all my energies into for the last twenty-five years, was utterly destroyed. Children are my life. Taking care of these tiny defenseless creatures means everything to me. I was crushed. Seeing my little gem shattered was the end of my world. Day after day, I went back to remind myself there was nothing I could do at all."

Rassmia Abbas Ibrahim is only one of the many bewildered people who simply cannot comprehend how an atrocity like this could have happened.

ER, after the looting, broken and bare

"It's as if everyone went berserk," Emaddin, a young doctor, tells me. "They were ripping intravenous drips from patients, dragging beds out from under the terminally ill, ransacking the pharmacies. And it didn't stop there: they took desks, blackboards, lights, shutters, tiles—everything went. Anything they couldn't steal was wrecked, with a fury and a violence I've never seen before."

I think back to the first time I visited the Ministry of Health. I remember climbing the ruined stairs and not being able to believe my eyes. There was nothing left. Everything lay smashed in pieces. Jim Haveman decided that reconstruction would begin right here in this huge building where more than two thousand people worked. Office after office, corridor after corridor, floor after floor, work steamed ahead and is now completed. The staff are beaming with joy, Rassmia included. She is the director of the new nursery. She is dying to share her happiness with someone and invites me to drink tea in her new office.

"I was only fifteen when my husband died. A fifteen-year-old girl with two children to bring up." Shock… fifteen? Did I hear her correctly? She smiles. "I was thirteen when I got married. My husband was forty. It's really not all that unusual here in Iraq. My oldest daughter was a year old and my youngest baby was just forty days old when my husband passed away. My life's path was decided."

With her mother's help, Rassmia was able to continue her studies, and after graduating from high school she found a job working as a baby-sitter at the Ministry of Health.

"I had enough experience with children for them to give me the job straight away. I had to look after employees' children during the working day," she says. "I started out with the tiniest of rooms, with a couple of toys and four children. Two of the children were my own!"

The Ministry of Health was, and still is, the only place in Iraq where women do not have to give up their jobs when they have a baby. Forty days after giving birth, they can get back to work while their child is put into Rassmia's care.

"I'm very proud to be the first in my country to go ahead with a project like this," she says, satisfied. "In 1979, I was given a large room opposite the ministry. I had ten children ages four days to four years. I knew them all, one by one. I was strict with my rules. Mothers could only come and visit their children for breast-feeding, they had to take off their shoes and hats before they could come in, and they had to respect my schedule!"

And Rassmia's schedule ran like clockwork.

"I prepared breakfast at seven, and then at eleven the children would have a nap while I prepared lunch. At midday we'd all eat lunch together and then, one by one, I'd take them to the bathroom. I'd change their diapers and then hand them back to their mothers all clean, sweet-smelling, and content."

In 1980, the war began against Iran. But instead of her numbers dropping off, Rassmia actually had more children to deal with.

"The mothers employed by the ministry were so happy about having someone to look after their children that nothing held them back from having more babies," she says. "Husbands were happy and didn't force their wives to drop what they'd studied for years. The mothers could feel fulfilled both as mothers and as working women."

Rassmia's activity grew. In 1995, she, along with ten other baby-sitters and seventy-five children, moved up to the third floor of the Ministry of

Health's main building. She was based here until the appalling looting that happened on April 25. And then, some nine months later, another memorable date: January 19, 2004. More than one hundred children entered the new ministry nursery. Five rooms, a kitchen, and three offices. Toys, rocking horses, cloth toys, colored pens, and bright picture books are scattered about everywhere. Tiny school desks with little wooden seats stand in rows, one behind the other. The blue walls are patterned with paintings of Walt Disney characters.

"And all this happened so quickly!" Rassmia continues. "In June, the Coalition advisors provided me with desks and carpets so I could start up again with my little angels. Less than a week later, I already had twenty children! Lots more joined them. Seeing this, the advisors decided to set aside some space for me. And this is it! I never thought I'd ever run a place like this. Not even in my wildest dreams. Look at it! Isn't it wonderful?"

Tears glisten in the corners of Rassmia's eyes. Tears of joy.

Your astonishment when you first set foot in Saddam's presidential palace is unparalleled. Yet soon, the golden doors, lofty frescoed ceilings, azure domes, mosaics, sumptuous divans, marble staircases, and bathrooms, all from the thousand-and-one-nights tales, become part of everyday reality for those who work here, and you soon forget the initial breathtaking marvel. Visitors entering through the main gate are greeted by immense busts of Saddam. They fascinate me. Each one is different. They are to be pulled down. For months there is debate on how best to bring them down without damaging them. I will never understand the reasoning of this decision. They mark part of a chapter of Iraq's history.

"I bet they'll put George W's bust up there now!" I tell Jon, sarcastically. He pretends not to hear.

The dictator's heads lie on the ground for weeks. One rests on its nose and proves to be quite a hit. For a couple of days, having your photo taken next to the fallen dictator is the main pastime here at the CPA. I have often wondered about the fact that these busts were toppled from the presidential palace just days before Saddam's capture. Sheer chance? A coincidence?

"DO NOT URINATE," orders a sign propped up next to the busts. The first time I see it I cannot believe my eyes. Another photo opportunity!

Only people with special permission can enter the Green Zone, where most of the CPA staff live and work. The "red zone" is considered to be dangerous, and venturing through it is unadvisable. How unfortunate, then, that most of the ministries are located in the red zone, which means that every morning, escorted by Humvees, we have to drive through the streets of Baghdad.

"This is Sniper Alley," Major Mike Smith tells me as we head to work kitted out in flak jackets, helmets, and rifles.

"Is there no other route?" I ask, a trifle alarmed. The name is hardly comforting.

"No," is Mike's dry reply. "It's the only way to get to that side of the river."

I will never get used to traveling down Sniper Alley, better known as Haifa Street. Driving through in the mornings and back in the afternoons, my vigilant eyes scrutinize the balconies and rooftops on either side of the wide, never-ending, tree-lined avenue. And then there is the gripping fear every time we pass under a bridge. You never know what might rain down from above as you drive out on the other side. This is the reason we switch lanes incessantly in the faint hope of confusing the "enemy"; hoping to guess the "right" lane as we surface on the other side.

"And then you wonder why we get to work exhausted," I muse, one morning after a particularly turbulent arrival at the ministry.

Goodness knows how many times we had to reverse in panic, then rear up onto the pavement to skirt past suspicious-looking blockages in the road. Everything seems to be permitted. Driving at full speed on the wrong side of the road, causing accidents, mowing down pedestrians, crashing into buses and donkeys. Survival of the fittest. The moment you sit at the wheel, every minor setback can make you lose your mind. Getting stuck in traffic is one of the most terrifying things that can happen.

"Snipers have all the time in the world to take aim," Mike explains, trying to justify his demonic way of driving, always seasoned with a torrent of swear words.

"Perhaps you could moderate your language?" I ask him, provocatively. "I've never heard so much vulgarity in all my life as when I'm in the car with you or Ralph. Sure, I'm happy that you're helping to expand my English vocabulary, but don't you think you're overdoing it just a little?"

After a couple of months I decide to take matters into my own hands. I want to drive.

"You're not able to deal with chaos," I tell Major Smith one morning. "You're confronting it with brute force. There are ways of doing it that don't involve disasters of cosmic proportions, smashed jeeps, deranged screaming, or guns being waved at people. Let me show you how it is done."

"Right, so where was it you learned to drive in a combat zone, signorina?" is Mike's cool, sarcastic reply. How he loves that term: combat zone.

"In Rome."

From that day on, I become one of the most popular drivers. Everyone wants to be my passenger, especially the English, who by now have adopted a coping strategy, keeping their eyes shut during the whole journey.

"She doesn't career about, yet does incredible things that seem perfectly normal," says Jon one day when questioned why he always wants to come with me. Only Dave Tarantino, a doctor who has spent two years in Naples, can beat me in the daily battle down the increasingly panic-stricken streets of Baghdad. And then there is also that hand gesture to contend with. I will have to stop doing it as soon as I go back to Italy, lest I cause a serious fracas.

"Well, aren't they all so rude?!" I can remember thinking, the first time I saw someone do it.

It took me some time to realize that the hand gesture, which in Italy means "what do you want?"(translated very politely), in Iraq is simply a request for someone to wait. Soon I learn to drive with my right hand on the steering wheel and my left at the window unremittingly making the

A $55 million cash run

signal: hand in a cup shape, thumb and fingers pointing upwards and touching at the top.

"Wait a moment, I'm coming through," is all it means here in Iraq. In other parts of the world, I would be in big trouble.

"Anna, I want you to drive one of the jeeps for our dash to the bank," Mike asks me one day.

"Wow! I am reaching dizzying heights on the social ladder." I tease him. "Even though I'm a damned civilian putting all your lives at risk, I sure am making myself useful," I say, mockingly.

I am referring to a confession that Jon made.

"When you entered the building for the first time we were all appalled to see you: what the hell was a blonde, well-dressed woman doing among us, we all wanted to know. I'll admit that it was only for the fact that you don't pose as Rambo and the shirts you wear with your jeans are decidedly more elegant than ours. Not to mention your shoes."

I smile at Jon's words. I had guessed something like this.

"She is going to get us all killed. She has no idea what it's all about. I won't hide the fact that each one of us disapproved of Haveman's decision to have you with us. We asked ourselves how it had happened. How the hell was a civilian going to make any difference? We were wrong. There is no one I feel more comfortable traveling with than you. You know these people better than any of us. You have a communal language with them. I can tell that you've spent a lifetime in these countries."

Perhaps Jon overlooked the fact that Arab blood has flowed through many Italians since their occupation in the eighth century. Every Sunday, clad in a dark chador and with my colleagues all wrapped up in improbable shawls hoping not to attract attention, I get behind the wheel of a black Suburban. We are going to withdraw the wages for all the Iraqi staff working for the ministry. It is cash we are dealing with, hundreds of thousands of dollars that we then have to carry back across the streets of Baghdad.

After a couple of what I like to call "death runs," I refuse to participate again. Far too dangerous.

"Enough! I'm done with this," I inform Colonel Charleston, as we pass through the last checkpoint before entering the Green Zone. I pull the chador off over my head. I am sweating. My heart is in my mouth. There is no point in me continuing.

"I agree that staff should be paid. But there has to be a safer way of doing this. I can't cope!"

"It's a great adrenaline rush, though," is the Marine's response.

I do not reply. There is certainly no lack of adrenaline here. There is no shortage of occasions to get yourself killed in Iraq. But there are priorities that often get lost along the way. It is easy to get caught up in sacred fire and forget what tops—and what must always top—the table of values: life! Life comes first. Everything else is secondary. I have had moments when I have lost control of the situation. I am thankful that the consequences were not irreversible. I have been lucky. I have learned my lesson. It only takes one time to go too far, just as my friend François did, though he was only shopping at the market, buying meat for a party we were having. One time too far, one spray of a submachine gun, a wife without her husband and two children without their father. François. There are many things that help keep his memory alive.

Our thoughts are often pulled in a certain direction, toward a specific person, a significant moment in our life, when we chance upon a particular smell, sound, sensation, or sight. We cannot stop it from happening. We are completely helpless before such an irrepressible phenomenon. The more we try, the less we succeed, and this is why I have decided to let my sentiments flow freely and let my tears fall when I hear that song. Because François is a song for me. A sweet melody. Moving lyrics. I have stopped trying to keep the lump from forming in the back of my throat when I hear it. I am sure that one day, this bitter lump will mellow into a soft smile: the same smile that lit up François's face when he heard "his song."

Because now this is, and always shall be, his song. I still remember the evening when he confided in me. Incredible for a man like him, reluctant to reveal anything personal. I still remember the surreal atmosphere in our jeep as we slipped through the streets of Baghdad in thick, black night. Nobody around. A deserted city, abandoned. Silence. Except for our jeep.

It was not just music: emotions and feelings filled the air. Not just notes. I will never forget it. How could I? It was one of those moments.

"Don't You Forget about Me" is the title of the song. How appropriate. How poignant.

I picture François, who asks us to remember him. When I heard the melody for the first time, I imagined it was his daughter, Chanel, behind the lyrics, begging her father not to forget her.

> *"Mom's sick. She says she can't get up. My little brother is getting hungry. I must go to the village to ask for some food. Would you help me?"*
> *"Sure, Conny. I'll help you."*
> *"I always feel good when you are with me."*
> *"You are my friend, Conny."*
> *"Are you always gonna be that when I grow up? Are you?"*
> *"Cross my heart."*
> *Don't you forget about me. Don't you forget about me. We were soft and young in a world of innocence. Don't you forget about me. Don't you forget all our dreams. Now that you've gone away, only emptiness remains.*

Evocative words, sad melodies. I have put them in my little private treasure chest that I'll open once in a while. I will let the powerful memories fly free. Just to remember, once again, my friend François. I know that he would like that. The man has protected me for months. The man whose duty was to keep me out of danger was the first to let down his guard. Through helping others, he lost sight of himself. We all feel guilty. His colleagues blame themselves for not having stopped him from going to one of the most dangerous zones of Baghdad—Kharada Street—to buy meat.

"It's the best meat in the whole city," he had said to Willy, who had tried to dissuade him. "It's the one time we have a party and I want it to be perfect! I've even had wine sent from South Africa!"

Stubborn man. Bloody stubborn man. Bloody perfectionist. I am full of remorse for having accepted that he organize a barbecue in our honor.

"A real South African barbecue," he says, as we return from the airport. "I want you all to fall in love with my country, and we'll start with the taste buds."

Dead for a barbecue. And we let it happen.

CHAPTER 8

A Tribe in Action

"Hi, how are you?" hundreds of people ask me along the presidential palace's never-ending corridors.

"Fine, thank you…"

I soon work out that nobody is really interested in my state of health or well-being. They ask the question, complete with a cheery smile stamped across their face, then continue on their way, without even slowing their step. Their not slowing down is probably a tactic to avoid having to stop if the person is not feeling fine and wants to speak about it. I spend the first couple of days trying to get my bearings in the labyrinth of this huge, extravagant palace. I give up. I will just limit myself to not getting lost, after the fool I made of myself on the first day.

"Pam, I haven't a clue where I've ended up."

I have done everything I can to avoid telephoning Major Pamela Evans, Jim Haveman's military assistant, to tell her I was stuck behind two doors that could be opened only with a combination code.

Photo: Planning for the Hajj

"Where are you?" she asks.

"I haven't a clue," is my wretched reply.

"Are you north or south?"

Silence. I am not equipped with a compass and even if I looked for where the sun is in the sky, I cannot imagine it would help. Orientation has never been my strong point. Nevertheless, I decided to give it a shot and stick my head out of the window.

"Anna, are you there?"

"Yes, yes. But I can't see the sun."

"The sun?"

"Uh huh. Oh, there it is! I've got it… er, I'm not sure what to do next, Pam."

Major Evans still does not understand what I am doing. She is working hard on it, but it has not clicked yet.

"Let me see… if the sun sets in…"

Pam bursts into a great guffaw. "No!!!" She cannot contain her laughter.

"Look at the number of the room in front of you. If it's marked with an S, you're south; if there's an N, you're north."

I step back from the window and…

"106N. I'm north."

I have to wait for a bit for Pam to come rescue me. She has brought me a map of the palace.

"Perhaps you should have this," she says, with a huge grin.

A couple of months later, I find myself in a similar situation.

"Men's toilets. Women's toilets are north," says the sign. I look around. I am outside. There is no N or S to help me out. Dammit!

"This time only the sun can help you," I can remember thinking to myself. "I'll give it a try!" is my conclusion.

"It's that way," a workman tells me, when he sees me scrutinizing the sky.

I have often wondered why the straightforward arrow system to indicate directions has not caught on here. Likewise, the system of bathroom keys.

"When the door is shut, it means it's occupied," an angry soldier explains to me, moments after I burst in as she is in the toilet. She is furious. I notice her rifle propped up against the wall next to the toilet. I decide this should not be a recurring error. Clocking the time gone by and waiting for someone to come out of one of those damned doors is ridiculous. Only to find out, of course, that after a series of polite little knocks, the toilet is empty.

Another absurdity is the KEEP AWAY FROM THE GRASS sign. I am in a rush. I notice a new sign, read it, continue, and then do a double take. Grass? Keep away from the grass? I must have read it wrong. I go back and check. Yes, I had seen it correctly. I look around, searching for something that might resemble a stretch of grass. Nothing, only sand. Lots of sand.

For the next couple of months, I, along with hundreds of other people, respect the sign and do not trample the sand. During a party, even Bremer enjoys ridiculing the oddities of this country, making particular reference to the ban of walking on flowerbeds. Then, one day, just as suddenly as it had appeared, the sign vanishes. Despite its removal, I notice that we all continue, quite unperturbed, to walk the long way around. You never know, perhaps one day a little tuft of grass might appear.

Tribe. This has been my first impression since the day I arrived at the CPA. I have been summoned here to form part of a tribe and should adapt to its customs as soon as possible. They probably chose me, as I fit the bill, despite some differences. Differences that are bound to become useful to them. If I think of what a unique occasion this is, to be part of such a tribe, how could I step away from such an opportunity? When will an opportunity like this come again?

A tribe can be defined as a group of people who share customs, language, and territory. The definition holds so far. We are enclosed in a fenced-off zone, we all speak English, and our days are ordered according to strict schedules. A tribe should have finite dimensions. Again, this applies to us. A tribe should also have limited relations with the outside world. This is certainly true in our case. It is not by choice, but we are not always welcomed by the outside world. Some of us do decide to venture out beyond the walls of the Green Zone, but lots more prefer to stay here in our pen.

To complete the definition, a large number of tribe members must have an ethnocentric, and therefore slightly distorted, vision of the world. This, too, cannot be disputed in our case, even if that limited view of the world diminishes over time—at least in what concerns the sub-tribe I also belong to, known as the Ministry of Health. To be more precise, I belong to two sub-tribes, the ministry sub-tribe and the Italian sub-tribe.

An example of our slightly distorted perception of things in the early days can be seen in the anti-smoking campaign. This was a campaign initiated by Jim, who in time realized its absurdity and let it fizzle out quietly. Thank goodness for that!

"Iraqis smoke too much. There's not a single person who doesn't have a cigarette in his mouth," he tells me one day, as we make one of our hospital inspections.

He is right. Doctors, nurses, patients, and relatives all have a lit cigarette. On seeing us arrive, they drop them instantly and stub them out with their feet, like children caught with their hands in the cookie jar. Then there is always someone who shoots off to raise the alarm of our arrival. Cigarette butts everywhere, innocent faces. It is so sweet! Jim, though, does not think so.

"Can't they see the NO SMOKING sign?"

I would like to tell him that we aren't in the United States. If you want to ban something here in Iraq, you need machine guns, not signs.

"We need to have a massive no smoking campaign," he states. "Anna, see to it. I'll give you a couple of days to come up with some ideas, and then we'll get everyone quitting as soon as possible."

I stare at him. I disapprove. And he knows it.

"Don't you realize that in ten years time they'll all be dead from lung cancer?" he asks.

"I would imagine they've already got enough problems to contend with, without contemplating their distant future," is my measured response. "It's one of the few pleasures in life they still have. Leave them to it. And this is a non-smoker speaking," I stress.

But this determined, Calvinist American of Dutch origins does not want to know. I am not going to insist. I do not want him to think my skepticism is due to laziness and an unwillingness to prepare the campaign. So I consult two Iraqi advertising and publicity experts, and then two days later I submit my proposals to Jim for his campaign against smoking and its harmful effects.

"What a mess," he remarks, disgruntled.

I know what he means. But after a brief advertising analysis on what attracts Iraqis' attention, this is the result.

"They like this sort of thing," I tell him. Look around you. They never just have one clear message or slogan. Their posters always have lots going on, crammed full of messages, plastered with lots of words. I would also prefer to have just one clear image. But that's not their style. They wouldn't even look at it."

Jim clams up with a pout.

"After all, we want the message to reach them, not us! That's if we still want to do it," I continue.

I manage to convince him, and Jim is a satisfied man. But my posters are never taken out of their drawer. He must have rethought the whole thing. He will never admit that his idea was outlandish in a country like Iraq. I, however, am quite content. In ten years' time, Iraq may have stopped worrying about its daily problems and will be able to focus on secondary issues. And who knows, perhaps my posters might get used.

Jim Haveman changes with the passing of the coming months. I have a snapshot in my mind of him, taken about halfway through his mandate. I do not think he is aware of just how much his hard edges have softened and how much his ethnocentric vision has mellowed over time. He is sitting at the head of a long, crowded table. Tension is running high. Everyone is overwrought and excited. Everyone but Jim. He leans back in his chair and watches the scene with apparent nonchalance: the frenzied comings and goings, the hustle and bustle of enthusiastic organizers, the rustle of maps. Maps of Iraq, Iran, Syria, and Turkey rolled out everywhere.

We are organizing the annual pilgrimage to Mecca. We should actually be helping the Iraqis with the final details of this voyage that every Muslim must do at least once in a lifetime. Jim Haveman has the arduous task of managing the operations. It is a challenge entrusted to him by Paul Bremer.

Moving thirty-five thousand pilgrims who are participating in the Hajj for the first time in their lives is not an easy task. Perhaps this is why the Hajj pilgrimage to Saudi Arabia was off-limits for all but a select few during Saddam's regime. It was the dictator himself who chose who could go, and the total number of pilgrims was extremely low compared to now.

During the meeting—one of the many animated Hajj meetings infamous throughout the CPA—everyone has a query or an insurmountable problem. Jim has that look on his face—I know he is just waiting for the right moment to speak.

"Why don't we all just calm down?" he says dryly. This is his tone of voice that inspires reverence and demands respect. "The Iraqis have been doing this for centuries. They know how it works. We don't need to teach them anything. They'll get there by themselves. Before Saddam got to power, they always got to Mecca and back under their own steam."

Everyone turns and looks at him. The English generals who have come up from southern Iraq ask what he means. They are very concerned, as they are the ones in control of the border that all the pilgrims will be passing through.

"Let's stop trying to do everything better than the Iraqis! We should be giving them a hand, not making their lives impossible!"

I look at him in admiration. Finally, he has got it! Jim Haveman is absolutely right. We'll do it his way. And the pilgrimage to Saudi Arabia could not have gone better. Everyone left, and everyone came back. Everyone is enthusiastic. And everyone wants to go back to Mecca.

Only in appearance is this American so hardheaded. He has just expressed what Thomas Edward Lawrence, better known as Lawrence of Arabia, said in 1917: "Do not try to do too much with your own hands.

Hajis at the gate

Better the Arabs do it tolerably than that you do it perfectly. It is their war, and you are to help them, not win it for them."

The transformation that everyone undergoes during the stay here in Iraq is quite remarkable. Again, always talking about my senior advisor, I have another clear snapshot, this time taken days before his departure for the United States. He has undergone a further transformation. Jim is a great example, as he perfectly embodies the clear-thinking American. The American who never doubts nor wavers. Jim's assignment was putting an entire health system back into shape, and so he devised an intricate plan to go about it. However, as soon as the plan met reality—the Iraqi people and their culture—it had to be radically changed.

Jim is a different man. He is fully aware of the effects that this entirely unknown world has had upon him. It will not be easy to return home with his new, amplified vision of things. For all the tribe members who have freed themselves, if only partly, from their ethnocentric vision, going back to their pre-Iraq worlds will certainly be traumatic. Unfortunately, only a few have experienced such transformations. Too few were open to discussion.

We are at Jim's last official ceremony. It is the inauguration of the new emergency room at the hospital complex in Baghdad. A perfect occasion to act on everything we have all worked toward for almost a year: the transfer of all responsibilities to the Iraqi minister of health. The Ministry of Health is the first ministry to hand over authority and reinstate Iraqi control.

Jim is at the back of the room. The ceremony has begun and he wants to stay on the sidelines. He is just a spectator. This is no longer his show. Taking a back seat cannot be easy, especially after having been the main player for so long. I do not know if I could do it. Ceding power must be difficult; once in possession, nobody wants to let go. He is repeatedly asked to speak in front of cameras. He refuses. He is asked to sit on the front row. He refuses. He is asked to cut the ribbon. He refuses.

And I am watching. Not what is happening on the stage, but him: Jim Haveman. At one point, I think I catch a flicker of a melancholy expression, but I cannot be sure. Perhaps it is only my imagination. I picture him, after a year in Iraq, accepting the challenge of coming here. No hesitation. No doubts. Not too many questions. And today, with no hesitation, no doubts and without posing too many questions, he decides to shrink away from the ceremony, leaving the stage for the Iraqis, the true actors of this show.

But let us get back to the CPA tribe. At dawn, most of the tribe's members go running or lift weights in the gym, their leader included. I must have bumped into Bremer many a time doing his morning jog flanked by a dozen bodyguards, as the sun rises behind Saddam's Victory Arch. The Victory Arch, a monument made with two huge swords, is where the dictator used to organize his grand military parades. People were forced to stand for hours under the blistering sun. Woe betide anyone who dared sit down! Ambassador De Martino told me himself about the horror of having to participate in such events when he came on visits.

I only subject myself to the ritual morning jog during my first phase here at the CPA, the acceptance phase. The moment I am fully accepted by the tribe, I adapt the hours I keep to my own biorhythms.

"Jogging at five in the morning is unnatural," I try in vain to explain to Scott, who knocks on my door every morning. "At such an hour, my body tells me I have to stay in a horizontal position."

What can I do? They love getting up to go jogging and arrange meetings at seven to avoid upsetting the day's plans. I have done my best to explain that this is clearly unhealthy and will mess up their psychophysiological equilibrium. No use at all. We are different.

"In the mornings, you are completely incapable of anything," remarks Jim Haveman one day.

In my frenzied dash for the helicopter, everything that can go wrong is going wrong, and what a disaster! I do not have time for a coffee. Luckily someone who knows me hands me a cup before I climb on board the Black Hawk.

"This isn't morning," I moan, "it's the middle of the night! Look, it's pitch black! And what are you all complaining about? I made it. I'm here now. Okay, maybe I'm not entirely with it, but…"

Jim is looking at me in that scrutinizing way of his. I know I amuse him. And he knows he is able to count on my punctuality, even if I might arrive a bit disheveled.

"Your hair's looking a bit more ruffled than usual," comments Bob. "You've got a tuft that's really being quite anarchic."

"Tonight at one o'clock, when I'm still firmly awake, all bright-eyed and bushy-tailed, I'll get you up on your feet. Then we'll see who's talking about tufts," I retort.

After jogging, there is a healthy breakfast consisting of eggs, ham, cereals, pancakes, bread, peanut butter, and marmalade. By now it is six o'clock and everyone is seized by e-mail obsession. At all times, day or night, we obsess over the thought of missing the arrival of a vital e-mail. Myself included. Even when we get back at the most unthinkable hours, I cannot help but drop past the office and check my inbox. It is an absurd fixation.

From this moment onward, everyone goes about on his own, always in a hurry, obviously. The lunch queue begins at eleven. I am never here for the lunch event, because at the Ministry of Health we work until mid-afternoon. The greatest shock for me is dinner. As an Italian, I absolutely refuse to start queuing for my last meal of the day at half past four in the afternoon. Even though I am now a tribe member, I still have my own requisites. Beginning with the first day, I always manage to slip into the last dinner sitting and show up at the canteen just moments before it closes. The Pakistanis who work at the chow hall know that I always arrive by the skin of my teeth. Sometimes they even leave a plate aside for me with my favorite dishes.

"Ciao, Italian girl!" they say with a smile. "We've still got a bit of chicken Kiev, if you'd like."

Then they laugh at my resigned expression as they hand me my cardboard plate.

"The mashed potato is better than ever today!"

They enjoy themselves with very little. I admire them for it. They do the same thing, day after day, week after week, month after month. Smiling. Happy to see friendly waves.

There is a whole assortment of different nationalities here at the CPA. Nepali warriors, Indian cooks, Pakistani servers, Iraqi translators, South

Green Zone Cafe before it was blown up by a suicide bomber

African bodyguards, American Marines, Italian carabinieri, English diplomats—there is something for everyone! And that doesn't include the Japanese soldiers who never set foot outside. They dress in elegant dark blue uniforms and are always intent on eating. The laundry area, on the other hand, is Kosovar territory. It is exceptionally organized. We are all given a white sack to put our dirty wash in. The sacks are often so crammed full with laundry that the only way to carry it is to throw it over your shoulder.

"Off to the seaside today?" Davide asks me one day. Davide is one of the ambassador's carabinieri escorts and I would reply if only I understood what he meant.

"Today you're all wandering up the corridors with sacks over your shoulders. You're really quite comical."

He points at my laundry bag.

"So what's in it? A towel, swim suit, and tanning lotion?" I laugh.

"Everyone, eh? There's not a single person without a sack today."

Davide is right. It is a Friday morning. On Fridays, we can all go to work a little later than normal. This does not mean we lounge around in bed. Things have to be done. The trailer needs cleaning; sheets need changing; soap needs buying. I look around me and it's true—everyone has a sack of dirty laundry slung over his back. If we were to go to the laundry room on any other day of the week, we would not have to stand in such a queue to hand over our washing. But I make the same mistake each time. Every Friday morning, I find myself waiting my turn.

Thursday evening is the big night out. We refer to it as our "social night" and make the effort to leave the office before eight o'clock to go somewhere for a party. It is a pity that the choice of venues is rather limited, although in time it does increase. The procession begins at Hotel Al Rasheed swimming pool and ends at its nightclub. In spring, however, two Chinese restaurants open up in the Green Zone, as do the Green Zone Café, a pizzeria, and an Iraqi restaurant. A real gust of fresh air.

Keeping my eyes open during these gatherings around the swimming pool becomes a real struggle. It is not that I find the evenings boring but because as soon as I start to relax and tension subsides, fatigue hits me and I find it almost impossible to keep my eyes open. In time, I will get used to my life here and will become better at managing my stress and surviving crises. Consequently, after a couple of months, Thursday evening becomes an appointment I cannot possibly miss. I still remember the first time I ever set foot inside the famous disco at Al Rasheed. Deafening music pours down from above a great marble staircase swathed in a sumptuous red carpet.

"This was Uday's favorite nighttime hangout," Colonel Gerber informs me. He seems to have read everything about Iraq. "You have no idea how many women he raped and threw off the hotel's roof."

The very idea makes me feel sick.

"People speak about a marriage that took place here. Uday saw the bride from his top floor room. He had her husband killed before her eyes, raped her, and then threw her out of the window. From that day on, nobody wanted to celebrate their wedding here."

Horrific stories and their echoes still lurk in the hotel's dark corridors. Bugged rooms, secret passages, places of violent amusements… and the disco where nobody wanted to set foot because it was known to be death's antechamber. But if Uday invited you, there was no way you could refuse. If Uday ordered a man to give him his wife, he should feel honored. If Uday wanted a man dead, he would not hesitate to do it with his own hands. How many crimes have been committed within these walls, how many horrors?

A man of wanton, unrestrained passion, Saddam's firstborn had hands stained with the blood of umpteen murders. His victims were often killed for no reason whatsoever, and many of the murders happened here, between the walls of the gray colossus of Hotel Al Rasheed. His passions included women and football. Those who knew him speak of the lengths he went to procure a woman. Uday had no qualms about using terror and violence; he literally eliminated women's relatives who did not accept his advances. If Uday took a fancy to a woman who lived abroad, she would be ordered to return immediately and her relatives would be given the death penalty.

And then there was football. Uday directed the National Olympic Committee as well as the national soccer team. There was trouble if his teams lost. He would take the defeat out on anyone, from the referee to the trainers to the soccer players. He battered referees to death if they did not favor his team; if football players let him down he forced them to play barefooted with a ball made out of stone.

So it is with some dread that I step into Uday's disco. I am engulfed in a red haze. Everything is flaming red. It is as if Satan himself has chosen the interior decoration—drapes, lights, fitted carpets, and small boudoir chairs. I feel quite panicky. I have never seen so many people crammed into such a small space. There is a tiny dance floor and hundreds of people writhing on it. They are almost exclusively men. There are only a few women, and this makes me feel uneasy. Everyone is staring at me. I would like to disappear but it is too late.

"Are you married?" a tall, good-looking guy asks me.

"No," I reply, marveling at the directness of his question.

"Okay, so I can chat you up!"

Verbosity is clearly not in fashion here! I roam about the disco. People speak to me but I do not hear them. I do not want to hear them. I am absorbed in my own thoughts. I feel as if I am in a film. There it is—the film reappears. If I thought that I had already encountered the different scenes, then I was mistaken. If I thought I had already arrived at the credits and the final "The End," then I could be no further from the truth.

On one corner of the dance floor there is a barefoot soldier in shorts. She is dancing slowly and sensually, driving the men around her wild. They have drunk too much. I leave. I feel numb. I do not know if I am disgusted by it all. I just cannot understand how they manage to be so oblivious to their surroundings.

We are in Iraq, dammit! Has anyone noticed? I need time before I understand and then I will be ashamed of how harsh my initial judgments were. Never judge something you are not familiar with. Especially not here in Iraq, where everything seems to follow its own path. A mistake I will try not to make again. You have to be here for awhile to understand that letting off steam is absolutely necessary. You cannot survive without being able, if only for a couple of hours, to escape or at least cut yourself off from the difficulties and atrocities that we all have to contend with. Everyone has his own way of doing it: going to a disco, working out at the gym, drinking a glass of whiskey, playing a game of cards, munching a tube of Pringles. Unfortunately our choices are rather limited here in Iraq. I only need a couple of weeks to catch on to this.

In fact I, too, will flee to this very same disco after my driver's assassination and after I have looked death in the face for the first time in my life. I will dance all night. By myself. Alone, surrounded by people I barely notice. Dancing in Uday's aura.

Isn't destiny ironic? Coming here, to this disco, to find comfort from the horrors all too often found on the streets of Baghdad, in a place where so much evil was perpetuated. Today we seek solace. Here, at Al Rasheed's nightclub, I will try to escape from the memory of the pool of blood, the interrogators, and the therapy sessions. And I will come to understand many things.

A Miraculous Escape

We leap into the jeep. We are in a rush.

This is our first mistake. Never be in a rush in Iraq. Things cannot be organized haphazardly in this country. Most times when people are killed or have a close encounter with death, they have underestimated something and have made a mistake. Mine was a close encounter. On that cursed September 30, some were lucky like myself; others were not.

There was someone, though, who tried to stop my madcap journey.

"Anna, you know the rules," Colonel Gerber warns me. "Two cars and four shooters." The stern-eyed colonel is usually unwavering, but today he gives in to my insistence.

"Anyway, it's nearby," I tell him, as I put on my flak jacket. I want to reassure him. For days we have been trying in vain to visit the most important tuberculosis treatment center in Baghdad; we would even go on foot.

"Walk? No way!" This time, Gerber balks. "I'll give you two cars and two FPS guards. Go and call the drivers."

Photo: With a friendly shooter

FPS stands for Facility Protection Service. In Iraq there are about forty thousand of these guards whose task is to protect the different government buildings. Each ministry has its own FPS and selects and trains its guards according to guidelines provided by the Ministry of the Interior. After they tried to kill me, I went on to read more about these mysterious figures. I learned that each FPS has to undergo three days of intensive training. Gosh! A whole three days of training! Everyone already knows how to shoot, but three days of training is a bad joke. The selection criteria require first of all that candidates demonstrate outstanding fitness. I don't think so. Most of these youngsters would rather get stuck in a lift for hours at a time than accompany me up flights of stairs. By the time they reach the second floor, most would be at great risk of having a stroke.

"It's dangerous to walk up the stairs. You could get stabbed. We'll take the lift," Marwan tells me one day. I protest vehemently. I would prefer to avoid being stuck in one of those horrible smelling lifts. I have already had one experience and am in no rush to repeat it.

"It's for your own safety, Sir!" persists the congenial FPS.

How many times have I tried to explain to them that I am not a Sir? What futility. It's their way of showing respect. I have to accept it, and yet every time I hear it I have to suppress a smile. I will miss it. Marwan has touched the right button, and he knows it.

"Security?" I ask him. "Let's get the lift."

What a pity that even climbing stairs constitutes a grave risk in one's life. Strange though, that when it comes to walking down the stairs, this risk seems to evaporate completely. I shake my head. Marwan grins. He has duped me once again.

The FPS selection process also requires that a candidate have good moral attributes and no criminal record. Interesting. I would love to know how they evaluate a person's moral attributes. Are they given a quiz? And how about criminal records? Everybody knows that in Iraq there are no records to document criminal histories. Saddam opened the prison gates and let all prisoners walk free. Thousands of killers poured out onto the streets of Baghdad. So just how does one go about recognizing a killer? Impossible. As long as they don't get caught committing another crime, and by then it's often too late.

The sight of an FPS on a ministry corridor, gun in hand (and often without the safety catch in place), makes my blood run cold. From now on, after this late September day, every time I come across an FPS, I will want to throw myself to the ground. The FPS guards are a courteous bunch. With their infantile smiles, they greet me each morning with a cheerful wave of their AK-47s, rather than a simple hand gesture. And I gape, eyes wide in terror, waiting for the blast to hit me. They laugh. They know that it takes every ounce of my courage to walk up the corridors. They all know about my misadventure. And they are sincerely sorry about what happened. So they wave their guns at me, eager to show me that they are not like the assassin who tried to kill me.

I must have repeated what happened on September 30 dozens of times, first to investigators, then to psychiatrists. I decide not to say anything to people at home. They will find out about it months later when everything is recounted in minute detail in one of the best newspapers. Nightmare situation! No one at home will ever trust me again, and who could blame them?

Almost immediately, I sense that to get over the shock, I must write it all down and reconstruct everything, detail for detail. This is my strategy, unlike my other colleagues involved in the tragedy who want to blot it all out. Everybody reacts in his own way. I am obsessed with the idea of understanding what happened to me that day.

"It was an accident," the investigator assigned to the case tells me.

Only a couple of hours have passed, and yet he's already made up his mind about what happened?

"An unfortunate accident. Something like this was bound to happen before long. I am sorry, Miss. In Baghdad you have to come to terms with things like this."

Before going to sleep, I want to see the Land Cruiser again. Chuck Fisher comes with me. He does not want me to go by myself. He is worried that I might break down. I look at the bullet holes in my headrest. I touch them.

"Be honest, Chuck. Was it an accident?"

Chuck does not answer me, but his silence betrays what he thinks. I go to bed. I relive the moments, again and again. I want to relive them, even if I am not sure that it is the right thing to do. Sometimes I break out of this masochistic rite. I feel as though I am fainting. When I wake up in the morning, I am resolute and clear-headed. Accident? I have never heard so much nonsense in all my life. I march into Colonel Gerber's office. He is not used to seeing me this early without a cup of coffee in my hand.

"Sir, I have to speak to you."

"When you call me Sir, it means it's serious," he says in an attempt to play things down. But he does not even need to look up. He understands immediately. He has also spent a sleepless night thinking about it. He knows that I don't swallow the story about it being an accident.

"You're right," he says. "The case hasn't been archived at all. On the contrary. Get ready for this. It's not pretty. We tried to keep you in the dark. We wanted to protect you. But at this stage I can't hide the fact that the secret services are working on the case."

Much to his surprise, I am relieved by this. If I have to come to grips with demons and anxieties, the last thing I want is to be mocked. I want to face up to things, not flee them. Psychiatrists are called in. They want to see me every forty-eight hours to monitor my health, both mental and physical. Often psychological stress manifests itself through physical symptoms. Nausea, vomiting, insomnia, dizziness, depression, panic attacks, fainting, migraines, the list seems endless.

I find my solace early on. I write. I write an e-mail.

"E-mail to myself" is its title. I will never send it. This is my way of freeing myself from the horror, fears, and uncertainties. I do not speak to anyone. I know that they are all worried about me. They are especially worried about all my silences, and for having endured the shock without any obvious repercussions. My behavior puts my colleagues on guard, even if I have won their unconditional respect. The way that I withdraw myself without complaint rather than vent my feelings in long outbursts makes them concerned, but in my shoes, they would do the same. I throw all my energies into my job. I smile. Life goes on, if only because of a miracle. I can say this with confidence: I have never received so many pats on my shoulders.

They observe me, often silently. I know it and am grateful. I do not think that I have ever told them how much they have helped me. I know that being able to count on the support of this close-knit group will help me to recover. I know that I do not even need to ask. They will be there for me.

I am sitting on the left side of the back seat in Mr. Haveman's white Land Cruiser. He is in Madrid for the International Donors' Conference and we have decided to borrow his car.

"How come every time I go anywhere you steal my jeep?" he moans on his return. "You wreck it every time, and this time is no exception. Look! It's in pieces!"

He is right. Last time he went away we had the great idea of fixing the side of the jeep. Jim gives me a big hug. He is moved. They have told him what happened, but until he sees the bullet holes, it does not sink in.

"I would never have forgiven myself. You know that, don't you?" It was I who wanted you here. I feel as if I have fatherly commitments to you. I have to look after you."

There are five of us in the jeep. Next to me, seated on the back seat, is Maurizio, an Italian doctor on his first day of work in Iraq, and the FPS guard. This young Iraqi guard is nervous. Our eyes make contact a couple of times before he glares fiercely out of the window, ignoring me completely. His behavior is hardly comforting, and both Maurizio and I notice it immediately.

"If he is nervous about protecting us, how are we supposed to feel?" I say to the tuberculosis specialist. "Let's hope that he doesn't need to do any shooting. He doesn't seem happy with that thingamajig," I go on.

We both laugh. Perhaps not a good idea. We have made him more nervous.

"I guess we should stop laughing. We don't want him to think that we are making fun of him. They've got delicate egos, this bunch, and when they're holding submachine guns..."

"Yes, but they've put us with some jumpy guy," continues Maurizio. "He can't keep still!"

We sit in silence for the rest of the journey. Then, as soon as we arrive at our destination, the FPS guard leaps out of the jeep.

"What's he doing?" Maurizio asks me.

"He'll be helping us park..."

I do not even finish my sentence before all hell is unleashed. An ear-splitting sound. I throw myself to the ground. I feel as though my head is being drilled into. My head is going to explode. Only when it is all over do I realize that the blow at the nape of my neck was not just in my imagination. It was the impact of two bullets smashing through my head rest.

Only the previous day Colonel Chuck Fisher had issued this warning: "The moment you hear something, get to the ground. Don't move! Don't look to see what's happening." I had listened to only the first part of his briefing. The next part, about what to do if your helicopter catches fire or crashes, washed right over me.

"As though these things are ever going to happen to me," I remember thinking. "It's not as though I'm a soldier. This Rambo always has to be at the center of attention. He loves terrorizing people."

But if I hadn't taken that superman's advice, I probably wouldn't have dived for the floor as fast as I did, and that feeling that my head was being blown off would have been for real. Horrifically real.

"Keep your head down!" I yell to Maurizio as he throws himself on top of me. He is trying to look around to figure out where the spray of shots is coming from.

"Don't! They'll kill you," I scream.

"They are going to kill us anyway," he answers in utter panic. "Shit."

But this is not what I had planned. How could this happen? Were they waiting for us? How did they know we were coming? These are the thoughts crashing through my head during these endless fragments of time: I can't stand this. That shrieking gun noise is killing me.

Later, during one of our collective psychiatry sessions, I will learn that each one of us was affected during the shooting by different experiences. It is my head that is echoing. I won't learn why until later, when I see the Land Cruiser. Mike, who was sitting in the front, is tormented by the smell of the gunpowder. Maurizio? I don't know. Out of the three of us, he is the one who struggles most to recover. But in fact, Maurizio hasn't recovered. He has what the doctors would call post-traumatic stress disorder; he is paranoid about simple things and sleeps every night in a different place, yet he takes huge and unnecessary risks when he could very well avoid them, as if his mind was all of a sudden surrounded by thick fog. And Mike will die of a heart attack in June. We find him dead one morning in his trailer. Working too hard? Too much stress? Too many difficulties to face? Probably. I suppose we'll never know.

"Anna, get out of there." This is Kees, my Dutch colleague, returned to Brussels, who calls me the moment he hears about Mike's death. Mike, his irascible Irish friend, was never afraid of speaking his mind, nor cared about the consequences. He always believed in what he did. He died dreaming. They had only just renewed his contract. He was over the moon and his heart just could not cope with such happiness. This is how I choose to interpret his death. Another friend to put in my casket of treasures.

"You and Mike were the veterans of the group. You've been there longer than anyone else. Look what happened to him. You don't want to go the same way, right? Get out!" Kees is genuinely worried. "I'm telling you this as someone who spent years in Afghanistan and got through all its wars. But this is different. I'm telling you. You need a break. Then, if you want to, you can go back."

But now I am still at that fateful September 30.

The window on my left has been blown out. I am covered in shards of glass. We are being shot at from my side. The shooting continues. It seems as though it will go on forever. I have no idea what the hell is happening in the front seats. Nobody speaks. Nobody screams. Nobody tells me what I should do. I only know that there is no way I can get out from my side of the jeep.

"If I try to escape from here they're going to kill me," I remember thinking. In my imagination, I see an army of snipers lying in wait for me on the roof of the house opposite us, waiting to send me my deathblow as soon as I set foot out of the jeep.

"We've got to get the hell out of here! If they hit the fuel tank we're going to explode." This is Maurizio speaking. He's decided to run for cover.

"No! Don't do it!" I shout.

It is too late. He is already running. I decide to follow him. I do not fancy the idea of being blown up. I would prefer to gamble my life with the snipers instead. I get out and run for it. This is the first time I am literally running for my life. I drop low, crouching. It seems to be the rational thing to do. I get to some building, run inside, and cower in the furthest corner from both the window and the door. I make myself as small as possible and wait, wait for them to come and shoot me at point-blank range. Outside, blood-curdling screams take the place of the gunfire. I don't move. There is no way I want to get out of my corner.

"Get out of there!" shouts Ziad, the driver of the other jeep. I do not move.

"I'm waiting for the American Force Protection," I tell him.

In my mind, it is only moments before the Apaches arrive to chase the criminals off the roof.

"We can't stay here. It's too dangerous," Ziad yells at me.

He makes me follow him. I have to trust somebody. Ziad seems to be the only one who has kept his calm among this hellish panic. Mike appears unexpectedly from a building where he had gone to find shelter.

"You left me behind, you bastards!" he rages.

Mike always finds controversy, even in these marked moments. It is only now that my eyes stumble upon the pool of blood. Blood is dripping out of the front seat of the jeep. I am motionless. I can't comprehend. Mohammed! An ambulance arrives. They throw the driver's lifeless body into the back and screech off, not even closing the door properly. Dangling out of the back are the legs of the young Iraqi.

"Get in the jeep!" Ziad orders me. "We have to get out of here!"

He is right. Around me things are happening that I can barely register. There is a young man lying on the ground. His face is covered in blood. He is being beaten. I will learn later that he is our guard. I am so dazed that I do not step forward to try to halt this seething mass of incensed people. Even Ziad jostles his way through and kicks the man. I do not move. Not even the screams of the young man are enough to lift me out of my torpor of numbness. It seems like one of Dante's rings of hell on earth.

The ambulance pulling away, the broken body shoved in as if the vehicle were a sack, the splotches and stains of blood, the screams, the violence, the faces contorted in cruelty. These are images that keep coming back.

Mike climbs into the driver's seat. We soon get lost. We are prey to the utter madness of it all. I don't know where we are, and don't even try to help Mike find the right road. It is such a relief to pull into the ministry. Down in the underground car park, the others are all waiting for us. I climb out of the jeep.

"You're covered in broken glass," a voice informs me.

"Are you hurt, Mike?"

"No, it's Mohammed's blood," answers the doctor.

For the next half hour, I wander about like an afflicted soul. First I seek refuge in the office. There I am suddenly seized by claustrophobia and want to be among people again. I get out my phone. I feel the need to speak to someone. No. I don't think this is a good idea. So I go back to the car park. I want to see the jeep. I want to understand.

"Where are you going?" demands Scott.

He is worried I might do something crazy. He tries to hug me but I step away. "Forget it, Anna. Don't go. It won't help."

He tries to stop me from seeing the bullet-ridden jeep and the blood. But I will not be stopped. Now I am looking straight at where I was sitting, and I understand. There are two holes, neat and precise, in my headrest. One is at neck height and the other one is slightly higher. I feel myself slipping away. That's why my head thundered with a screeching noise.

The ground is sliding away from me.

"A miracle!" I gasp as my chest heaves.

"You can say that again. One day you'll tell us how you did it. You definitely can't say that you have slack reflexes," says Scott, stuck to my side like my shadow. I begin to cry, relentless, uncontrollable tears. This is the first and last time I lose control.

"Kid, do you think you can go out? You have to go back urgently to the CPA."

I nod my head. I put on my flak jacket. They are still hosing down the jeep, cleaning away the blood.

"No, get another jeep. You can't get back in that. That's enough for today."

"If God kept me alive in this seat a couple of hours ago, I can't see how he would let me die now," is my adamant response. Such foolproof reasoning.

That Land Cruiser would later become mine. Haveman would give it to me even if he wasn't happy that the bullet holes were good for me. I am convinced I was saved by a miracle and thus the holes cannot be anything but beneficial. They might even stop me from going after more trouble. I know myself too well.

The jeep's roof is riddled with bullet holes.

"This is yours," Ziad says, holding out a bullet. "It got lodged in here. I followed its trajectory. You're a lucky woman, Anna."

I take the bullet and touch it for the first time. It is the first of many times. We'll get to know each other well, before it gets confiscated from me in Amman airport. It will become my inseparable companion for my following nine months in Iraq.

It is not easy to explain what is going on in my head in the coming days. I don't cry. I don't lose heart. And it's not a mask that I decide to put on. I'm not pretending. I go about work with a smile on my lips even if what happened is never far away in my mind. But I am aware of how much I am keeping myself to myself. I'm fine when I'm in company. But when I'm on my own, I have my worries, and the phantoms reappear.

A good thing about this place is that nobody is ever alone. Even when we would quite like to be. The concept of privacy is a remote mirage that we all dream about, yet we all forget it very early on. The total lack of privacy is difficult for everybody and gets worse when the Al Rasheed is destroyed and we all have to pile into barracks or into the palace's chapel. At certain times, though, it is a great relief to not have to be alone. Is this running away? Perhaps. But survival is the important thing and everyone has his own way of going about it. There are no magic wands here. Everyone has to stake out his own particular path.

I remember a conversation I had with Andrew Burns, a young advisor for the Ministry of Finance. The memorial service for François has just been held and I have withdrawn into one of my silences. No tears, no sobs, no heart-rending scenes.

"How are you doing, Anna," Andrew asks.

He knows how much I liked my South African bodyguard. Now he wants to be close to me in a moment that cannot be anything but difficult. The umpteenth of a long series of difficulties.

"Fine," is my reply. A little too curt to be believable. "I'm fine."

Andrew is getting frustrated.

"Do you really think that you can hide every time behind that ready-made phrase? Do you want to stop dodging reality?" he demands, angrily. I want to tell him to leave me alone, but I know that he is trying to help, and deep down I'm grateful.

"I'm not dodging anything, Andrew. I just cope differently from others. I'm looking ahead," I tell him.

"Coping by not facing the facts," he insists.

"Why do you say that? Just because I don't cry or break down in public, does that mean that I'm not facing the facts? What would you know? How do you know how I am in private?"

"I just know that sooner or later you are going to have to face your demons."

"Says who? Where does it say it?"

"Everyone knows it!" asserts Andrew.

"Now you're the one with the ready-made phrases. Everyone knows it. Who knows it? You are speaking rather oversimplified psychology here. Things are much more complex."

The conversation has taken an awkward turn. I know it and would like to repair the damage. I certainly had no intention to argue with Andrew, who is really only trying to be a friend.

"I'm putting it all in my casket of treasures," I try to explain to him. "The casket that I spoke about during the service," I continue.

"A casket that sooner or later you're going to have to open," he remarks.

"No, that's not what I intend to do. Not at all!"

"So what would you like to do?"

"When all of this is over, once I've finished with Iraq and its dead, I'll go to the sea and release it as the Indians release the ashes of their dead into the Ganges."

Andrew looks at me perplexed.

"I think it's nonsense," he concludes.

"Not for me. One day, when I'm back home, I'm going to take my little casket and, with a smile on my face, I'm going to let the waves of the sea take care of all of my friends."

I'm certain about this. Just the idea that one day waves will cradle my casket kindles in me a sense of serenity. Andrew is like a younger brother to me. It strikes me as odd that this time it is he who is trying to help me. Andrew is brokenhearted and he wanders awkwardly through a world that is too difficult for him. He is the protagonist of a common love story cast against an aberrant reality that leaves no space for broken love. His girlfriend left him when they met up in Turkey. I remember Andrew's enthusiasm when he left to meet her, and his lost, hopeless look when he returned from that holiday.

"I wanted to marry her. But she left me," he tells me wretchedly.

"How long were you together?" I ask him.

"We'd known each other for a couple of months," is his reply.

I don't think I heard correctly. What? A couple of months? Marriage? But Andrew is quite a character. He is religious almost to the point of exasperation, and it seems that everything revolves around his church in the United States. A trait that to me is typically American. It was at church where he met the alleged woman of his life and he did not hesitate in asking her to marry him. Thinking about it, she decided to escape from such serious intentions. A textbook case.

"Sir, I want to see my assassin," I announce to Colonel Gerber.

Any other request would have been more expected. He looks up and winces.

"No!"

If the colonel thinks that I'll leave just like that, then he is quite mistaken. Even if his response does not exactly leave space for discussion, I'll at least try to get him talking and wrangle things a little. A curt "no" might work with fellow military, but not with me.

"I insist," I tell him. "If I want to get over it, I'll need to see him."

After his refusal, Gerber turned back to his work and does not notice that I am still standing behind his chair.

"You still here, Anna? Don't you know that I hate it when people stand behind me?"

"Luckily I've only been here a moment, Sir. But I'm not going anywhere."

"You stubborn thing! What on earth are you saying? What do you think you might solve if you go to prison to find him?"

Colonel Gerber is convinced that the motivation behind my request is a desire for revenge. Well, I may not be a saint, but that is not my intention. I am also amazed by my reaction.

"I only want that man to look me straight in the eye and admit that he made a mistake," I attempt to explain.

By now the whole office has turned to listen.

"I want him to know that everything that he might have heard about us is not true. Or at least not in my case. I am an Italian civilian who was only going to a hospital. I want to explain to him what I do."

This is the first time that I have spoken about the evil act for days. They all listen to my outburst. They do not approve. I can see it in their eyes. They probably think that I would lunge at the killer's throat and try to kill him.

I get the impression that the fact I am a woman irritates him. He is irritated that a woman can push others around. I'm sorry about this. But this is not what I had in mind.

"Anna, he had already decided to kill you, even before you laughed at him. You said yourself that he was nervous," Gerber points out.

"Anyway, we are speaking about people who have been brainwashed. The only way to get them to change their minds is to meet them. I am asking for your help. I want to meet him."

"I can't possibly imagine how it could do you good to meet the man who wanted to kill you. I know you're strong. But don't push yourself too far in that direction. Once you have crossed the line and fallen over the edge, there is no going back."

The colonel is seriously worried.

"You are useful here. We need you. We don't want to send you home because of psychological disturbances" he goes on. "We all think that you will cope just fine. The psychologists are also positive about your state of health. We're all amazed at how you've managed. But you have, thank goodness. So forget about your crazy idea about going to find that man in prison."

And with these words, the colonel, who had a miraculous escape himself only months ago, gets back to work. He knows what he is talking about. The scar that runs down the left side of his forehead does not let anyone forget. The bullet literally grazed him. If he had not turned to speak to Major Hanlon, the bullet would have struck him head on. It would seem that we who work for health care are protected by a loving guardian angel. An extremely busy angel, who would probably enjoy a moment of ceasefire.

"Anyway, I've had enough of this case!" he says just before I leave the room.

Who can blame him? As well as pursuing this investigation, Gerber has also been roped into something decisively bizarre. "Not only does he shoot at us," he tells me. "But then we also have to pluck him and his family out of danger!"

There would have been a bloodbath had the colonel not intervened. He somehow managed to stop the dead driver's relatives from heading to the assassin's house, looking for revenge.

"It would have looked like a slaughterhouse. It's one of their ways. If you kill my son, I'll kill yours, and perhaps another one for good measure,". Gerber explains. "But money solves everything," he adds with a glint of irony. "A generous handout and everyone is happy! So they say. And the pain wanes."

I will never see my killer. I stop insisting. I don't know how I would react. Best not to tempt fate. I'm here to work, not chase demons, which luckily have decided to leave me alone.

At least for now.

CHAPTER 10

Father of Strangeness

Ex-political prisoners and disabled people. These are to be my friends for the coming months.

"We need to start thinking about how to help the thousands of torture victims scattered all over the country. Yesterday evening, I met a really interesting character. Anna! Jon! I want you to speak to him and decide how we can give him a hand. He's an idealist!"

Once again, Jim does not waste words. He does not expand further. Neither Jon nor I have really understood what he is talking about, but we refrain from asking him for clarification. I get him to jot down the character's phone number and then disappear into my office.

Abu Ghraib death row

"I came back to Iraq to help people like myself who were tortured under Saddam's regime. Abu Ghraib was my home for a long time," says the voice on the telephone. "I am a psychiatrist. I think I could be useful to you."

I cannot wait to meet him. Jon, too, is impatient. We have been visiting Abu Ghraib for months now, trying to get its heavily damaged hospital back into working order.

"It would be good if he'd accompany us to Abu Ghraib, as long as he's happy to do so," I say to Jon.

"Phone him and ask."

"No, I don't think it's a good idea. He probably never wants to set foot in that place again," I say.

"It never hurts to ask," Jon points out.

"Visiting the death chambers with him would be quite something," I muse.

My wish is granted. The following day, Jon, the psychiatrist, and I are on our way along what is considered to be the country's most dangerous road, heading to one of the darkest places in Iraq's history. Saddam has gone, but Abu Ghraib prison still rises up threateningly amidst a desert plain. Abu Ghraib is intimidating and ferocious, its outer walls punctuated with high towers. This is the prison that, sadly, has become infamous.

Abu Ghraib. Every single Iraqi knows this name well and still shudders at its mention. Saddam is gone, but Iraqis are still reluctant to venture near.

"Father of Strangeness" is the literal translation of Abu Ghraib, Iraq's largest prison. Dr. Badea Khalaf is willing to go back despite the fact he has many a reason to stay away. Condemned to life imprisonment as a political prisoner, this psychiatrist is a lucky man, as his name was among those to whom Saddam granted an amnesty after the Iran-Iraq war.

"My older brother wasn't so lucky. Saddam ordered his execution in 1976," he relates. Badea had to flee to London but has since returned to his homeland to assist in reconstruction.

"My younger brother was also imprisoned here," he continues, as we near the prison's walls. "He was only sixteen years old when the Secret Police came for him. His crime? He'd spoken words against the regime during the funeral for our executed brother."

It is hard to hear Dr. Khalaf. He has a deep voice and speaks so quietly that his words seem to disappear as though they had never been uttered.

"I was accused of organizing a coup. It was not the first time I had landed in serious trouble," he says. "I had been arrested back in 1978 for being a member of a secret organization. I was tortured for seven days and was forced to sign a statement saying I would not participate in any illegal activities."

Dr. Khalaf's voice does not waver as he speaks. Even when he starts describing his tortures, his tone remains steady. Badea Khalaf does not give details. He does not want anyone's pity. His brilliant eyes, his soft smile, and charming manners do not reflect his unimaginable sufferings of the past, but speak of his iron will to forge ahead. An iron will to go forward and assist in reconstruction efforts, despite the tragic past.

"I was forced to join the army during the war against Iran when I completed university. After I'd fought for two years, I was arrested in 1986. I'd been an active member of a political opposition group since 1980. It was an underground movement and was completely wiped out. I was held at the so-called Security Headquarters in Baghdad for seven months and was subjected to daily torture and harsh interrogations."

Once again, Dr. Khalaf does not dwell upon details that he probably feels are of little importance. He is well aware that people who have never lived in Iraq have an almost morbid curiosity about the torture practices inflicted on Iraqis. He is careful to avoid letting the conversation slip into such superfluous details.

"I was put in front of the Revolutionary Court. This was a secret yet official court created by Saddam in 1969. It operated right on up until the regime collapsed. I clearly remember the row of judges, all clad in military uniforms! Their sentence was clear—life sentence."

Badea Khalaf was taken to Abu Ghraib.

"I was glad," the psychiatrist continues. "Being taken to prison meant an end to the relentless torture!"

Glad! Badea Khalaf was glad to be taken to one of the most horrible places on earth. Glad to share a tiny cell with twenty people. Glad to have thirty square centimeters of space to move in. Glad to see his family twice a year. Glad to be able to wash once a week. Above all, glad to be alive.

"As long as there's life, there's hope, and I never stopped hoping that I'd be freed one day," he says. "I am a Sunni Muslim. That is the only reason I wasn't sentenced to death."

In 1988, after one year in Abu Ghraib, Badea Khalaf was released.

"But it was like being transferred from a small prison to a larger one."

By now, we have almost arrived at the prison gates. Dr. Khalaf continues his story.

"I had to sign in regularly at the local police station, which meant that, being a doctor, I was unable to work."

In 1991, Dr. Khalaf fled Iraq.

"Once again I was lucky." An odd concept of luck. "Aziz, the officer who was in charge of me, urged me to flee to Jordan. Immediately. Saddam was re-arresting everyone he had released after the Iran-Iraq war. I paid $300 for a fake passport and crossed the border in a taxi. It was July 2, 1991."

Dr. Khalaf worked at a private hospital in Amman for ten months and then received a message from his family telling him to leave Jordan.

"My life was in danger. They had tracked me down. I managed to get a visa for Russia and spent nine months living at a friend's house in St. Petersburg. Then I received an offer from Riyadh's Central Hospital to work as an internal medicine physician," he says.

But Saudi Arabia was certainly not the place this psychiatrist was looking for, even though initially he had hoped there would be a real opportunity to overthrow Saddam's regime by joining an Iraqi opposition group. After the Gulf War, more than thirty thousand Iraqis fled to Riyadh.

"All the restrictions in the name of religion were all too familiar. I couldn't stand it. If I had to put up with such restrictions, then let it be in my own country!"

Dr. Khalaf went on holiday to England. He didn't return. He received his degree in psychiatry in London and married an Iraqi woman who lived in the United States and worked in a London hospital.

"I continued to follow the events back home, although I knew that the time was not right for Saddam to be overthrown. But finally, in March, the moment we'd all been waiting for arrived. I was certain of it! I joined the Iraqi Reconstruction Development Council in the United States and decided to go back to my homeland."

Jon and I look at each other. Now all those prison cells have acquired a new meaning in our eyes. We have already made our decision. There is nobody more suitable than this sensitive but resolute man to take care of the thousands of torture victims in this mangled country. Thirty-five years of Baath party rule and three major conflicts have taken their toll on the Iraqi people.

"Torture leaves deep wounds that can be cured with the right treatment," says Dr. Khalaf. "But torturers often aim at mental suffering. Psychological wounds are the more personal, intimate, and long-lasting results of torture that can have devastating effects on the victim and the victim's family alike. Invisible scars that cannot be detected by objective science or through testing. Torture can profoundly damage relationships between partners, parents, and children as well as between victims and their communities."

Words seem to pour out of Dr. Khalaf's mouth like water down a stream.

"Torture victims were the most forgotten and neglected group of society. They were forbidden to complain or seek clinical help. They were not even permitted to speak about their ordeal to friends or relatives. Torture victims are survivors who have looked death in the face, and many of them will need medical or psychiatric treatment that has been denied to them for decades. Even those who manage to deal with their traumatic experiences themselves will benefit from speaking about it. I would be very happy to support my fellow 'companions of misfortune' by providing a listening service. I could help communities in their efforts to rebuild fractured networks."

Jon and I become great friends with Badea. We pass many an evening talking about Iraq in various restaurants around Baghdad. We have to be inconspicuous and go in disguise. Badea invites us to spend Fridays in the countryside with him and his family. Yet every time, he changes his mind.

"It's too dangerous, guys," he tells us one day when I complain that he has stood us up for the umpteenth time. "I would love to spend the whole day with you. But I'm not someone you want to associate with. They're following me and making threats. Forget it. We'll do it another time, when the waters have calmed."

Up to now, this moment has yet to happen.

We will spend months sorting out the hospital at Abu Ghraib. During these months, Jon and I visit the prison at least a couple of times a week.

"Now the prisoners are making up excuses to stay here as long as possible. Look at him there," says a nurse, pointing at a middle-aged man with a long beard. He looks like a Taliban to me. "He's perfectly healthy. But the moment he thinks he's about to be sent back to his cell, he causes so much trouble that we'd prefer to keep him here."

Indeed. I'd also prefer to avoid confrontation with him, the man with the blazing eyes.

A short time later, Abu Ghraib makes front-page news. An inquiry is launched into the events that have taken place in the Father of Strangeness both before and after Saddam's capture, and the results are revealed to the world, stirring up much indignation and furious debate. I speak about it to Jon, who has been back in the United States for a couple of months.

"I feel guilty that I never looked behind the scenes or noticed anything amiss. We had even toured the prison. We knew some of the inmates. Okay, so we didn't have access to all the areas, but that was understandable," I say to him. I remember the day when my curiosity was given a rude awakening.

"Those are the maximum security prisoners," one of the hospital's doctors tells me. He has seen me peering into the distance, trying to make out what is going on. "Al Qaeda prisoners—you know what I mean."

I start to pull out my camera. It has a powerful zoom lens that enables me to capture images too distant for the naked eye.

"No! Do you want to get me sacked?" he says, frightened. I put my camera back into my rucksack. This does not stop me from going closer, however.

"It's not a good idea, Madam," warns a U.S. soldier from the turret. "You never know, they could throw something and you could get hurt."

They sleep in tents under the baking sun and wander around the camp like tormented souls.

"Their normal wing is undergoing reconstruction," the soldier tells me. "What you're looking at is a temporary arrangement."

Temporary or not, the sun is beating down. My attention is drawn toward a surreal scene. I still shiver today at the thought of what I saw: a sad, single file of maximum security prisoners. There is something harrowing and heartbreaking about their long, slow procession toward the helicopters, here to take them away to some unspecified location. Each man's hands are placed on the shoulders of the man in front, and with shackled legs they shuffle toward the gaping doors of the aircraft, before being enveloped in the clouds of sandy dust kicked up by the helicopters' blades. There are armed guards everywhere making sure no one tries to escape.

"Seeing as you're quite happy about going to prison, why don't you go on a tour of one of the villages for disabled people?"

Jim does not waste any opportunity in making jokes about my frequent trips to Abu Ghraib. On the blackboard where everybody's daily tasks are chalked up, my name is almost always next to the prison.

"Watch out, signorina. It's a dangerous place," Major Mike Smith tells me every time.

This time, my senior advisor speaks in all seriousness. If the victims of torture were completely ignored for decades by Saddam's regime, then disabled people certainly fared no better. And eight years of war with Iran created many more victims. Forced to live all together in compounds, hidden out of sight from everyone else, these people have lived isolated lives.

Now Jon and I must decide whether these people should remain a little longer in their villages or be allowed to leave—and bear all the consequences this might entail. After all, living in ghettos hardly seems like a modern solution. We discuss it at great length with those directly concerned and eventually arrive at a conclusion. We decide that uprooting disabled people from their known reality would not be a welcome move at present. Although confined and restricted, their world is nevertheless cushioned and protected. For the moment, we will focus on improving their living conditions. Later, it will be up to them to decide their own future.

Mohammed Al Najar is one of the leaders of the Iraqi Handicapped Society. This, the country's leading advocacy group for disabled Iraqis, takes care of both the military and civilians. He tells a story that unfortunately is familiar to many Iraqis.

"June 22, 1986. I will never forget that day," Mohammed says with a smile on his lips and a cheerful lilt in his voice.

"That's when it all began. When my life crumbled apart."

His artificial left arm speaks for itself. Mohammed, who is married with two daughters and one son, was seriously wounded in the Iran-Iraq war.

"The funny thing is that I'm not a soldier and I've never been trained to be one," he says. "I was studying engineering at Baghdad University when Saddam ordered all students to join training camps. We had to be ready if we were needed to go and fight in the ranks of the People's Army."

The Iraqi People's Army was made up of civilians who were usually forced to join, whereas the Regular Army was made up of career soldiers.

"I arrived at the camp on June 22. I had no choice. If I had refused to go, Saddam would have had me expelled from the university," says Mohammed.

The Iran-Iraq war lasted for eight years, between September 1980 and August 1988. Casualty figures have still not been ascertained, although estimates suggest one million war-related deaths, many more wounded, and millions of refugees. The Iraqis suffered an estimated three hundred seventy thousand deaths and sixty thousand POWs. Figures for Iranian loss-es indicate three hundred thousand deaths and fifty thousand wounded out of a total population that stood at nearly sixty million at the war's end.

"Shortly after I arrived at the training camp, my father was struck by typhoid fever and, since I'm his only son, I went home for a few days to take care of him. Unfortunately, I did not know that anyone leaving the camp for more than seven days would be subjected to severe punishment on their return," Mohammed continues brightly.

"When I rejoined my unit, Saddam issued Order No. 720. I was trans-ferred to the Regular Army and sent to the front line as punishment. Of course nobody had informed me of the consequences of my trip to see my father before I left. They probably weren't even aware of it, because it was one of Saddam's new laws."

So this is how Mohammed found himself at the front line on Iraq's southern border with Iran along with seven thousand other students. Cannon fodder.

"I'd been in the army for four months. It was my first major battle. A bomb exploded, I lost consciousness, and when I came round, I found myself at Basra Military Hospital," relates the now middle-aged Mohammed. From there he was taken to the Baghdad Al Rasheed Military Hospital, where they discovered that his left arm had turned gangrenous and amputated it straight away.

"After fifty days at Al Rasheed, I was taken to a rehabilitation center for soldiers. I had to turn up once a month to fill out papers. This was all my government was prepared to do for me."

Next, Mohammed was sent to the Al Ikrima Center for the disabled, which now cares for more than thirty-six hundred veterans. Because he had been injured as a soldier, Mohammed was able to have a prosthetic arm fit-ted. Civilians did not have this "luxury."

"I even managed to graduate," he says proudly. "In order to be readmit-ted, I actually had to resort to underhanded measures. I had written seven letters asking if I could complete my studies. I only needed a year more to graduate. Finally, my application was accepted, thanks to a clerk who took up my cause."

This is Iraq. Infinitely cruel and infinitely generous people.

Now Mohammed is a salesman. "I buy and sell gold and antiques for my living," he tells me. "But now that I'm a founding member of the Iraqi Handicapped Society, I'm trying to give as much time as I can to the disabled cause. We also work for disabled civilians, as they have been completely pushed away and ignored up until now by the Iraqi government."

Mohammed's dream is to take care of his disabled friends, particularly those who are worse off than himself and who are in need of full support and assistance. He hopes that life improves for them all.

"Disabled people should have the same opportunities in work as every other citizen and should be able to enjoy a more satisfactory social life," he insists.

Unfortunately, nobody in Iraq has ever paid heed to the problems that disabled people face, and so nothing has been done to tackle them.

"Just look at the outhouses," he says, with an edge of contention. "No ramps, no special staircases, no adequate bathrooms, no handholds. Disabled people who use wheelchairs usually get stuck in the doorways, which are far too narrow," he says.

"We need a special law that takes care of us and protects our rights." Mohammed's face lights up as he speaks. "And I will do my very best to make this happen," he concludes with conviction.

I pass many a happy morning at Shamook Village, one of the six villages for disabled people in Baghdad. By now they know me well, and I go from house to house, drinking tea, eating baklava, and chatting with the residents. I am almost embarrassed to say I am here to work.

Children come running over as soon as they see me arrive. They are so beautiful. This might sound like a cliché, as children are always beautiful. But these children seem more special than others. They push their fathers happily around in wheelchairs—fathers who, knowing my passion for Iraqi tea, hand me cups of it even as I am still climbing out of my Humvee. There is no other place in Iraq where you hear so much laughter.

"We are renovating the mosque's minaret," Ahmed informs me, proudly.

His three-year-old son is seated on his lifeless legs and his daughter Samira is pushing them both around at top speed. Enthusiasm. This is the magic word. So much enthusiasm, despite all the suffering.

"Come see the clinic," he tells me. "It's almost finished. We can't wait for you to see it."

"We expected you last week," Majid interrupts. "Why didn't you come?"

It is hard to explain to people here that it is not always easy to move around Baghdad, or that by continuing to come here, I often have to put aside security measures and orders issued by my superiors.

Disabled in Shamook

"I'm risking my life to come here!" I would like to tell them.

But I could not tell them. One glance alone at their living conditions makes me feel guilty. I do not even try to explain. They would not understand. And I would not want them to misinterpret my apprehensions and concern as a lack of willingness to support their cause.

Banners made out of sheets thank the Ministry of Health for thinking about them. These people are proud of their creative spirit. "Thank you MoH," I see written everywhere.

We feel satisfied. The problem of disabled people is certainly far from being resolved, but I feel confident in saying that huge steps forward have been taken. I stopped believing in miracles a long time ago. Even distributing wheelchairs to these people was a Herculean task. A wheelchair can change a disabled person's life, yet unused wheelchairs had sat in huge warehouses for decades and nobody had ever taken the trouble to distribute them to those in need. There are some things I will never understand. I vividly remember the shining eyes when we handed out these most appreciated presents. Kisses, thank-yous, invitations to dinner—all signs of gratitude.

"But we're not doing anything," I say to Chuck Fisher, who had discovered one of the vast warehouses. "We're only giving them the wheelchairs they should have received years ago. Was there any point in keeping them all shut away?" I will never get my head around such things.

They kiss my hand. They cry with gratitude. I am feeling uncomfortable. We are not saints. We are only doing our work. The inauguration of the Shamook clinic is a touching event, as is the opening of the swimming pool, which will enable rehabilitation programs. Theirs is a gratitude, however, that tends to evaporate at the first obstacle. This, too, is typical Iraq.

"Anna, we don't like the doctor you assigned to us," rails Ahmed, the spokesperson for Shamook Village.

"In what way don't you like him? Has he made some error?" I inquire.

"No, we don't like him," is his brusque reply.

"You're going to have to give me a good explanation, Ahmed. I can't just send him away," I try to explain.

A good explanation? Ahmed has no idea what I am talking about.

"You have a clinic, a swimming pool, access ramps, and a doctor. What more can you want? Either you give me a good reason for us to replace the doctor or else I won't even think about it," I say.

Ahmed is not used to seeing me annoyed. But my anger does not seem to bother him.

"All right then, we will come and protest. We will call for a demonstration across from the ministry's central offices," he states with conviction.

My jaw drops. A demonstration? Did I hear him correctly? A protest because they've taken a dislike to the doctor? With no good reason whatsoever? I burst into laughter.

Ahmed looks at me suspiciously. Then his children start laughing. They do not understand what we are talking about, but they find my laughter contagious.

"Okay, so I did tell you to feel free to complain. And to keep me informed of any quibbles or concerns you may have. I can see that you're following my advice to a T, but let's not exaggerate!"

Ahmed begins to smile.

"Anna, are you angry?" he asks, with childlike surprise.

"Absolutely! I'd certainly think so. You've threatened to come and find me at the ministry and protest because you don't like Dr. Samir. Of course I'm not exactly delighted! Bearing in mind everything I've done and not forgetting that at the moment I'm trying to get hold of a coach to take you all to Mecca!" I retort. "But

Never without Chai!

perhaps if you were to offer me a good cup of tea, I might just be able to forget. You just concentrate on behaving yourself here and getting on with the doctor!"

Iraqi tea. Sometimes I think it is a magic potion, able to put everything back in order.

Sometimes. But unfortunately, not always.

CHAPTER 11

A Bleak Christmas

The winter begins under less than favorable auspices. Every evening, at about the same time, we have to run and seek shelter in the bunker. The "giant voice" wails almost daily. A long, lugubrious sound that makes me shiver. We do not have time to contemplate this. At the first shriek of the alarm, we each sling on a flak jacket and helmet and run following a series of motions that has now become automatic. When the windows rattle in their panes we throw ourselves to the ground, the siren sounds, the Marines arrive, and we have to flee underground. Always the same rigmarole, night after night.

"Jon, we're going to have to change our routine. Every time we go to the gym we get missiles thrown at us. I've had enough of spending hours in my sweaty clothes in the cellar!" I suggest to my friend Jon Bowersox. Jon and I go to the gym every day on a stress-beating mission during our work break. "Either we go earlier or later to the gym. This way, when

Photo: Bunker nights

their charming little presents clatter overhead we will be at the office. We can't keep this up. It's so monotonous, isn't it? They never change their schedule."

We cannot keep going on like this. We are barely sleeping.

"If they keep it up, I'll surrender. They will have won. I'll go back home for the simple reason that I'm too tired. I can hardly stay on my feet. And then it is too dangerous to go around in these conditions. Sooner or later they'll shoot us," I moan one morning, after spending the umpteenth night underground.

"Are you tired, Anna?" Aurora asks. Aurora is a Kosovar doctor, and even after all these months she is still an enigma. Despite my best efforts, I will never understand her real reasons for being here. She will not go to the ministry because she says it's too dangerous, but then she goes out shopping in the streets of Baghdad. She will not go to the military hospital's dentist, preferring instead to go to an unknown dentist she saw advertised on a street sign. The result of this ingenious move: an abscess so bad that she has to be sent back home. This morning, as I drag myself into the office, Aurora really is in form.

"Why are you tired?" she asks, wide-eyed.

"You didn't hear the bangs last night?" I reply. "The whole place was shaking!"

"Of course. I was in the bunker until this morning," she tells me.

"And so was I. That's why I'm tired."

"No, no, I don't think so. I reckon it's the change of season. You're just suffering the change of season," she concludes, proud of her discovery.

Change of season! Clearly she does not want to face reality and see how things are getting worse, that we are completely done in from the strain, that we are risking our lives. And that if it continues like this, they are going to get us, sooner or later.

"A day here, a day there. Always closer. Yesterday an uninhabited shack, today the parking lot. And tomorrow? We've been lucky up to now. But how long can our luck hold out?" These are the words muttered over and over again during the never-ending hours in the bunkers. We all know that with every day that passes, our chances of getting hit increase. Yet despite this, we all plow on without batting an eyelid, journeying toward whatever destiny has in store. Hoping that destiny is merciful. Praying to be in the right place at the right time.

"As long as we've got Prouse with us, we'll be okay," Ambassador De Martino says one evening.

We run underground when the alarm goes off, resurface when the "all clear" sounds, and get back to work as if nothing has happened. As time goes on, we get so fed up with running down the stairs that we continue working regardless, locking ourselves into the office so as not to get caught by the Marines.

"Anyway, they've already fired their worst," we tell ourselves.

I have a book ready on my desk. I grab it before I flee. Time goes by so very slowly when you have to sit still underground.

"They could hit the palace head-on and we wouldn't notice a thing," Maurizio comments one evening. The explosions outside seem to be particularly heavy, and we are never told what is going on. Telephones are cut off, Gurkhas run past wearing yellow fireman hats with their radios switched on, the Marines come past wearing their full combat gear—but not a word is said to us. We have to wait until we are allowed to return to our offices, then we immediately connect to the CNN website to find out what is going on. Some of us have laptops; others discuss work; some try to catch some sleep; yet others pace up and down with CD players. We really are a comical assortment of individuals. People too tired even to notice the absurdity of the situation. We go forward, automatons, myself included, hoping things will improve tomorrow.

But they do not.

"Anna, we would like you to carry a lit candle to the altar. We are all going to carry a candle in honor of our fallen companions."

I am speechless. I feel privileged to lead a procession to the altar in honor of Ivan, one of the carabinieri killed a couple of days ago in Nassiriya. It is the Tuscania regiment boys who ask me. I am touched. It is the most surreal ceremony of my life. It is difficult to imagine anything more moving. A dark church. The flicker of candlelight. Dark shadows projected through the high windowpanes. Shadows clad with guns, flak jackets, and earpieces. And we are sitting in church. Down here we are praying; up there they are shooting. What contrast!

We are in the middle of the red zone. We wanted to show our defiance. The dead deserve it. Ambassador Bremer is in the first row. We squeeze hands. He is moved. I am grateful for his presence. The deafening throb of the helicopters makes everything even more unreal. And I am struggling to stay on my feet. This is the effect of the drugs. That's right, I have been pumped full of powerful painkillers to get me through this ceremony. If not, I would still be in my hospital bed.

"Kidney stones," pronounces Ben Gonzales, the doctor who manages the military hospital's first-aid department.

"I know. I've had them before," I reply.

They attach me to an intravenous drip. I am not getting any better. I am writhing in my bed.

"Jon, tell them I've had it before. Tell them I was operated on. Tell them one of those little pills is not enough… I need more than a little intravenous Coca Cola!"

Ben comes back with some sky-blue pills in his hand.

"Viagra?" I ask him, trying to laugh.

I've suddenly got an image in my mind of the recent statistics on the most widely sold pharmaceuticals in postwar Iraq. The exponential rise in the sales of these magical love pills gave us in the ministry a good giggle. They say it's one of the effects of stress.

The stabs of pain are increasing.

"Two?" Jon intervenes, aghast.

"You can't give her two of those. They're like bombs! They'll knock her out completely!"

"And that's just what we want, isn't it?" answers the friendly doctor, whose hobby is flying.

"This way we can conduct all the necessary tests without her thrashing around in agony," he finishes, before I am whisked away into the labyrinths of the hospital.

I am finding it hard to stay on my feet. I have no energy left in my legs; it left along with the pain.

"I want some of those pills to take back with me. We don't get them this strong in Italy," I say to Ben. "It's wonderful. I'm floating in another world."

I am not able to finish my sentence. Speaking is too exhausting. They leave me on a camp bed for a couple of hours. The kidney stone takes its time to pass. Suddenly, I hear groans coming from next to me. I did not realize I had company. I turn round and am shocked by what I see. I pull myself up. I can't believe my eyes.

"What's the problem, Anna?"

I am horror-stricken. I cannot speak.

"He is part of a bomb squad. A mine blew up in his hand while he was trying to defuse it," Ben explains. "He's twenty years old. He's going to make it."

The boy's face is completely burnt. He has lost both his arms. His wheezing makes me shudder. On his chest he has a tattoo: SUSAN I LOVE YOU. Block capitals. I stare at him. I gaze at his nonexistent features.

"Who made you come here to ruin your life?" I would like to ask him.

"As soon as his condition is stable, we'll send him by Medevac to Germany. Maybe tomorrow," Ben continues. Scenes like this must be pretty standard for him by now.

"After a year's work here, this is why I have to go back home," he goes on. " I want to go and fly. Dream. I can't stay here any longer. I've learned a lot. But now this is enough. Day and night, they send me cases like this. From all over the country. By the way, I am very pleased about your carabiniere. He has made it."

Doctor Gonzales is referring to the only Italian man from the Nassiriya attack who was operated on and recovered here at the 28th Combat Support Hospital. He survived the tragedy and was sent back home. He had only three more days left to go until the end of his stay in Iraq.

"Ben, I have to go," I say to the doctor. "I'll phone and get them to pick me up. The memorial service for the Nassiriya fallen takes place this afternoon. I can't miss it."

"Don't you realize what state you're in? You can't even stand up. You're drugged up enough for the next week. I'm not even going to discuss it with you."

By now, though, I have already dialed Jim's number.

"I'll send a security detail," says Jim. "Go and change and we'll take you to church."

Ben and my bodyguard have a long discussion. The doctor is worried that if something happens, I will not have the presence of mind to react and escape to safety.

"You're going to have to carry her on your shoulders," he explains to my bodyguard. "She's completely out of it. She won't even be able to open the jeep door. Imagine she's drunk five liters of wine," he finishes. They look at me.

"I'm going. Even if I have to go on foot, I'm going," I respond, resolute.

He does not have much of a choice. And this is how I find myself in front of hundreds of people, trying to keep upright, with a lit candle in my hand. The path from the pews to the altar seems never-ending. I have to remind myself that the blurry shape far in the distance really is the altar.

I will be ill for the next couple of days. But I am able to take part in one of the most moving ceremonies I have ever attended. No hysteria, only a profound, resonating silence and people who understand the meaning of death. No clichés. Only emotional intensity.

I have never received so many hugs as in those days following the attack at Nassiriya. They made me feel proud to be Italian. It was wonderful to feel the warmth of my American colleagues. To understand the compassion they had for our fallen men.

When I speak about my Iraqi friends and colleagues, I try to let them speak for themselves. I try to limit myself to the role of the intermediary between them and the reader who knows little about them. It may be true that people are sick of hearing about Iraq, but few pause to think about the real people involved.

But I cannot let Saba speak for herself. I have to speak for her. This time, my feelings are too deeply entangled to maintain a cool distance. This time I cannot simply be the intermediary, ferrying between Saba and you, her audience. I cannot because Saba is dead. Assassinated.

December 18 will be a date for all of us at the Ministry of Health to remember. None of us will forget that terrible moment when we heard that Saba had been killed. None of us. It is one of those moments that will stay in everyone's mind. The knotted throat, that deeply private feeling, will stay with us forever. We will never be able to speak about it or share it with anyone.

Saba had just graduated with a degree in biology. She was twenty-four and literally brimming with enthusiasm for life. I had wanted her to be one of my protégés, a little hero. Everyone who cannot be here should know about this character. She was perfect. You would have loved her.

Saba is a heroine. Although not in the way I would have liked her to be—a lively, educated Iraqi woman who believes in the future of her country and is prepared to fight for her dream with everything she has. Was she ready to die for this post-Saddam Iraq? Can a girl in her early twenties be ready to sacrifice her life? Unfortunately, the answer is yes. Saba was a dreamer and, like most dreamers, she would do absolutely anything to fulfill that dream.

Only too often heroes are created when it is too late. My biggest regret is not having had time to make Saba a living heroine. This is a mistake that we writers often make. I hope this will be the last time.

Saba was on my schedule. Schedule—what a cold, lifeless word. I had planned to chat to her about her secrets and hobbies the following week. Planned is another soulless word. Now it is too late. Too late for interviews and informal chats. Saba was due to marry shortly and was a huge fan of anything from the United States. She loved American films and owed her perfect English to Jim Carrey, her favorite actor. As a result, she spoke English with a strong American accent. The first time I met her she was wearing a headscarf. A couple of weeks later, she was running down the ministry corridors in jeans and a colored sweater. She loved tuna sandwiches and nail polish. This is almost everything I know about her... unfortunately. And now it is too late to change things. Or possibly not? Perhaps not, if I let one of her good friends speak for her. Someone who knew this courageous Iraqi better than anyone else.

Lieutenant Scott Svabek was one of the first to hear about Saba's death. This is what he had to say:

"I joined this mission in Iraq wanting to do a good job and then go home. But then we realized that our success would rely largely on the support and the will of the Iraqi people. One of these people was Saba, a young woman who sacrificed her life for her country in the hope that she would one day live in a better world. She didn't do it for money or for fame. She did it for a simple reason: the dream of a free Iraq.

"For twenty-four years, this girl had lived in fear of tyranny, torture, and persecution. I'm happy that, for at least four days, Saba lived to see her dream fulfilled. I say four days, because my friend was killed four days after Saddam was captured. But it hurts me to think it was only four days. On December 18, Saba was assassinated doing something she believed in. The cowards who killed her did not just shoot her. They went up to her and emptied an entire magazine of bullets into her body. This Iraqi treasure. I call her treasure because she was a delight and pleasure to work with. Day in day out.

Saba—a cherished memory

"I know that some of those cowards could still be prowling about the corridors in the ministry. I hope that they'll get caught one day. Now I feel that my task is to let the world know how special this girl was for her country, for our team, and for me. I owe it to everyone who never had the fortune of working with her and who can never hope to meet such fearless Iraqi men and women. They work without protection, without flak jackets, without bodyguards, without weapons.

"Saba was my interpreter at the beginning. But by the end, she was so much more. She was my assistant, my right arm. But above all, she was my friend. I hope this testimony helps you to get a better appreciation of our Iraqi friends."

Saba's death hits us all hard. We had received several letters threatening to assassinate a list of people if the Ministry of Health pursued its anti-corruption campaign. Saba was the first name in this list.

Corruption permeates Iraq's entire health system, especially its pharmaceutical system. Scott is the person in charge of purchasing Iraq's pharmaceutical products and, having chosen not to purchase exclusively from those companies aiming to monopolize the market, he has made himself many enemies. His assistants are also caught in the crossfire. First was Saba. But the death of this girl does not discourage the others. The assassination of their friend seems to have had the opposite effect.

Maysaa has never wavered in her determination to make the new National Formulary for Pharmaceuticals a masterpiece; now she is unstoppable. The system of purchasing and distributing medicines was so corrupt under Saddam's regime it succeeded in keeping most Iraqis from getting what they needed. Not only were medicines of poor quality, but most were available only on the black market. A team of consultants from the U.S. Department of Defense's Pharmaco-Economic Center has now been sent to Baghdad to tackle the chaotic state of the pharmaceutical industry. Aided by Iraqi pharmacists, their aim is to introduce a modern national formulary. They face thousands of difficulties, and we all enjoy witnessing their nervous breakdowns as they try to come to grips with this utterly illogical system.

The experts in pharmaceutical formularies have made many discoveries. In order for a new formulary to be successful, it must reflect the locals' customs. So thanks to our Iraqi friends, we discover Iraq's various medical preferences.

To begin with, Iraqis love injections. They prefer injections to pills, lozenges, and inhalers. A doctor's success is based upon the number of injections he administers. After injections, Iraqis love syrupy medicines. Give an Iraqi a choice and he will go for an injection or a sweet, sticky mixture rather than an easy-to-swallow pill any day! This is only one of the many bizarre details that the American experts came up with, helping them to compile a formulary based upon the real needs and preferences of the people.

Without the help of a young pharmacist from Baghdad, they would never have succeeded. The pharmacist is Maysaa Hillal Mahmood, and she can be credited with bridging the gap between the American experts and the complex Iraqi system. Maysaa and her brother run one of the hundreds of pharmacies that line the streets of Baghdad. There are literally pharmacies everywhere. There are whole districts of the city that live off this business alone.

"During Saddam's regime, government salaries were only a dollar a month. To get by, people opened their own private shops," Maysaa explains. "We would work for ourselves during the morning and for the government in the afternoons."

This would explain why there are more than thirty-five hundred pharmacies scattered all over Iraq. Most of them are tiny, a counter, and shelves piled high with medicines that people just come and grab for themselves. Customers don't even wait for the pharmacist's assistance.

"In the past, pharmacists relied on favors from doctors to survive," Maysaa continues. "The system was totally corrupt, but now that salaries are rising, pharmacists will no longer have to rely on their own businesses. One hopes this means that corruption will stop and the quality of service will increase."

There were two major problems with the Iraqi pharmaceutical system. First, there was an excessive number of medicines on the old formulary, which was full of unnecessary duplications. Second, prescription of the drugs was wholly inadequate.

"The formulary we've been using up until now had more than twenty-six thousand different types of medicines. Comically enough, most of them were not even available," Maysaa goes on. "It was pointless to have all those medicines. This is why we've been working day and night to improve the formulary. Our aim was to cut the list without compromising quality and to ensure that all of the selected products are available."

When the American specialists got hold of the old formulary, they realized just how unfamiliar they were with Iraqi medicine.

"Although they had lots more experience than I and other Iraqi pharmacists had, they had never worked in my country," explained the short-haired brunette.

"They often stared at me, utterly clueless. They were the first to admit everything here is completely different from anywhere else in the world. I admire them for acknowledging that they needed help from me and my colleagues. They made us feel proud to be Iraqi, even if we know that we've still got a lot of catching up to do."

As well as guaranteeing the Iraqi people the reliable availability of effective medicines, the ministry experts decided to provide guidelines to improve the treatment of certain diseases. It is vital that the country use the various medicines in an appropriate and safe manner.

"We finally have the opportunity to change the inefficient pharmaceutical system. This will bring nothing but benefit to the entire medical system," Maysaa enthuses. "It's up to us to get things going on the right path. I have never been so excited in all my life!"

In December, Maysaa left Iraq for the first time. During Saddam's regime, no pharmacist could leave the country. She would never have returned.

"I was chosen to represent Iraq at the Alzahar Third International Conference for Pharmaceutical and Biological Sciences in Cairo," she says. "I had a thirty-minute presentation to highlight the conditions of the pharmaceutical industry. Everyone was looking at me—me, an Iraqi pharmacist. Just think, there were more than one hundred people from different countries, mainly from the Arab world, listening to me. It was the first time in decades they heard a voice relaying the situation in Iraq, which had been thoroughly isolated from the rest of the world. It was a unique occasion, both for them and for me."

This was finally an opportunity for Maysaa, a young, timid pharmacist, to get in touch with different cultures, opinions, and backgrounds.

"I realized just how much damage isolation can cause. It had had such an impact on my country. We had fallen far behind, and our technology was pretty nonexistent. Making up for lost time will be quite a task," she says with a determined tone.

"But the first step to reconstruction is recognizing that we are at least thirty years behind. This recognition should spur us on and inspire in us a wish to demonstrate to ourselves that it's possible to leave the past behind. Don't forget, Anna, that Iraq is not a developing country. Iraq has resources and educated people. It has suffered greatly, but it is also ready to combat its years of isolation and embrace the future with hope. I am thrilled. It is an amazing opportunity. I love challenges. They make me feel alive. Finally I am alive!"

I have no words. Maysaa's enthusiasm is contagious and moving. And, if I had been plagued by doubts after Saba's death, chatting to this vivacious pharmacist has rekindled my spirits. Shouldn't it be me giving *them* a hand?

Christmas and New Year are among the saddest days for me and my colleagues here in Iraq. Apart from Saba's death, however, there is no real reason for our despondency. Maybe it is because of our sheer tiredness. Not a single rest day, not a single day when we can pull out the plug, not a single moment when we can relax. Christmas day began with a dash to the bunkers. To tell the truth, I did not even shake myself out of bed. I let the others run for safety. I had decided that if I were to die, it might as well happen while I am lying in the comfort of my camp bed.

"Anyway, by the time we get down there, it's all over," I say to Amina, a girl who sleeps next to me.

"Perhaps. I've only got a couple of days left here, though, so I don't want to do anything rash!" she says, struggling to fasten up her flak jacket.

"Goodness, I've put on so much weight," she complains. "Or maybe the straps have just gotten shorter," she giggles. She is a lovely roommate.

The barrack is beginning to get on my nerves. Even if you wanted to, it would be impossible to sleep past a certain hour in the morning. Seventy people really is quite a lot. Our cramped quarters should have lasted a matter of days, or perhaps weeks. "A temporary arrangement," they had told us. By now, two months have gone by and not a word more has been said about other accommodation.

"Anna, what's going on?" Ambassador De Martino is on the phone, checking that I have not been hit by rockets.

"A couple of hits, that's all" I say, sleepily.

"Are you in the bunker?"

"No."

"So where did you end up this time?" he asks, pretending to be annoyed.

"I haven't moved out of bed."

"Yes, and yesterday evening were you on the treadmill when everyone was running for shelter, by any chance? Don't you think that perhaps you're overdoing it?" he hounds me.

"I am fed up with running down there. And now that it is the Marines standing guard, you can't get through at all. At least before, with the Gurkhas, there was some room for discussion. After awhile they would let you go back up. But there's no way with the Marines. No way at all. If they've been given orders to keep us down in the cellar for hours, nothing will make them budge."

In time, I learn to appreciate their witless—or better, their faithful—way of sticking to orders. Although it is a draining experience when they're on checkpoints, I learn that working with them at the upper end of their hierarchy is a pleasure. After all, there are only a few of them and they have been carefully selected and trained. When the kids working on the checkpoints receive an order, they stick to it to the point of absurdity.

"Ma'am, can you show me your ID?" the same Marine asks me every morning at the same checkpoint. For some time now, you have had to show some ID as well as your CPA badge.

"It's always the same me!" I mutter, as I search desperately through my rucksack.

Then, once we have established who I am, the next question: "Where are you from, ma'am?"

"From the same country I came from yesterday, and the day before yesterday, and the day before that!"

I am sorry but in the morning, my sense of humor leaves much to be desired.

"Anna, there's no point getting angry!" Jon tells me. "You can't expect too much from guys used to conquering beaches," he points out. "Because that's what they do—conquer beaches!" Once again the old sibling rivalry among the U.S. Air Force, Marines, Navy, and Army. They never waste an opportunity to have a go at each other, no matter where or when.

"Seeing as I couldn't get to sleep this morning, either, I really don't think I'll make it through work today," I tell Jon on this overcast Christmas morning. From nowhere, once again, Jon shows me his affection.

"It's no big deal, Anna. It's symbolic," he says as he slips a little packet into my hand, wrapped up as best as he could.

"Dog tags!" I cry. "I've been wanting some for ages!"

"Oh, I didn't know. It's a way of saying that to all intents and purposes, you are now officially one of us. You deserve all of our respect."

"That's why you asked me the other day what denomination I am!" I say. "And my blood group, too."

I am touched. People who don't live here cannot understand certain things. I will treasure these dog tags forever. I will not go anywhere without them. Not even at night. Anyway, today, December 25, 2003, Jon Bowersox is taking all my cares away.

"I like you so much, Jon. Thank you."

I get a lump in my throat when I enter the office. I go down for a coffee, but all the chimes, Christmas decorations, immense cream cakes, and Christmas songs do nothing but increase my sense of desolation.

I sit down at a table with Cornelius, Blacky, and Willy, three of the South African bodyguards, seemingly intent on gobbling down uninviting looking porridge. I think back to the first time I saw them. Scars everywhere, icy eyes, and hard-nosed gaits. Cornelius has an obvious limp. I do not want to ask why. The fewer questions I ask, the less I know and the better it is. Who knows what they have experienced, what intense lives they have led, how many tragedies they have witnessed.

The number of South Africans in Iraq increases daily. In time, there will be four thousand of them scattered throughout the country. Despite the fact that South Africa is not part of the coalition, it has the largest presence here after the U.S.A. and the UK. Even on the only flight that shuttles between Amman and Baghdad, the pilots and flight attendants are all South African. Seeing them makes me understand just how dangerous it is to fly above the skies of Baghdad. They are competent people, used to this type of war. They know how to fight urban street battles and employ guerrilla tactics, and they get paid more than $1,000 a day. That is their reason for being here. They do not hesitate to admit it.

Absorbed in my thoughts, I sip my coffee. I am not hungry.

"Those chimes are hateful, I could shoot them down! I can't put up with them anymore. They've been ruining all my meals for weeks. Meals, what meals? Bloody chicken Kiev and porridge." I've lost my patience. The other three can see, jokes aside, that I really am on edge, and they try to lighten things up.

"Shoot them down?" asks Cornelius. "But you don't even know how to hold a gun!"

"Well, if nobody teaches me, how the hell am I supposed to learn to shoot?" I retaliate.

"You've been telling us for months you'll come with us to the shooting range. But you're always working and never have time to waste. It would not be you're afraid, by any chance?" Cornelius continues.

He is right. They have often tried to convince me that knowing how to hold a gun might one day come in handy. I, however, do not share their beliefs.

"I would probably shoot myself in the foot!" I tell him. "And I'd never be able to shoot a human being. I can't even kill a cockroach!"

The story about Anna trying to save one of those horrible black insects during the middle of the night, soon got round the whole CPA.

"All right then, I'll come and shoot just to show you that even if I'm a woman I still have good aim," I conclude, defiantly. Blacky, Cornelius, and Willy get up in unison.

"Let's go! Right now. No excuses. It's Christmas and you can't possibly work today!"

Christmas. Going to a shooting range on Christmas. Picking up a Beretta pistol and an MP5 on our most sacred day. No, I cannot do it.

Then I look around me. There is little sacred here. What with the armed-to-the-teeth soldiers and the ready-for-anything mercenaries, the concept of "loving thy neighbor as thyself" has lost a little value. And so I make my decision. Rather than sit here sniveling in my office achieving nothing, I decide to follow my three "teachers." But I had not reckoned with the memories and phantoms that reemerged with the first dry crack of gunfire.

Cornelius is demonstrating how to shoot. My heart suddenly starts to beat wildly. I am on the verge of a panic attack. My chest tightens and I feel breathless.

"Anna, are you okay?" Blacky is worried.

"Yes. Just give me a minute. That day has just come back to me."

I walk away from them. The air is crisp and there is light rain.

"Okay, I'm ready now, boys. Tell me how you do it," I order them when I come back. They are already packing up to take me back to the base. They start grinning.

"Always the same stubborn mule!" says Cornelius, as he loads my MP-5.

So this is how I end up learning to shoot. I do it as a sport. It is a challenge between me and the targets, there in the distance. When they ask me to go around armed, though, I refuse point blank. Even if, by now, I have learned to get by.

Christmas shooting

"It's against all of my principles," I can remember saying, "I came to Iraq in civilian clothes. I am proud to be a civilian, and if I'm not able to go about my work without the aid of a pistol, it means that the time has come for me to go back home."

CHAPTER 12

Iranian Resistance

"**I**talian lady, seeing as you like the wild life, I've got another challenge that'll be right up your alley!"

Dr. Shakir bursts into my office. I smile at him. This Iraqi doctor always puts me in high spirits. He overflows with initiative and will go on to become the vice-minister at the Ministry of Health for the new government. He is right. What with tortured ex-prisoners, disabled people, and a mass of pilgrims, recent months have been quite a rollercoaster. I am sure I have never been more deserving of a holiday!

I am a bit apprehensive about asking what he has in mind. I still have not recovered from the Mecca pilgrimage, even though it could not possibly have gone better. The great success of the exodus to Saudi Arabia has filled everyone with enthusiasm, not only we at the ministry and the participants, but all the Iraqis who did vital work preparing the way for the great undertaking. How many times have I wondered what would have

Photo: The woman's brigade at Camp Ashraf

167

Wafa, flight surgeon

happened if the whole escapade had ended in disaster? Personally, I expected it to go wrong, with the eyes of the world watching.

I remember the joy the pilgrimage brought to Wafa, Iraq's first female aeronautical doctor. She is an incredible woman who has managed to combine her two great passions, medicine and flying. She graduated with a degree in medicine from Mosul University and then had a long wait before being able to specialize in the Faculty of Aviation Medicine.

"I spent my childhood in Saudi Arabia. My father was a lawyer in Riyadh," Wafa recounts. "But Saudi Arabia is certainly not the place for an ambitious woman. I wanted to study. That's why I decided to come back to my country."

Wafa is married and has two children. An azure blue dress and gold jewelry brighten up the dark headscarf she wears around her head.

"Once I graduated in medicine, I was no longer permitted to leave Iraq. In the meantime, my two brothers had left Saudi Arabia to go study in the United States. A short time afterwards, my parents went to join them. I was left alone."

In spite of being left alone, Wafa decided to pursue her childhood dream even if it meant following a tortuous path. Having to wait years before she could be admitted to the Aviation Medicine Program at Baghdad University, Wafa worked for five years at Dahouk, a city in the Kurdish zone of Iraq.

"Only in 1998 did I finally get permission to attend the course. I specialized a year later," she says. "By this time, I had married my father's cousin."

But the future for aeronautical doctors was not particularly rosy during the last years of Saddam's regime. There were no air links with Iraq, and as long as Saddam was in power there was no hope for any change.

"I had worked hard to achieve my objective, but then my assignment was extremely frustrating and hardly stimulating," says Wafa.

She stops here. She knows what I am about to ask.

It is quite evident that Wafa is far from inundated with work. There are very few flights coming and going from Baghdad International Airport, no aircrew needing medical certificates, no meal inspections, no sick patients, no disease checks or measures.

"I know what you're thinking," she says.

"My two rooms are empty. I know. But let me tell you something. By the end of January they won't be big enough to hold all the people who'll be coming to see me."

Wafa is right. At the end of January there is the Hajj pilgrimage, and thousands of Iraqis will be journeying to Mecca, either overland or by air. Every year, hundreds of thousands of believers from seventy different countries flock to Saudi Arabia for the Hajj. This year they will be joined by the Iraqi pilgrims. More than two hundred thousand Iraqis participated in a lottery to enable fair and democratic selection. For the first time in decades it is not Saddam who decides who can and who cannot go to Mecca.

"The flights bound for Saudi Arabia should leave at the end of January," Wafa explains. "Whereas the pilgrims going by coach will leave a little earlier. What an impressive sight it will be—thousands of people in my airport!"

Dr. Wafa Saleh Tahir had been a calm, composed woman until now. She suddenly bounces forward in her chair as if she's revitalized by the thought of seeing her clinic full. She is quite clearly excited. Everything she has fought for her whole life, the dream she has doggedly pursued, is about to become reality.

"And don't forget what an important role my country played in history!" she continues, sweeping me up in her enthusiasm. "We're talking about Mesopotamia!"

Wafa is on fire.

"Hordes of tourists will soon be arriving to visit Baghdad, Babylon, Niveveh, Hatra, Ur, and other historical and archeological sites that are all over the country. By the way, did you know that the Bible names Ur as Abraham's home before he set off west?"

She is right. "But I can see that the idea of Iraq as a mass tourist destination is perhaps a little too radical for you," she says, provocatively. "A couple of weeks ago I would have thought the same, had someone told me that thousands of pilgrims were about to come through that door!"

Now Dr. Shakir unfolds his fiendish plans.

"Mujahedin. Does this mean anything to you?" he asks me, out of the blue.

"Of course it does," I reply. "No, Shakir! You're not getting me involved. Whatever you have in mind, you can forget it. I refuse point blank."

"No, no, you don't refuse. You love the Iranians and you'd never let an opportunity like this pass you by," he retorts, always laughing. Then somebody enters my office. The doctor suddenly breaks off. I realize that we have to change the topic of conversation. Oh dear! Does this mean it's something confidential? I am honored that he trusts me. There is a moment of silence while we are both frantically thinking of something to talk about. We have got to seem as natural as possible.

"So, did you remember to bring my book?" I say, thankfully having thought of a topic.

"Shakir pulls a book from his bag and opens it up at the page he wants me to read.

> "The young doctor came back alone. He was plump, with thick black curls. As a postgraduate, he began to ask me routine questions. He asked me the correct questions and checked my reflexes and my pulse meticulously. He, like all the other doctors, seemed resigned and tired. I could imagine how much they'd had to do over the past six weeks."

These are some of the words Dr. Rhonda Cornum has used to describe Shakir Al Anaji in her book, *She Went to War*. Rhonda was a flight surgeon and met this surgeon during Operation Desert Storm. Rhonda was taken as a prisoner of war, suffered severe injuries, and was treated at a military hospital in Baghdad. She was treated by Shakir, who at the time was a young doctor with gentle manners and is now a director general at the Ministry of Health. Neither his manners nor his professionalism have changed. His wide smile still lights up his round, cheerful face.

Dr. Shakir, Jon Bowersox, and the book

But something has changed since that distant day in 1991 when Shakir treated Rhonda Cornum. His hair is definitely different. Today, no black curls frame his face. An obvious, but minor, difference. There is also something else. Years of war would eat away at the strongest, most steady man, especially if this man had never taken a moment's rest from the tragic events that have rocked his country. His strong sense of justice and duty and his immense dedication have meant he is always ready to assist those most in need. He did not care if they were Iraqi, American, or Iranian. And now the corridor outside his office in the Ministry of Health is a testament to his unwavering desire to help everyone.

Never-ending queues—people stand patiently waiting their turn. They are convinced that this orthopedic surgeon has the key to paradise and can resolve all their problems. He is the director general of clinical operations and is responsible for all Iraq's specialized health services. He was chosen for his energy, his problem-solving skills, and his enthusiasm for getting the job done. No inshallahs, no God willings.

Dr. Shakir is a practical man, appointed to tackle some of the most complex health issues. In the evenings, he continues his surgical work, performing operations. He has a wife and two children. I have eaten many a dinner at their house. His wife, Sahad, is a pediatrician who has decided to take time off and dedicate herself to her family. She makes the best hummus in the whole city. She has tried, in vain, to teach me the tricks of the trade. Hours in their kitchen have taught me to make it, but I haven't yet discovered the secret of making the chickpea paste so velvety.

Dr. Shakir is tired. Tired, but not resigned. He is a fighter. He has always been a fighter. And now that things are beginning to take shape, now that his country is beginning to get on its feet, he is certainly not about to hang up his gloves. His eyes, his expression, his whole posture are testament to this determination. Only his voice does not seem to fit his character. It is soft and delicate, even when he loses his patience. Thirty-five years of Saddam's regime taught him to hide his emotions. This is how people were able to survive under Saddam's iron grip. This is how Shakir managed to keep working as an orthopedic surgeon in his own private clinic.

Perhaps time itself will bring some change in his tone, which is always so carefully controlled. But one thing is certain: decades of dictatorship have not been enough to dampen the flicker in his eyes. This is something that the great doctor was never able to control, and sooner or later his defiant expression would have betrayed him.

He could work as a professor for the University of Baghdad. They have asked him several times. He could work full time in his private clinic. He could be a renowned surgeon, highly successful, in any country of the world without the difficulties and dangers he faces daily in Iraq. But Dr. Shakir wants to stay in his homeland. He has chosen to work for the Ministry of Health. He chose the most exhausting option. The option, though, that will have a real impact on Iraq's future.

"What? What were you saying about the mujahedin?" I ask, excitedly.

The intruder has left. We close the door behind him.

"It's the PMOI, the People's Mujahedin Organization of Iran. Maybe you know them by the name MKO, the Mujahedin-e Khalq Organization?"

I shake my head.

"They've been put on the U.S. list of terrorist organizations, but they enjoy the support of numerous figures within the Pentagon. Their support may be crucial in the future if the U.S.A. wants to put pressure on the Tehran government," he says, in a whisper.

"No, stop! I don't want to know. I'm just waiting for you to get me in some sort of trouble. Prisoners are acceptable. Terrorists are not. Doctor, you're crazy!"

"If you'd let me finish, maybe…" Shakir jumps in.

"No, I'm not going to let you finish. If you go on, it'll be all over for me. I know you. You can be so damned convincing. I don't want to hear anymore!"

Shakir looks at me. He knows full well that the story does not end here. He knows I am dying to find out.

"Terrorists, did you say?" I ask him after a couple of seconds of reflection.

"Yes, about five thousand of them. I visit them twice a month on Fridays when I'm not at the ministry or at my clinic. They live in a camp at the gates of Baghdad. I spoke about you to the women combatants and they can't wait to meet you."

"Women combatants?" I stare at the doctor. I do not understand.

"Yes, when I told the mujahedin women that I have an Italian friend who's spent a lot of time in Iran and who doesn't do anything else but sing the praises of Iranians, their eyes began to sparkle and they asked me to bring you to their camp. They're waiting for you," the doctor tells me.

"Mujahedin? Hang on a minute! You visit the mujahedin? They're here in Iraq?" I ask astonished.

"Certainly. Somebody has to look after them. There're lots of them, I've known them for ages."

"But what are they doing here?" I'm still baffled.

"The Iranian mujahedin were armed and encouraged by Saddam's government to fight against the regime in Tehran. In fact, they were given a heavy arsenal of weapons to take part in the war against Iran. In exchange for their efforts, they were given camps to live in. After the war they were added to the list of terrorist groups."

I open my mouth in a vain attempt to interrupt Shakir. But he is in full flow. He really has decided to land me in trouble!

"When the Americans entered Iraq, they had to deal with a delicate problem. Sending the mujahedin back home would be sentencing them to death. How could the Americans do anything but offer them protection in Iraqi territory?"

"Obviously, they were disarmed so now they're quite harmless. They certainly couldn't have been left with all those guns and tanks. Their hatred for the mullah regime in Iran, however, is still intact."

Now I am beginning to understand. My imagination is playing cruel tricks. Mujahedin, women combatants, people ready to commit the ultimate sacrifice. I would love to understand what goes on in their heads, what it is that pushes them to martyrdom.

"When are we going?" I ask.

"Tomorrow morning. Early. Wear a chador. Nobody should know you're a Westerner. I'll come pick you up outside the gate. Opposite Assassin's Gate. We'll take an old, ruined car. We've got to be inconspicuous," Shakir tells me.

He already had a plan in mind. He *knew* I would go along with it.

"Outside Assassin's Gate? Can't you come inside? I'd rather not get blown up while waiting for you," I say, worriedly.

"I'll be there waiting for you. I'll phone to let you know when to leave."

"You don't want to come inside? You *really* don't want to?" I ask, pleadingly.

"Do you really think I'll get through the checkpoint into the Green Zone with an old Berlina that's falling apart and with this face?" he gestures, jokingly.

"You're right. It hadn't crossed my mind."

In modern Persian, mujahedin means "freedom fighter." Since the People's Mujahedin Organization of Iran was formed in 1965 by university students, its members have fought to establish a democratic government in Iran, one that respects human rights. The group was suppressed by the shah and then driven out by Khomeini, after the group had begun military operations against the Khomeini regime during the war with Iraq. Today it is the largest anti-fundamentalist movement in the Middle East and proposes a democratic and modern interpretation of Islam. The secretary general of the organization is a woman, Mojgan Parsaii, a scientist in her forties.

The PMOI is the first mass Muslim movement to try to demonstrate that there are no contradictions between Islam, modern civilization, and values such as democracy, tolerance, and a pluralist society. As a political organization, the PMOI believes that it can fulfill its aims peacefully. Its members maintain that they would give up their armed struggle if free and democratic elections were to be held in Iran. They assert they would respect the outcome of the vote, regardless of what that might be. More than one hundred twenty thousand men and women have been killed over the past twenty-five years in this fight against the mullah dictatorship in Iran.

This is how Shakir and I end up visiting Camp Ashraf, about one hundred kilometers northeast of Baghdad, which is where all the mujahedin in Iraq live. Tyson is at the wheel. I call him Tyson because of his resemblance to the famous boxer. Even if he would prefer to be

Tyson, ready to roll

likened to the famously arrogant Ferrari race car driver, Schumacher. In Tyson's attempt to emulate him, we risk many a collision.

I still remember our trip to Iraqi Kurdistan. After hours and hours of desert, the mountains suddenly appear. It is the first time Tyson has ever seen them.

"He's from the south," Shakir tells me. "He's never been in the mountains before."

Unfortunately, with his enthusiasm for the mountains, our Formula One driver is unable to keep his hands on the wheel. He tackles the hairpin bends with his hands clawing at his hair in excitement or else takes photographs with the new digital camera the doctor gave him. Many a time we come close to ending up in ravines.

"Given that I have no intention of dying in Iraq," says Kristie Wahler, our friendly gunner, "I would be seriously pissed off if I snuffed it because some idiot doesn't know how to drive. If I'd wanted to kill myself, I wouldn't have bothered to come all the way out here!"

Tyson's English is certainly not the best, but he understands well enough when it suits him. Being insulted does not go over well with him, especially as it is by a woman, even though it is quite obvious that he has a weak spot for Kristie. So our lovely big baby of a driver concocts the worst possible punishment for us—he plays the same damned cassette of local Arabic music over and over again. For the rest of the journey, the breathtaking scenery is accompanied by a hellish lullaby. Our pleas are useless. Even Kristie's apologies are not enough to sooth the wounded pride of our friend Tyson. What a laugh. This will be one of my favorite memories of my time in Iraq.

Waiting for us at the gate of Camp Ashraf are two men and a woman. At the American checkpoint we are not even searched before going through. Two huge marble lions greet visitors. Lions are the symbol of Iran. I am speechless.

"But these people are rich!" I say to Shakir in astonishment.

Luxurious parks, beautiful small villas, palm trees, flowerbeds in bloom, statues of heroes of the resistance, tarmac roads, fountains. Everything is clean and perfectly organized.

"I feel as if I'm in Switzerland!"

"I wouldn't know," the doctor replies. "I've never been."

The people even look different, certainly distinctive. Iranians are taller and more athletic-looking than Arabs. Iran is not an Arab country, even if lots of people think it is. Iranians do not speak Arabic, but rather Farsi, an Indo-European language that sounds quite similar to French. Nothing like Arabic at all.

"I feel quite at home," I say to the doctor.

I cannot help it. I have always felt at ease with Iranians. And these do not seem very different from the ones I have met in the past. A man walks over and in perfect Italian does the honors and welcomes me to the camp.

"I lived in Italy for years," he says, noticing my amazed expression, "in Rome."

"Yes, I can tell!" I laugh.

It always makes me smile to hear a foreigner speak Italian with a regional accent. With his flawless spoken Italian, anyone mistaking this well-dressed young man as an Italian would be forgiven.

"Before you meet the women mujahedin, we'd like to take you around our museum," says a woman with soft features.

She is Camp Ashraf's director. Her hair is covered with an elegant headscarf. Thick glasses add an intellectual air. She speaks very calmly, almost in a whisper. She is clearly educated, as is everyone we have met so far. They offer us tea.

"You wouldn't have some Iranian sugar lumps, would you?" I ask.

I want to impress them by showing I know their customs as well as their country. It works perfectly. They stare at me, stunned. Moments later, my beloved sugar lumps appear. In Iran, you do not use powdered sugar to sweeten tea. Instead, you put a sugar lump in your mouth—sugar lumps that are much harder than ours—and sip the tea. The sugar dissolves slowly in your mouth as it meets the hot tea. Mmm…it's heavenly, especially for those of us with a sweet tooth.

"Shall we go?" the woman asks.

"Oh, I love this place—women in charge!" I say to Shakir. "I wonder if they've got room for me too!"

On a sign outside the museum are the words "Museum of Martyrs of Iranian Resistance." The museum is dedicated to everyone who has sacrificed his life for the cause. I enter a hall brimming with glass cases, photos, paintings, and statutes. Suddenly, we are pitched into darkness. The lights have been switched off. Horrific images are cast onto the wall opposite us. They are projecting a "video shock." My heart is beating heavily.

"I'm never quite able to relax in your damned country," I whisper to Shakir.

Death by a firing squad, death by hanging. I can cope with that. But when there is a scene of a limb being amputated—an amputation without anesthetic—it is hard not to turn away. "This is only one of the means of torture," says a girl standing next to me.

The video plays for a while longer. Parts of it are truly grisly.

"If you were to show this in Italy," I say to the girl, "half of the audience would faint!"

The video is interesting. There is no doubt about that. But it is unilateral. Watching this video would make you think executions happened all the time in Iran. I spent months there and never once stumbled across a hanging. I am not saying that Iran is paradise on earth, but it is also not the hell on earth that they are trying to portray. A lot of progress has been made in what was once ancient Persia. The times of Khomeini are now over, and gradually the country is picking itself up. Slowly, slowly.

Bullet-ridden jackets worn by heroes of the resistance at their execution, clothes ripped off during torture, letters written by prisoners sentenced to death, and all sorts of personal items are displayed under glass. Everything is very well presented. I stop in front of one of the photos of a martyr. It is a woman. It is as if I know her.

"It's my mother," says the young woman who has accompanied us from the beginning. I look at the picture again. Her daughter is a perfect likeness.

"They killed my whole family. I am here for revenge."

Revenge, vendetta, hatred. Why do people rationalize in these terms? Certainly, it is easy for me to pontificate. I can only begin to imagine what it is like to have your entire family wiped out.

"I was young. My parents had put me under a relative's charge in Sweden. That's where I lived before I decided to come here and dedicate myself to the struggle. I'd had enough of the easy life. I wanted to go back to Iran!"

"I would too," I tell her. "It's an amazing country."

By now we have left the museum.

"The women mujahedin are waiting for you," says my chaperone with the perfect Italian. Shakir seems more excited than I am. A little nervous, too.

"Let's hope they really have been disarmed," he whispers in my ear.

We enter a vast hall filled with beautiful girls who smile when they see us. I am intimidated. I did not expect to see so many people. Everyone's eyes are on me. They rise to their feet and welcome me warmly. I am ushered to a seat next to Shakir and the movement's older leaders. They are all young women between eighteen and twenty-five. The one in charge wears a green headscarf; almost all the girls wear similar colored scarves. Underneath their veils, jeans and the latest sandals peek out.

"They're beautiful," I whisper to Shakir.

"I told you," he hisses back.

"They don't look dangerous at all," I continue. "I can't exactly see them firing Kalashnikovs. They look so sweet…"

If I'd expected to find a pack of snarling women wrapped up in black chadors ready to overthrow the Tehran government, I couldn't have been more mistaken. Or at least, partly mistaken. Appearances sometimes deceive.

The women who are quite clearly the leaders take the floor. They have prepared themselves well for this meeting and outline the aims of their organization. I listen to them talk as I look at them, one by one. I listen in silence to the accusations they level at the mullah government and their stories of slaughtered parents. It is all very interesting, but somehow it feels stale. It needs a bit of spice. I decide to try to unleash the devil in them.

"I know Iran well, the cities, the countryside. How is it possible that in all the months I lived there, I never once saw an execution? I know it happens, but not as you're trying to have me believe!"

A thunderbolt unleashed upon us could not have caused more damage. I glance sideways at Shakir. He buries his face in his hands.

Well, that did the trick! All their beautifully crafted speeches about democracy. We the poor victims, they the evil who should be eliminated. Let's not forget, though, they are armed to the teeth: a rosy concept of democracy.

I can tell by the doctor's expression that he wishes he never brought me here.

"I should have known that you'd raise hell. Just for the sheer pleasure of inciting people to anger," he says, sorrowfully.

"I want to see what these sweet little girls are made of," I tell him, satisfied with the reaction I produced. Up until a couple of moments ago, the mujahedin had been sitting gracefully behind their desks, politely waiting their turn to speak. Now they are spitting fire. They all want to speak and yell their version of truth at me. They leap to their feet, wave their arms, and shout, trying to get their neighbor to shut up at the same time. Yes, now I can imagine them with Kalashnikovs. Now I can see them at the wheel of a tank, heading for Tehran. What a performance!

Calming everyone down takes some time. I want to hear everyone, one by one. So, following the order of raised hands, I try to deal with the repressed rage hurled at me. But they do not let me respond. They are talking among themselves. Everyone has a more convincing argument.

"If you want to teach democracy, perhaps you should apply it first to yourselves," I say, coolly. Shakir squirms in his chair. He is envisaging our frenzied escape from the camp, chased by hordes of enraged women freedom fighters.

What wrath, what passion, what intense expressions. If only it could be channeled in the appropriate way, great results would be achieved. They are young and beautiful. They could have chosen an easy life in Sweden or Canada, but instead they chose to pursue their ideals living here, in a fenced-off camp in the middle of a mutilated country. Although I challenge their methods, I cannot help but be in awe of their impassioned ardor, shining eyes, and trembling voices. When do you ever find such passion in the West? How many young people would abandon their comforts in the pursuit of an ideal? Few. Very few. But here there are crowds of them. What a shame they are all furious with me!

I calmly try to explain my perspective to them. Slowly, slowly, I manage to recover the girls' favor. Even if we still have our differences.

"Are you sure that a change in Iran can only come about through force?" I ask them. "You don't think your country has already seen enough revolutions and suffered enough violence? You want to face more of that?"

Silence.

"It's the only language they understand!" a girl blurts out.

"Are you sure?"

"Yes, violence can only be met with violence. Then we'll be happy to lay down our weapons."

I do not agree.

"You certainly can't dispute that Iran is better off now compared to the Khomeini days. Khatami has made a lot of progress in your country."

"Khatami is too slow," they interrupt.

"And he's a mullah just like the others."

"Of course he's religious. If he wasn't, he'd never have been elected. But he's a reformer, a moderate. If you don't support him there's a risk that the extremists will take the reins of power again. And then your chance would be lost."

I go on. This time it is *me* who does not let *them* speak. At times I too have trouble accepting the concept of democracy. I admit it.

"You don't have faith in your compatriots," I tell them.

"They've been brainwashed," a girl cuts in.

I am tempted to tell her that she has also been brainwashed. I am tempted to tell her that although some more and some less, we are *all* influenced by the society we live in. But I do not want to go too far.

"But if you don't even know your own people?" I reply to her. "You said earlier that you grew up in Sweden and you've never set foot in Iran. How can you claim to want to invade a country if you don't even know how it works? How are you going to go about appealing to the hearts of people you don't know?"

This seems to be a totally new concept

"Iran is a stupendous country with fabulous people," I continue. "You Iranians are educated. This is your winning weapon. Do not underestimate it. Your people are fighting. Not like you, but in a quieter way. They are frightened, but it's understandable. They do not know anything but dictatorial regimes. Why do you only speak about Khomeini? What do you have to say about the shah?"

They stare at me. Nobody speaks anymore.

"The shah of Iran was equally damaging for your people as the various ayatollahs are today."

Silence. I sense that this is the moment to lighten things up.

"Isfahan. How many of you have climbed up the minaret of the Immam mosque?"

Magic words.

"I come from Isfahan," says a girl on my right. "You've been there?"

"Have I been there? It's my favorite place in the whole world. There is nowhere more delightful."

Finally, I am winning them over. Shakir stretches out his legs and lets out a sigh. The older leaders, who had stayed away from the discussion, serve us Iranian biscuits.

"Do you also go on picnics on Friday afternoons?" I ask, as I taste a sweet pistachio pastry.

If there were some girls left who had not warmed to me, then this was the winning stroke.

"Of course!" a chorus of voices reply.

"I thought you would. I love your outdoor picnics. You even have them in the middle of Tehran traffic. You're fantastic."

We go on to speak about their country. It makes me smile that they're asking me where they should visit when they can go back to Iran. Or when they have conquered it.

"Why don't you stay with us for a couple of days?" they ask me.

I cannot deny that part of me wants to. I am really quite tempted! I look over at Shakir, who is violently shaking his head.

"And who will keep the Force Protection at bay?" he asks, concerned that I would even entertain such an idea.

"Next time I want to come when you're having a picnic. Maybe for Noruz," I say.

Noruz is the Persian New Year that is celebrated on March 21. It translates literally as New Year. I have always longed to be in Iran on that day. I have not succeeded yet.

"You know Noruz?" they ask me, clearly delighted.

"Come and celebrate it with us. You'll have a great time!"

Here it is, the same enthusiasm that so frightened me earlier. At heart they are just young women genuinely infuriated by the current state of affairs. But their ideals are mighty, as are their dreams to live in a better world.

CHAPTER 13

Kurdish Rap

"So is this the national tire-burning festival?" asks Colonel Matt Mulhern, looking out of the window of the jeep that is taking us to Iraqi Kurdistan.

I laugh, looking at the mountains of burning tires that surround us. Thick black smoke clouds the otherwise bright blue sky on this beautiful late March day. For the first time so far in Iraq, we have decided to take a couple of days off and go and celebrate the Persian New Year—Noruz—in the Kurdish zone. It was Jim's idea and we readily took him up on it. If you exclude the South African bodyguards, there are equal numbers of men and women present. This will guarantee us a certain amount of frivolity, something I'm really quite looking forward to.

Sitting in the back, I try to make myself as small as possible, wedged between two lumps of men, Jim Haveman on my left and Matt Mulhern on my right. We are all wearing flak jackets, which help to make the journey

Photo: A peaceful moment in Kurdistan

that extra bit more comfortable. Kristi and Viki and Bob follow in the jeep behind ours. We are a great little group, eager to liberate ourselves from months of stress.

I am amused by the thought of National Tire-Burning Day, but I'm not convinced. I cannot, however, come up with a more plausible explanation. It would not surprise us at all if the Iraqis had also invented this as an excuse to party. And as long as they do not take out their rifles and start firing wildly, it is fine by me.

The farther north we get, the more fires there are. My confusion deepens.

"Tire-Burning Day—don't be silly," I say to the colonel. "It's the Eternal Fire of the Zoroastrian."

"Zoro what?" Jim asks me.

"Have you never heard of the Fire Worshipers?"

No answer.

"You're a real American, aren't you? I've got to teach you everything." I am deliberately winding them up.

"But until a minute ago, you were going along with Matt's theory," Jim retorts.

Kurdish rap

"Yes, but then I rummaged around through the great sack of cultural baggage that I lug around with me and found the solution."

Two well-placed elbows, one from my right, one from my left, put me back in line, reminding me that you cannot joke around with a senior advisor and a colonel from the Marines.

"C'mon, we're all ears," Matt says.

He cannot wait to find out what this black smoke is all about. I have to admit it is quite unsettling to see great bonfires surrounded by manic people. My explanation should soothe our anxieties. It should silence those demons that have been dogging us ever since various television networks transmitted the horrific images of exultant Iraqis celebrating after committing an attack. Images that traveled the world. Images that we cannot dislodge from our minds.

"All of these fires are related to Noruz," I say. "Do you have any idea what the Persian New Year symbolizes?" I ask.

They shake their heads.

"It's related to the spring equinox, which was celebrated for more than three thousand years in what was Mesopotamia. The Noruz rites, which are still performed today in Iraqi Kurdistan, Turkey, Iran, and Afghanistan, have their roots in the Zoroastrian faith, which was the religion of Ancient Persia before the advent of Islam."

I break off. I can see the others are interested. Even Richard, one of the South African bodyguards, appears to be eavesdropping, though he pretends he is not.

"The Zoroastrians believed that guardian angels came down to earth to visit the human beings whom they safeguarded. All sorts of festivities and celebrations were organized to welcome these divine beings in the grandest possible way. Huge bonfires were lit on the roofs of houses. The fires signaled to the guardian angels that the humans were ready to receive them," I finish.

"And so all these fires with people dancing round them are a legacy of those festivities?" asks Matt.

"Yes. We shouldn't forget that the only religion professed continually since ancient times in Iran is the one founded by Zarathustra."

"I've never heard of it," Jim says.

"Persepoli. Have you ever heard that mentioned?" I ask.

"Yes," he replies.

"Well, the Persepoli complex was designed for one single purpose—the Noruz festivities. The Persepoli palaces were built especially for the Zoroastrian festivities that celebrate the coming of spring. That's where the famous Persian New Year reception was held and where the representatives of all the nations that formed part of the Persian Empire met to pay their homage to the great king."

"Well, I can't wait to get dancing around a bonfire, then," says Jim. "I was up here over Christmas and I got started. Now I'm a professional Kurdish rapper."

We burst into laughter. The idea of this big man, who is hardly renowned for his grace, cavorting around a fire cracks us up.

"Sounds great! So you know, then, that at one point during the festivities everyone starts leaping over the fire as a cleansing ritual."

"Right, well, I'll sit out that part," Jim concludes.

It is wonderful how we are able to joke around now that we are far from our daily anxieties and concerns—Baghdad, sick patients, the handover have all been momentarily set aside. It is the first time I have seen Jim not at work, and I have to say, he is a different man.

As we gradually climb upwards, the landscape becomes more and more impressive. The great dull barren expanse slowly gives rise to greenness, then to hills, then to mountains.

I think back to the last time I came to Iraqi Kurdistan. When I saw all the caves strewn across the mountains, the impenetrable nature, the inaccessible rocks, and snowy peaks, my mind had begun to wander. This is the very land of the renowned Peshmerga warriors. How very cold the nights must be up here. Long nights, hostile like the terrain where these warriors have spent most of their lives. An existence born from fighting.

This is northern Iraq. A fascinating place, forgotten by God and man alike. A place where sunken caves served as hideouts during the day for the real masters of this mountain chain. "Ready to die" is the translation of Peshmerga. Legendary men ready to face death and protect their land. Historical protagonists of bygone times; stories of rebels who would fight to the end with guns, knives, and their bare hands.

Mosul Kurds

Among the Peshmerga was Omar Nasrulla.

"In 1985, I decided to go and join the Patriotic Union of Kurdistan (the PUK). I went to live in the mountains. I slept during the day, and in the night I attacked Baath party centers with my companions," he narrated to me one day.

"I washed once a month and ate when I could. I lived like this until 1993," continues the gentle-looking man who is now the director of a rehabilitation center for prisoners in Sulaymaniyah.

"Most of us fought either for the PUK or for the Kurdistan Democratic Party, the KDP."

I watch Omar as he speaks. I am almost disappointed that he is not ravaged by scars from his decades of bloody battles or that he does not carry Kalashnikov bullets on his belt. Myths aside, then, who are the real legendary Peshmerga?

"The KDP, led by Barzani, and the PUK, led by Jalal Talibani, each had about thirty thousand warriors. Many of them were combat veterans, either against Saddam Hussein's regime or against each other. The alliance of the two parties was a recent event," relates Omar. "Most of the combatants were men, though within the PUK there was a female battalion with five hundred well-trained women, led by a twenty-seven-year-old lieutenant, Sirwa Ismael."

Following the division of the Ottoman Empire after World War I, the Kurds, a group of about twenty million people of non-Arab origin who are now scattered across four different countries, did not receive the state they had been promised.

"The Kurds were not the only victims of Saddam, but we bore the brunt," Omar continues. "The people of this region, and especially the Peshmerga, paid a high price for having opposed the Baath party's racist and totalitarian regime. Now we are waiting for a reward. We want to be repaid for the decades of sacrifices we made and the genocide we faced. We want our legitimate rights to be recognized.

"At the end of the 1980s, northern Iraq was almost completely destroyed. The Iraqi government razed more than forty-six hundred Kurdish villages. Official figures document that more than a hundred eighty thousand unarmed civilians, including women, children, and the elderly, were driven from their homes and deported to southern Iraq. Many of them were thrown alive into ditches."

"We were forced to abandon our villages. Saddam wanted us grouped together into urban centers where it would be easier for him to keep an eye on us. Soon these areas became extremely crowded, and living conditions became unbearable. My family had to live in two rooms with twenty other people."

In 1993, Omar Nasrulla enrolled at the Kurdish Police Training Academy, and six months later became part of the Arbil police force, before being transferred to Sulaymaniyah prison and clinic.

"I am the right person in the right place. Being treated as a criminal for so long myself, I can well understand how the prisoners feel. They, too, are human beings—men or women who have done wrong. Sometimes they have committed a serious crime, but once they have paid their dues, they should be given the opportunity to be reintegrated in society. My job is to ensure that this happens."

The Sulaymaniyah prison really is the right place for Omar. There are three main blocks: male rehabilitation, female and juvenile rehabilitation, and administration. Everything is surrounded by gardens and playgrounds where prisoners can meet their families twice a week. Organized games are held weekly for their children, as are volleyball games and football matches for the inmates.

"You can't imagine how enthusiastically they train," Omar narrates. "It gives them a goal within this tiny community. For the non-sporty types, we organize computer courses or English lessons."

Brightly colored murals painted by the prisoners depict waterfalls, wild animals, mountains, chalets, and characters from fairy tales. Snow White and the seven dwarves are a big hit. Kurdish, English, and Arabic books fill the shelves of the recently built library. Daily and weekly newspapers are stacked up on a table at the entrance, and a group of men sit reading on the wooden benches. Some of them look up when we enter, but only for a second. They smile and then are drawn back to their books, clearly absorbed in their reading. Some of them have only just learned to read. I am amazed and moved by their enthusiasm.

"We've set up three work groups for those who want to learn a new trade. This will ensure them a place in society upon their release into a normal life," says Omar.

"At the moment there are about fifty prisoners specializing in all sorts of crafts. The necklaces, paintings, shoes, hairpins, and shirts they make are then sold at the market, and the money raised will be theirs when they leave the center."

Among the two hundred thirty inmates, there are five women and three juveniles. In their well-looked-after little corner, there are photos of their children, posters, books, magazines, and televisions, all neatly arranged. The windows look out onto a rose garden, and the sunlight streaming in lights up their faces. They are not the faces of suffering. They smile at me and we strike up a conversation. In the background we can hear children laughing and shouting.

"It's Friday today," one of the inmates tells me. "It's picnic day!"

In a corner of the courtyard, a young couple are flirting under a tree. Opposite them, a social worker is chatting to a group of prisoners. Life in Iraqi Kurdistan goes on.

"We're delighted you came to see us today. You couldn't have missed the Noruz celebrations." Dr. Alaa Abir gives us a warm welcome.

"Did you see the bonfires along the road? And have you seen the mountains? You can see every single village from miles away."

Recognizing the doctor was not easy, as we are used to seeing him in a jacket and tie. He wears his Kurdish outfit proudly and is quite charming in his *sherval*—the wide trousers they wear here—and his open *zobon* and *ssaya*, a heavy shirt and vest. His hair is wrapped up in a turban.

"This is the first time I've ever dressed like this. These trousers are so bloody wide I feel as if I'm naked. And the turban! I don't know if I've got it on correctly. I know it's bad luck to take it off, but it's so uncomfortable. It's making me sweat."

He introduces us to his friends, who burst into fits of laughter when they see their friend dressed up as a Kurd.

"I'm an Arab," Dr. Alaa explains. "That's why they're ridiculing me. These Kurds don't miss a single opportunity." They all laugh together. It is wonderful to see how naturally cheerful the people are here. We, however, are flabbergasted.

"Kurds and Arabs? Aren't they supposed to hate each other?" Matt whispers to me.

"Yes, I don't understand."

The doctor has overheard us. He smiles.

"I'm from Karbala, a city that's fervently Shiite. My family courageously opposed Saddam's regime. Years ago, I had to flee, and I found refuge here in the north," he explains. "I graduated with a degree in medicine from Mosul and then transferred to Sulaymaniyah. I had to earn the people's respect at every step, and it was not easy. But then I was rewarded and now I've been chosen by the Kurds to manage their Ministry of Health in Sulaymaniyah."

Unbelievable! An Arab representing the Kurds?

"Now, after the fall of the regime, I'm not ever going to go back to my birth city. But it's not because the people wouldn't welcome me back," the cheerful doctor says.

"Karbala is an extremely religious city and I would have to readapt to a way of life that I'm not accustomed to. I go visit my family every so often. But that's all."

In the darkness of this spring night, with pinpricks of light from distant fires shining like stars, sweet melodies fill the air. Kurdish songs drift from everywhere, echoing across peaks. A surreal atmosphere, even for Iraq.

"Listen! We have not sung like this for decades. There weren't many reasons to rejoice, especially for the Kurds," says Dr. Alaa. Tears of joy appear in his eyes.

"This will be a Noruz to remember. Finally we can stop mourning for our dead and can look toward the future with hope."

Peshmerga, retired

Silence. I had no idea how important this festival was for people.

"Look over there." The doctor points at a group of people. "They sing and leap through the flames. It's a purification rite."

I glance at Jim and nod over at the fire.

"Don't even think about it," he warns.

"Popular belief says that leaping through the flames frees you from sickness and bad thoughts," continues the doctor, brimming with enthusiasm. "Another fundamental part of the Noruz ritual is called Haft Sin. We have to set a special table with seven specific items. In ancient times, each object corresponded to one of the seven creations, as well as the seven divinities that protected them. The seven objects all begin with the letter S in Farsi."

The words tumble out of the doctor's mouth. It seems he is finally able to forget that two of his brothers spent years in jail for the simple crime of being related to him.

"Wheat and barley represent growth," he goes on. "A bowl of goldfish, and water, must be present on the table. Today we also add mirrors. Lit candles symbolize the eternal fire and are placed in front of the mirrors. Wine has been replaced by vinegar, because the Islamic creed prohibits alcohol. Decorated eggs, the universal fertility symbol, represent Mother Earth. Fresh garlic is another recent addition that wards off the evil eye. Samanu is a thick wheat and nut paste that is also a recent introduction to the ceremonious spread. It replaces Haoma, a sacred herbal mix known for its healing properties. Fruit and coins symbolizing wealth and prosperity are also placed on the spread."

We all marvel at the doctor's tale. How do such ancestral traditions manage to survive intact in this day and age? The people around us let themselves go at these frenzied celebrations. Like us, the doctor cannot wait to get going too.

"I want to be able to live in Kurdish Iraq. From now until eternity. I want to build a farm with a view of the mountains and a river running nearby. I want a wife and children to look after," he finishes with inspiration.

What an honor to be invited to take part in this Noruz, this incredible celebration of life that clashes with the belief some have that death and martyrdom can be at the center of religious ritual. Will these ancient Persian traditions continue to survive? A good question, especially when you consider this is a land whose people are fighting so that different creeds and faiths can live with mutual respect. The songs and the laughter we hear are real and are proof that not all treatment takes place in hospitals or clinics. We will party all night long. It is a great boost of much needed optimism.

Jim does not leap through flames, but does throw himself into frenzied dancing. We follow, despite making real fools of ourselves. We stand out a mile. Not only do we not know the steps, but we just do not seem capable of moving as they do. I am sure they have music flowing through their veins. Only Matt will manage to retain a little self-respect and will avoid making a total fool out of himself.

"Somebody needs to immortalize this craziness," Matt shouts to me, as I bounce around the campfire. He is grinning like a madman with a digital camera in his hands. "Well, it's clear that none of you have any inhibitions. We'll see tomorrow how much you're going to cringe when I show you evidence of your artistic performances."

"I would love a bit of milk in my coffee," says Jim.

We are a complete mess. Only a few hours of sleep and we already are back to pursuing our Kurdish adventure.

"I've tried to ask for some," I tell him. "But no one understands me."

We are having breakfast at an inn. We slept in two big rooms, the women in one, the men in the other. The innkeeper does not speak English. Not a word. He stares at Jim, smiling. A friendly smile, but not one that helps to make milk appear on our table.

"I'm sure they've got some," says Jim. "We've just got to find a way of making ourselves understood."

So an amusing, if not utterly bizarre, game takes place at our table. Everybody starts waving their arms, pointing at the most improbable objects. Kristi focuses her attention on the butter, before passing to the cheese, then the coffee, then even the calendar, and in minutes all sorts of things have arrived at our table. But no milk. Jim leans back in his chair and observes the scene.

It is difficult to describe what happened next in this little inn in northern Iraq. A group of people want a drop of milk in their coffee but all their best efforts at communication are in vain. Kurds run about from all corners. It seems as if the whole village has been summoned to try and help solve the puzzle. They are all giggling in the hopeless attempt to fulfill their guests' request.

Jim has that look on his face. He has got something up his sleeve, I am sure of it. I know him well by now. Suddenly, he rises to his feet with a huge grin stamped across his face. What a show. How will I ever forget Jim's fantastic impression of a cow? Pure inspiration. Moments later, a jug of milk appears on the table.

"It's the result that counts," he purrs, satisfied.

I cannot believe it. Is this the same man who never smiles? Who strikes terror in everyone's hearts up and down the corridors of the CPA? Yes, but here we are in Kurdistan, and the people's easy laughter has infected us all.

We spend the day in the mountains, fording rivers on the most precarious rafts, participating in all the picnics we are invited to, with lots of dancing and singing. We also visit villages destroyed by Saddam and listen to horrific tales of carnage, gassings, deportations, and mass graves. What a contrast. But this, too, is Iraq. And this is why I am in love with it. This is why I cannot tear myself away.

As we pass the city of Arbil, a sign flashes by: Emergency.

"We've got to STOP!" I yell at the driver.

"I've got to go and see them. They're Italian. They do the most fabulous things. Oh c'mon, just a little hello," I cajole. "There're so few of us Italians here in Iraq. You surely wouldn't deny us a little chitchat in Italian."

I am excited. The thought of speaking some Italian literally fills me with joy. My travel companions finally relent. "I can't say I'm against the idea of some spaghetti," says Viki.

We enter. The hospital is deserted.

"They're outside," an Iraqi boy informs us. "They're out playing football. It's serious stuff."

We head over to the football grounds.

"We lost. They were much stronger than we were."

Mario Ninno looks exhausted after the match that has only just ended on the new playing field in front of his hospital. Today's impressive lineup here in Arbil: Emergency Surgical Center for War Victims against Rizgary Hospital.

Doctors, patients, cooks, attendants, nurses, cleaning staff, and locals are all gathered around the field. The players are dripping with sweat and covered in dust and sand. Nobody seems in any rush to go have a shower. They are all far too busy having wildly animated discussions.

"You should've passed the ball to me instead of hogging it," wails a young man. He sports a mustache and a formidable physique. "I'm much better than you at scoring. You should just do the running up and down and pass the ball to me whenever you can. But no! You never bloody stop, do you? You run straight up the field and miss every time."

He is so agitated that he just cannot

River rafting

stay seated on the bench with the others. He paces up and down, jumping from one language to the next. His rage at the crushing defeat is best expressed in Kurdish. However, he also wants Mario, his Italian manager; Heidi, a Finnish nurse; Zihad, a Pakistani surgeon, and his fan club of patients to understand him. The result—English mixed with Italian peppered with Arabic and Kurdish words—is truly hilarious. It has everyone in stitches.

"He is one of the cleaning staff," Ahmed explains to me. Ahmed is one of the surgical center's anesthetists.

"I'm happy I made it through the game in one piece. It got a bit nasty at times. Tomorrow I have to leave for Afghanistan, where I'm needed for a delicate operation. Then I'll be back here."

There are two hospitals run by the Italian NGO Emergency in Iraq. Both of them have been active since 1995 in Iraqi Kurdistan.

"Here at Arbil, just as at Sulaymaniyah, we have one hundred beds and we treat victims of war and mines. During recent years we have also specialized in burns," Mario relates. "Here at Arbil, for example, we treat forty-five children on average a month. Usually they are less than twelve years old and suffer minor or severe burns."

In Iraq, particularly in the rural zones without electricity, people are forced to use open fires for cooking and heating. It goes without saying that there are lots of burn victims. In addition to the hospitals Emergency has set up in Iraq, it has set up twenty first-aid stations, each one managed by a doctor and six nurses. They are located in critical zones, such as the villages at high risk from mines along the border with Iran, or where the conflict between the PUK and the KDP is greatest. The organization is perfect. Thanks to ambulances, once a patient is in a stable condition he is taken to Arbil or Sulaymaniyah.

As we have been talking, the football players have been dispersing. Patients have been taken back to bed. Staff are back at work. Spectators have gone home.

A football. Once again, an old, battered, almost flattened black and white football has been the hero of the day. Once again, this simple round object has managed to bring together so many different people. It has managed to entertain them. It has made them laugh.

"The doctors and paramedics are ready to stand on their own two feet," says Mario.

"We've been working in Iraqi Kurdistan for more than eight years and we've succeeded in teaching them everything they need to know. Time after time, they prove to be well-trained professionals and great workers. Now they are also self-sufficient and capable of taking forward what we have built together in these years. Over to them. Inshallah."

CHAPTER 14

Top of the Class

March 28, 2004. It is a hot and sunny Sunday in Baghdad. Everything appears to be ready. Ambassador Paul Bremer, Dr. Khudair Abbas, and Jim Haveman are all present. We are about to transfer the authority of the Ministry of Health over to Iraqi leadership. Of all the ministries, we are the first to meet this objective.

Everybody is seated, waiting for the ceremony to begin. I confess that I am not feeling particularly excited. My mind is too absorbed in daily problems. I am elsewhere. Until the ceremony has actually begun, I have not had time to think about what is about to take place. Then, as I am looking at the podium, it suddenly dawns on me that my coach, our coach, Jim Haveman, is standing next to the man who is going to replace him as the leader of the Ministry of Health. Somebody stop the clock. What a grand moment. I am honored to be part of the team handing over the scepter to our Iraqi counterparts.

Photo: Minister Abbas flanked by Jim Havemen and L. Paul Bremer

Counterparts. This is what they were at the beginning. But then they became our colleagues. And now? Friends. Close friends with whom I have spent more time than anyone else. I know their families. They cook me my favorite Iraqi dishes while I play soccer with their children. I watch them. They seem moved by it all. Just like me. Perhaps they are also feeling a little confused—not fully aware of the occasion's importance.

The great design comes back before my eyes. The great design we have all worked so hard to complete for a year. This is the crowning moment of all our efforts.

Many of my colleagues are not here today. Some of them were injured and sent home against their wishes. Some of them left before completing their mission. Some have had to wrangle documents to be here; even though their mandates have finished they still wanted to be present at possibly the most important ceremony of their lives.

I think back to the day the previous spring when I first set foot in the Ministry of Health. Completely ransacked—no windows, no doors, no fixtures or frames, no desks, no lights. Everything had been stolen or destroyed. I remember the sense of utter desolation as if it were yesterday. And now? Iraqi mosaics sparkle in the sunlight, and beautiful wooden doors greet visitors. Desks with computers, new furniture, a nursery center. If my mind runs back through the year spent here in Iraq, I think of how much we have accomplished. And this is only the beginning. I know this. My Iraqi friends and colleagues will do the rest because they, as Jim stresses in his speech, are the most important resource Iraq has. They are ready for it. We must get out of their way.

But now the question is: am I ready? Am I, Anna, really prepared to give all of this up? Leave my second family? They do not need me anymore. But how about me? It is as if roles have suddenly been reversed, and I was not aware of it until today.

What a powerful moment. Both impressive and poignant. Perfectly appropriate for what Dr. Abbas, the Iraqi Minister, describes as a day blessed by God." From now on, as Ambassador Bremer said, it will be Abbas "at the wheel on the road to sovereignty."

I will not even try to convey the sensations and thoughts of everyone present. But I am sure of one thing: today is a memorable day, not only for the Iraqi people, but also for every one of us who has worked so hard to make this transition of power possible.

Jabur is sad. He hugs me in the corridor. All of this commotion has upset him. He does not quite understand.

"So you're going away?" he asks with wide eyes.

"Why would I be going away?" I reply.

I know full well what he means.

"Well, haven't you just had the handover ceremony? That means you're all leaving." he says, sorrowfully.

"Yes, Jabur, we're leaving. But I'll still be here for a couple of months. Don't worry. And then I'll always come and visit. I wouldn't be able to cope without your tea."

Jabur Hasan, the Ministry of Health's tea man, greets me every morning with a good cup of tea. He is seventy-five years old and has worked at the Ministry of Health for forty-five consecutive years. I have fond memories of one of the many long conversations we had in his kitchen.

"Airplanes!" he says as I take up my usual place next to the fridge. "What an enigma. I've got to find out how they don't get lost up in the infinite heavenly space."

Welcome to the world of my friend Jabur. A world made up of sweet dreams and great imagination.

"And then there's something else that intrigues me with these huge flying birds. I can't help but wonder how they refill with petrol. And what would happened if they break down," he continues with that mischievous smile that never seems to leave his lips.

"I didn't dare ask the others," he confides to us after the ceremony. "None of them seemed particularly interested in a problem that for me has become a question of life and death. After mulling it over for ages, I've

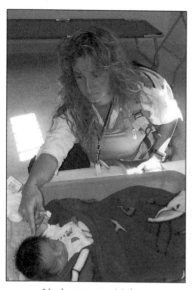

Newborn awaiting Medevac

come to a conclusion. Promise me you won't laugh. Ehi! Come on, don't laugh," he orders, authoritatively. "Ehi" is Jabur's favorite noise.

We all fall silent. A hallowed silence falls upon my friend. We are stunned. That tone of voice does not suit Jabur at all. He breaks the silence as he bursts into hearty laughter, and we follow suit. Jabur has witnessed the birth of nine other ministries, but until recently, had never been on a plane.

"In my rather fantastical mind, airplanes flew on roads to avoid getting lost. I was quite convinced that the sky had a network of roads linking one place to the next. Petrol stations along the way resolved the problem of fuel," he says. "But there were no mechanics. Otherwise, how would you explain the accidents?"

Roads in the sky. Petrol stations sitting in the clouds. What an elaborate solution to a problem that most people would not even consider. We all collapse into giggles, and the ministry's kitchen, Jabur's undisputed kingdom, fills up in moments. Everyone wants to know what is going on.

"Ehi! Yes, this is what I thought. It's logical. Come on, I'm a simple-born man with no grand education." he says, never losing touch of his natural sense of humor.

His friends pat him warmly on the back.

"Ehi! Stop it. You're all annoying. You're hurting me!"

Observing this man who has managed to retain a positive attitude toward life despite everything that has happened in the past makes me aware how spoiled we are. We have so much to learn, used as we are to taking everything for granted. We see airplanes tracing their winding paths through the sky yet never bother trying to come up with an explanation. We never pause and think about how things are. We don't need to.

"But now I know how they really work. Ehi! Last month, I flew to Saudi Arabia for the pilgrimage to Mecca. What an experience." says Jabur. "I was frightened. I'll admit it. Especially on our return. The airplane kept hopping about. Sometimes I would be squashed against my chair; other times I would be thrown up. I thought it was because we were overloaded."

An interesting explanation. How funny to imagine this old man climbing up the airplane stairs for the first time. I wish I had been there to see his enthusiasm, his happiness, and his astonishment. He, the man who wanders up and down the corridors of the Ministry of Health serving tea in his fatherly manner, finally made it to Mecca. He, who constantly cheers everyone up with his round pewter jug offering little cups of chai or hamouth—Jabur's special blend of dried lemons—finally saw his dream come true. A childhood dream. Not in his wildest imaginings would he have thought it would come true.

"I prayed for days and days. I prayed for my family, my six daughters and three sons. I prayed for all of you here at the ministry," he says. "You are all so friendly to me. Nobody has ever treated me so well. Nobody has ever done anything for me. Helping me go to Mecca was the best present you could have given me."

Now, not only can Jabur go visit the sacred sites when he wants, he is also free to pray.

"I come from a religious family. For us, praying is our duty to God. But Saddam killed my nephew and one of my brothers for their religious devotion. He could not bear the idea they could believe in an authority superior to his."

Jabur smiles. He has lost his front teeth. It makes his mouth look even bigger than it is and makes his expression more keen. His white hair and mustache are tidy. His bony, sunburnt hands tell tales of life-long hard work. The most striking thing about Jabur, though, is his eloquent eyes, sparkling and melancholic. Jabur loves having his kitchen full of people. This is when he really feels satisfied. People come to find him when they are in need of a warm, noble heart and ready ear to listen to their daily successes or failures, or when they need to vent their frustrations. Jabur fits the bill for this, too. It is a way of diffusing the accumulated tensions, and he knows it.

There is always a teapot on the stove. Clouds of steam fill the room. There is a homely atmosphere in here, in Jabur's realm, the most comforting place you can imagine.

"May God bless Iraq. A free, peaceful Iraq," he says, thoughtfully. "And may Allah bless you. You could be my daughter, Anna. I would love you to be one of my daughters. But it doesn't matter. Put it like this: I am your Iraqi father."

The power of imagination.

Another key player here at the ministry, a woman who certainly does not lack imagination, is Layla. She is the right-hand woman to John Walker, a financial consultant at the Ministry of Health.

"I've got time right now, if you want," she says when I walk into her office to ask for help.

Now? Hearing this word here in Iraq is really quite something. Now? Not tomorrow? Or the day after? Or when God wills? Now? Not after chai? Layla Kuleib has time. Now. It is not just her words that come across with authority but also her tone of voice and her entire posture. Layla is known here at the ministry for being a young woman with clear ideas. She is an indefatigable worker who rushes up the corridors carrying stacks of paper and never takes a moment's break.

"Compared to you, we Iraqis don't work much at all. Just from nine in the morning to two in the afternoon. It's difficult to get things done in such a short amount of time," she says. "That's why I can't ever stop. I don't have time to waste in useless chatter."

Her deep dark eyes inspire calm. She shakes out her black hair as she talks, an automatic gesture when she has finished work, when the moment has come to relax a little. She crosses her legs, and her calf-length denim skirt rides up a little. Black ankle boots and a colored pullover add to her sassy, carefree look. She has crossed her legs but she does not show the soles of her feet. I notice this straight away. She is certainly Westernized, but she does not forget local customs. Showing your soles is considered disrespectful in Iraq.

"Nine. My favorite number is nine," she says in a brisk, brusque manner. "I couldn't tell you why. Number nine makes me feel at ease. I have no idea what this means. Perhaps one day I'll find out."

Layla is definitely unique. And it is not just her passion for the number nine. This twenty-eight-year-old does not seem to care about other people in the room when she talks about herself. This attitude is extremely rare in a country like Iraq where people still have apprehensions about speaking about their private lives, passions, and intimate feelings.

"I was offered a two-year scholarship in the United States. My parents didn't want me to take it," she narrates. "It wasn't easy to give in to their wishes and not go to the country I've always dreamed about. But I didn't argue. I already enjoy sufficient freedom, and I didn't want to undermine their trust in me."

Trust, respect, freedom.

"After graduating from high school, I wanted to study French," she continues to tell me.

"I had fallen in love with French literature and the language. But my parents opposed my wishes and so I opted for English. Now I'm happy that I took their advice."

Layla really enjoys working as John's assistant. "I began by being his interpreter," she says. "Now, after almost a year with him, I help him with all the decisions. I've learned so much that now I'm able to stand by myself in almost all situations."

Layla began working for the ministry a year before the war. She had to translate medical journals from English into Arabic and had to check that nothing was ever printed that criticized Saddam Hussein and his regime.

"It was wearing, painstaking work that left no room for error or distractions. Foreign journals openly criticized the Iraqi government, but I couldn't let a single negative opinion escape my attention. One single mistake would have been enough to—I don't even want to think about it."

People in the room have stopped working and stare at Layla. They are all engrossed, listening intently. Layla does not even seem to notice their stares. They are stares of admiration, not disapproval. Her colleagues are impressed by her courage and would probably like to follow her example.

"I have a recurring dream," she says.

We laugh. First numbers, then dreams.

"I dream about riding a bicycle."

Riding a bike? This does not strike me as a particularly exciting dream.

"I haven't been on a bicycle since I was thirteen. In my dream I never fall off. I'm convinced that I won't even fall in real life either. And this is why I want to do it."

In all honesty, riding a bike really does not seem like a difficult dream to satisfy. Get a bike, sit on it, pedal, and you are on your way. But not in the eyes of this young Iraqi woman.

"Another thing I adore is the smell of rain," Layla continues, continuing on the theme of likes. Who knows why she decided to speak about this to me? Numbers, dreams, feelings, what else?

"Riding a bicycle in the rain. What a wonderful feeling that must be!"

"It's horrible," I tell her. "Especially if you get caught in the middle of a storm when you are dressed to the nines or heading for work."

But Layla would probably be blissfully happy.

"Or drive a jeep through a sandy desert," she says.

Poor Layla. She is trying all possible ways to win my approval and say something I agree with, seeing as so far she has not had much luck with the bike and the rain. I must admit that her dream of driving through the desert is much more comprehensible than being soaked to the skin on a bike.

"I have never seen snow. I would love to see a beautiful snowfall on Christmas day," she says, decisively.

Christmas?

"I love Christmas. It's a Christian festival, I know. And I'm Muslim. Devoutly Muslim. But this doesn't stop me from being happy at

Christmas," she stresses. "I pray five times a day. I'm very disciplined when I'm at home. Here, at the ministry, I certainly can't just stop working. I couldn't disappear and then come back as normal in the middle of a meeting. It would be impossible. And could you really see John waiting for me while I go and pray?"

I laugh at the thought of her boss and friend, an ex-Marine of few words, famous for consuming the most Coca Cola and cigarettes in the whole of Baghdad, waiting for her to come back from prayers. He would be going absolutely crazy.

"So this is why I have adopted a strategy I call 'invisible praying,'" she continues. "I think about God and try to behave in a way that corresponds with his wishes."

God's wishes. Allah's wishes. We are speaking about the same almighty force that lets people kill themselves and others, claiming they are following God's will.

"In Iraq, just as all the other Islamic countries, too many people use religion to their own benefit," says Layla, reading my thoughts. Her tone of voice is hard, unyielding. "They use the Koran, our sacred book, to serve their personal needs by changing its content and distorting its verses. But this is an affront to Islam itself. It has nothing to do with the God I pray to. These are the people we Muslims should be afraid of. Look at my parents. They are simple people who work, take care of their children, and wait patiently for things to happen."

Layla is tense. She cannot bear the thought that many of the criminal acts carried out in her country are perpetrated in the name of Allah. But thinking about her family, her six brothers and five sisters, brings her back to her usual calm self.

"I would love to go bungee jumping!"

Yes, here she is, the cheerful, bubbly Layla we are in love with.

"Although I don't think the bridges in Baghdad are high enough. But who knows? Maybe they'll build one so that we Iraqis can hurl ourselves off it with our feet attached to a bungee and dunk our heads in the Tigris," she says, happy with her new plan. Well, you never know. In this crazy world, everything is possible.

"Layla, are you ready? Let's go." It's Zainab entering the room.

"Oh, and your partner in crime too. How are you doing, Little Miss Engineer? What are you two plotting?" I ask the two girls.

Layla and Zainab burst into giggles. It is difficult to not to attract attention when you have Zainab's green eyes and smile. This is true in any part of the world, but even more so in Iraq.

"We walk home together," they explain. "That's all."

"That's all, eh? Say that to someone else," is my response.

If Layla is self-assured and easy going, then Zainab is sophisticated yet natural. Both her dress and her headscarf are elegant, with colors that match her eyes perfectly. She has a gap between her two front teeth that gives her an impish look. I hope she does not mind me telling you that she is only twenty-three. Because of hard living conditions, Iraqi women rarely manage to retain their youthfulness and light-heartedness after the age of twenty. This does not mean that this young civil engineer is frivolous.

"I graduated just over a year ago, and shortly afterwards I was given work at the Ministry of Health," she says. "Honestly speaking, as I'm a civil engineer, I'd hoped to go work at the Ministry of Construction. But it didn't happen like that. I didn't have any choice."

Zainab is not a rare case. There are lots of girls who decide to study engineering, but all too often it is considered a male profession.

It depends on which branch you enroll in. Three-quarters of Iraq's environmental engineers are women, whereas mechanical engineers are mostly men. In the department of civil engineering, the male-female ratio is fairly balanced, she tells me.

"Education has always been important in my family. My mother teaches mathematics at school, and my father graduated in fine arts. Now he is a manager at the Ministry of Oil but has passed on his passion to one of my brothers, who is currently studying at the Faculty of Fine Arts here in Baghdad."

Zainab has two brothers and a sister. She is the eldest. They all still live at home.

"In Iraq, you leave home only when you get married. Never earlier, and I'm not married."

Silence. The conversation has taken an interesting turn. It is up to her whether we continue or whether we backtrack.

"Three men have proposed to me, and three times my parents have refused them," she says, accepting the challenge.

"One was a forty-year-old widower with two children, the second was

Eyes bright with future promise

not especially well-off, and the third was my cousin. All of them were eligible, but my parents sent them all packing."

Eligible. This is the word Zainab skillfully chooses to avoid the use of the crucial word—the word she probably knows very little about—love. Women marry at about twenty in Iraq, even though official figures say that difficult economic conditions have brought about change. Today there are a million women under the age of thirty-five who are not married. Getting married is not easy, neither for the woman, who must wait passively for a proposal, nor for the man, who must raise a dowry, buy a house, and shoulder all the costs that a family entails.

"Women who have studied find it difficult to find a husband. More difficult than others," says Zainab. "An Iraqi man prefers a woman whom he can impose his authority over, not one who knows her rights and can contest him, expressing her own opinions."

Young women in this country do not stroll down the streets, do not go out for dinner, and do not go to the gym. It is therefore at the office, in school, or at the university that men and women have the only opportunity to meet and get to know each other.

"Dinners organized by the respective families is how it's done," she explains. "Whether you decide to accept your parents' decision or not depends largely on your education."

If young women cannot go out about town, participate in sports, or go to the cinema or concerts, what do they do in their free time? How do they manage to survive the endless afternoons and boring evenings cut off from the rest of the world?

"Tolstoy is excellent company. Did you know that?" says Zainab.

"I adore the Russian classics: Dostoevsky, Gogol, and Chekhov. They are my favorites along with Shakespeare. I have devoured all his plays. Romeo and Juliet, I could read it over and over and never get bored with it."

Her distinctive, mischievous smile reappears on her lips.

"Do you like Brad Pitt? And how about Daniel Day Lewis?" she says, turning her attention from literature to cinema. "I could watch 'Legend of the Fall' or 'The Last of the Mohicans' a thousand times."

Zainab's expression changes, reflecting a shift in humor. Her thoughts dwell once again on the daily difficulties that characterize her life.

"We young engineers didn't have many rights in the past. We had to do routine jobs for minimum pay. The senior engineers made money by taking commissions on the contracts they won" she explains. "But now I work hard, and I like it."

The gap between her teeth is revealed once again. "I've still got lots to learn, but I've found people who trust me and are happy to let me do things my way."

"Anna, have you heard from Emaddin?" Jim asks me. "He's disappeared. He's not answering his phone, and there's no one at home," he adds.

"He'll have left," I answer, sarcastically.

The Emaddin story has worn me out. He leaves, reappears, disappears again, back again. Oh, now off again—he has gone too far.

"Well, now that I think about it, a couple of days ago I had a missed call on my mobile phone. It was Emaddin," I remember.

"And what did he say?" Jim asks, excitedly.

"It was a missed call. I didn't answer it."

"And why not?"

"Because it was three in the morning and I was asleep. I saw the missed call the next morning and thought I'd see him here at the ministry, and then I forgot all about it. Oh dear! Maybe he needed to speak to me urgently."

Emaddin is a real puzzler. I have even marked down the dates that he has disappeared and reappeared, hoping to see a pattern. Unfortunately, you worry the moment you do not hear from someone in Iraq. And now it seems that doctors are targets and we are more anxious than ever. In the last month alone, more than thirty doctors have been kidnapped just in Baghdad. Most were released within a few days, after their families paid the ransom. So far none have been killed.

"I am the protest leader for the young Iraqi doctors." This is how the good-looking doctor introduces himself to me the first time I meet him. Rather unusual, especially here in Iraq where it takes some time until people open up. When they meet someone they do not know well, they prefer to speak about their family, their age, or their studies. But this young man gets straight to the point.

"That's why I admire Americans most of all. They don't speak much, just the bare essentials, and then off you go, back to work. Here, though, people love never-ending meetings that wind up in a hearty lunch. Even if we young people are starting to be different. But the older generation does not seem to catch on."

Emaddin complains that few of the key roles at the ministry were given to the younger generation.

"When the war ended, lots of us were fed up with seeing the same old faces still in the same important positions. That's why we decided to unite our forces and protest against those who supported corruption during Saddam's regime," he says. "We wanted more rights, and it was the first time we had ever freely expressed our opinion."

Emaddin represents the young Iraqi postgraduate council, a group that did not exist during the Baathist period.

"It was hard at the beginning. Everyone came to me with enormous, urgent, unimaginable problems and demanded that I resolve them immediately. Everyone thought his problem demanded more attention than the others.' I ended up with thousands of problems piled on my desk earmarked as top priority," he relates.

"The Iraqi people want rapid change. Most of them thought when Saddam went, all their problems would evaporate as if by magic. But this is not a fairytale. This is real life and things don't work like this. In Iraq we are not used to the concept of democracy, and the first step is to learn to use it correctly," explains Emaddin. He is twenty-nine years old and was chosen by the Ministry of Health to participate in a two-day conference in New York organized by the United Nations.

"I was chosen to go to New York after I'd worked for you for barely a month. This would never previously have been possible."

Emaddin is right. For years, only a couple of doctors had permission to leave the country. Most of them were fervent supporters of the regime and knew Saddam in person.

"Don't get me wrong. I have nothing against the senior doctors, especially those who have studied abroad. They have an open mind and treat us young doctors as they treat their own children. I have respect for almost all of my older colleagues, but the moment has come for them to take a step down," says Emaddin.

"They were happy when all decisions were made by a centralized power. But now the scene is radically different, and they feel lost in this new phase where enthusiasm and passion are the essentials for a successful new Iraq, a country made of new people."

Emaddin is married, with one son and a newborn baby girl.

"I want my children to be able to reap the benefits of what I will do for my country. But they, too, will have to contribute and work hard. I want them to learn to live in a democratic system. I want them to be able to hold open discussions, where all participants can express whatever they want."

"October 22, 2003. Emaddin Al Kubaisy has left Iraq," is what I wrote in my diary. Along with his enthusiasm, he packed his bags, deciding London was the best place for him and his family. The bright lights of New York were too glitzy for this young Iraqi dreamer.

"When I landed in New York, I just could not believe my eyes," I can remember him saying to me, on his return from the trip.

"What a night skyline. You can't imagine what it meant to an Iraqi who had never set foot outside his country, who has lived his whole life obsessed with one man. I was thrilled. Finally I was happy and excited. I wanted to see everything. I didn't want to miss a single thing. On the very night I arrived, I left my bags in the hotel and went out for a walk around. Everything was so new, so immense, so grand. Clean streets, gigantic buildings, lights everywhere, cars, people, women and men walking together. Everyone was happy. They danced and drank. In a free world."

This are precisely the words Emaddin used to describe his first night away from Baghdad. I only hope all that glitter and sparkle does not disappoint him. He seemed to be missing the patience he had preached so much about. Who knows? Maybe one day he will return to the young Iraq that, for now, will just have to make do without him. Without a young, courageous man who, tired of fighting, did not have the courage to stay and continue to suffer. Nobody can blame him. Especially those who have seen how much Iraqis suffer. History, then, is made not only of heroes.

"October 27, 2003. Emaddin has returned," says my diary. Everyone stares at him incredulously when he makes his appearance at the ministry. We were all convinced he had left the country.

"You didn't believe all those rumors, did you, Anna? Oh no," he cries, almost disappointed. "I'd just taken a couple of days of holiday, that's all," he explains. "In Iraq we are so used to people disappearing into thin air that we always think the worst. We never disappear because we're on holiday. Either we've been sent to prison, or we've been killed or we've successfully fled the country. It's difficult for us Iraqis to free ourselves from this way of thinking."

Emaddin has decided to stay. Baghdad, the city of unbridled rumors, can count on him, even if surviving in Iraq is more difficult and dangerous than in any other place in the world. But this is their homeland.

April 4, 2004. Emaddin has disappeared once again. I do not know what to say. I have no idea if he will reappear in my office in a couple of days as if nothing happened. I can already picture him in my mind, with that devious smile, inviting me to drink tea or go for a picnic along the Tigris.

Whatever he decides to do, Emaddin will also remain a courageous man for me, a hero. And if he has chosen to leave the country, I can say only that I will miss him.

Break a leg, Emaddin.

CHAPTER 15

Full Power to the Iraqis!

"Don't go, Maurizio. Forget it."

"I can't, Anna. I've made up my mind," he replies.

"You're so bloody stubborn! Well, if you get yourself killed, you won't see me crying," I rage, on the verge of despair. I do not know what else I can possibly say to stop him from going to Fallujah.

"Yesterday they killed my bodyguard. I don't know if I could cope with another death," I plead, hoping pity might work. "Please, I'm begging you."

"I'm sorry to hear it, Annina. I didn't know. I realize a lot is going on for you."

Maybe this has done the trick. Maybe my friend's death will dissuade him from going. I continue down this path.

"He was shot dead in a supermarket. He left a wife and two children behind. This country is always becoming more dangerous. It's no joke."

"Well, you think about getting me out of trouble if something happens. You'll be right there in the American headquarters. You're best positioned

Photo: Wisdom disguised as humor

to intervene if necessary. And then, I don't have a family. I don't have as much to lose."

I give up. Maurizio Scelli has made his decision. I am just getting myself worked up. Usually I have a soft voice, but now it is getting harsh and uncompromising. I really want to try to prevent his mad plan. Maurizio is also getting agitated, probably disappointed that he has not won my approval. But he will never get my approval, and the more we talk the more it is clear that we are not going to make any progress; neither of us is going to budge.

I am in Jim's office, and he is listening to the fiery telephone call. This is the first time he has seen his Anna lose her patience. And on the other end of the line, Maurizio's voice sounds more and more serious.

"I've got to go now. Ciao."

This is how it all ends.

"Wow. What a temper. I feel as if I've just seen a gun battle," Jim says, with his usual controlled tone of voice.

They all look at me with raised eyebrows.

"What's going on?" Dave asks me. "I've never seen you in such a state."

I tell them that my rapid Italian was aimed at Maurizio Scelli, the Italian Red Cross high commissioner, and I explain briefly what he is about to do.

"Crazy Italians," Jim mutters. "I just hope he knows what he's risking," he says, a little puzzled.

"By taking water to Fallujah he's risking his own life and jeopardizing the Red Cross's entire mission. Why doesn't he get the Iraqis to do it? There's no need for him to go." Dave is right, but he is missing a piece.

"Our hostages are at the heart of it," I explain.

"Ah, now I understand. So he has decided to go to Fallujah to try to negotiate their release. Has he thought about what will happen if he and his men get kidnapped too?" he asks.

"Then we'll have to get five or six hostages released instead of three," I retort, curtly.

I decide to go and let off steam in the gym. But I can't. I'm too agitated. I want to be at hand should something happen and they need a speedy response from me. Every quarter of an hour, with my heart in my mouth, I dial the number for Baldassarelli, the director of the Italian Red Cross in Baghdad. And every time the answer is the same: "No, Anna, nothing yet."

I am getting increasingly anxious. I go down to Bremer's office to let them know that the Force Protection might be needed to go rescue my Italian friends. Thank goodness I had said I wouldn't cry. Just the thought that something might have happened makes my eyes well up with tears.

Then, finally, the telephone rings.

"They've made it, Anna!"

Baldassarelli is as relieved as I am. But then the same scene repeats itself every other day for almost two weeks. One day, having not received notice for hours, I even alert the Force Protection. Luckily they stayed on standby and were never actually needed.

"Anna, what's Scelli up to today?" I am asked every morning by Ambassador De Martino. He hopes, in vain, that my answer does not contain the word Fallujah. My reply rarely puts him at ease.

What a huge sigh of relief when the news comes through that the three hostages have been released. It is June 8, 2004. It is exactly a year since I landed in Baghdad. What better way to celebrate this incredibly important anniversary for me? In the office everyone is delighted, probably celebrating the fact that I have stopped pacing up and down and tearing out my hair.

Slowly, we are getting closer to the fateful date: June 30, 2004. Who knows what will happen? Will things improve? Or get worse? Once again, I'm thrilled at the thought of witnessing such a crucial part of Iraq's history. An Iraq that by now I am very fond of, and that I am gradually beginning to understand.

Jim Haveman has left, along with many of my other colleagues. There are four of us left to hold the fort. Dave, a young doctor; Ken, a colonel in the Air Force who liaises with us; the Iraqi minister; and representatives from the U.S. Department of State had arrived in a second wave toward the end of December. Jim left the reins with John Walker, the financial advisor, who has been here since the beginning. Like myself. Every so often, I feel a bit melancholy working all alone in room S200. Once I was jostling for elbow space, it was that full. There were at least twenty of us, and only Colonel Gerber's well-known shouts could maintain order.

But now, surrounded by empty desks, unused guns, scattered flak jackets, dusty maps, and stacks of paper, I cannot help but feel abandoned. I start thinking about old times. From time to time, a newly arrived U.S. State Department reconnaissance man drops in.

"Could you please give me the telephone numbers of the Iraqi hospitals?" A man in a suit and tie suddenly appears in my huge office.

"Phone numbers?"

I think I have misunderstood him.

"Yes, Washington wants them. They need them to complete paperwork."

I open my mouth. I shut it. I bite my lips. I do not know what to say without making him feel silly. Without offending him. One part of me would like to suggest that he go home. The other part of me remembers my first day here, what a clumsy oaf I was. I had no clue about this country and its people. But this man standing here, dressed elegantly enough for the White House, leaves me quite perplexed. He repeats his question.

"I can't give you the numbers because I don't have them," I answer coolly.

He looks at me with an air of superiority, as if he is about to ask me what I have been playing at all this time if I have not even put together a list of phone numbers.

"You don't have the numbers?" he makes certain.

"No. It's not that I don't have them. There are no phones here in Iraq."

Calm, breathe in breath out, keep calm. I take a deep breath and start from the beginning.

"The land lines haven't been installed yet," I explain. "We have MCI cell phones to communicate between ourselves and the Iraqi doctors from the ministry. The telephone lines of the new company, Iraqna, are only just beginning to work. But we haven't quite got there."

"So what do you do when you need to speak to a hospital doctor urgently?" he asks.

His flabbergasted look speaks volumes.

"Well, we hop in a jeep and set off," I reply.

"Hop in a jeep? But it's dangerous out there."

I stare at him. I am speechless.

"I'd like to know one thing. Do you really think you can stay shut in here for the whole time you are in Iraq?"

By his expression, I reckon my question has caught him off guard. I realize that this distinguished-looking man does not have the slightest intention to set foot outside the Green Zone.

I do not wait for his answer. I am worried about how I might react. And then, who says he is wrong? He just has a different approach from mine. And from everyone else's here over the last year.

"How do you think you're going to sort things out while penned up in here? If you want to understand Iraq, you need to get out, meet the people, and see things with your own eyes. Oh, forget it. Tell me, is there some other way I can help you?" I ask, trying to be courteous.

In fact, I cannot wait for the moment he leaves my office. This place that once bustled with excessive zeal. Rightly or wrongly.

"Addresses. Seeing as you don't have the phone numbers, could you kindly give me the hospitals' addresses."

I think I am going to scream. Asking for addresses is even more ludicrous than asking for phone numbers. Next he will want a telephone directory.

"There are only a few roads with names in Iraq. Main squares and major roads. Nothing else," I reply.

Were you awake when you drove here from the airport? I would like to ask. Did you notice all the sandy roads that don't even have tarmac, and all the dead-end alleys? I realize that I am tapping the tabletop nervously as I speak.

"So, what do you do?"

I should have expected this. With a magic bolt—Abracadabra—I grab the GPS on my desk and wave it at him.

"We use this. I can give you all the grid coordinates of all the hospitals and clinics in the country if you want." I look at him. "But do you know how to use it?"

This time he realizes. "Yes, yes, give me the coordinates. It's better than nothing," he says, hurriedly.

"Don't hesitate to pop in again if you need anything else," I say, as he leaves the room. How two-faced of me. I never see him again.

Other than these characters who clearly find it hard to settle in, I have a continual flux of Iraqis who are desperately trying to leave the country. They turn up, presumably all on death's door and all requiring urgent treatment abroad.

"My friend is gravely ill," a boy says to me. As he speaks, he points at the middle-aged man next to him who is wearing a suitable expression for the occasion. I recognize this expression. I have just had the conversation about hospital phone numbers. I am hardly in the right frame of mind to try to solve whatever problem he may have.

"Please go ahead and tell me. What's the problem?" I ask.

"He's really ill. He can't go on like this," the boy explains. "He needs to be cured abroad," he adds with conviction.

"We are the ones who'll decide that," I interrupt. "You need to show me a medical report that states his need to leave Iraq for treatment. Do you have any documents to show me?" I ask.

The two mutter between themselves.

"No," says the boy. "My cousin was taken to Italy for the same problem," he states, not knowing that he is speaking to someone who knows quite a bit about the Italian Red Cross's "acceptable diseases" policy.

"And so what is it?"

Silence. A moment's embarrassment. The dying man looks at his feet. I really do not think he is about to keel over and die. Still, you never know.

"He's impotent."

Here we go. He said it. I gape at him. I try to hold back the giggles that are shuddering through me. It is not easy.

"But people don't die of impotence," I say, trying to control myself. "Okay, it's not great, but it's not a life-threatening condition."

I do not want him to think I am belittling his problem.

"But my cousin was sent to Italy by the Red Cross," the boy insists.

"Look, you're speaking to the wrong person. I personally deal with all the Medevac patients who get sent to Italy, and I can assure you that nobody with your friend's condition has ever left Iraq for that reason. I'm sorry."

The boy translates what I have just said to his friend, who looks at me sorrowfully. I smile at him. He is very sweet.

"Perhaps if you bring me the medical report I'll see what we can do," I add, in an attempt to cheer him up. Giving false hope is not something I deem correct. But this time, I just do not know how to get past the impasse. It appears there is no way out.

"Impotent," I mutter to myself.

Well, it is a good sign that people are starting to worry about normal complaints and conditions, I suppose? I am glad the world does not consist of only of burn patients and children with leukemia or birth defects.

My life here in Baghdad is made up of bizarre days, but I decide to polish this particular one off with a real event, a classical music concert.

I enter the office of the financial geniuses to ask if anyone is interested in a cultural evening. They are more wound up than normal. And that says it all. George, the senior advisor, is standing on a chair trying to fix a sign up on the door.

It reads "Don't bother asking us for money. We don't have any. Keep out of our way!"

Rather intimidating. Usually he is cheerful and jovial, but today George is not in the best of moods.

"Can you see the sign?" he barks. "If it's money you want, then get out."

I shake my head, then turn to Matt. "Did you remember the concert?" I ask. "Are we going?"

"Oops. I completely forgot. Sorry, Anna, I can't make it. We're having a crisis. Maybe I could catch up later."

"You've stood me up. Don't waste your breath," I answer. "And anyway, you people are always in the middle of a crisis. I think a little classical music might be good for your nervous system."

I walk down the marble staircase and past another ministry, where full pandemonium is also usually in full swing. This is the Ministry of the Interior.

"Satan! I think the devil himself is here today and is in no rush to leave," I hear him yelling when I am at the door.

"Ciao, Anna, how're you doing?" But the advisor does not wait to hear my reply and continues to rant and rave and swear and shout at the devil, who seems to be having great fun with the whole ministry.

"Ok, I get it. I'll go by myself," I say, in a whisper.

One final attempt with Viki, a fellow Noruz Kurdish rapper. She works for the Ministry of Transport.

"Locomotives from Russia. Tell me, Anna, what on earth am I supposed to do with fifty locomotives from Russia?" she rages. "We keep getting sent stuff we don't need. Locomotives? There are hardly any train lines and yet they're sending me locomotives!" Viki's words make me think of the red double-decker London buses that brighten up the streets of Baghdad. Were they a gift from Her Royal Highness?

This is a fairly typical day here at the CPA. I suddenly feel a bit mournful. I'm going to miss all these crises that would seem absurd in any other part of the world. But here they are just run of the mill. All in a day's work.

"Are you corpse hunting?" I ask Alex when I bump into him leaving the palace. Alex is a consultant at the Ministry of Foreign Affairs and is in charge of repatriating bodies. Black humor, yes, for the man who does one of the most unpleasant jobs imaginable.

"What with all these attacks and kidnappings, I spend all my days hopping between the mortuary and the airport. I can't wait until I leave.

They've found me a place in Thailand. I'm leaving in a couple of days. Bye-bye, Iraq. Do you promise to come visit me?"

I nod. I decide not to bother asking him if he wants to come to the concert. I think I am the only person interested in the Baghdad Philharmonic Orchestra's first performance since the end of the war. I certainly do not want to miss it. I really am quite curious.

The musicians make a triumphant entrance. The world's television crews are here to capture this grand event on film. The hall is not packed at all. But even if this were not their first official concert, it would still be worth a trip.

"Well, they don't exactly have the proper build," whispers the woman next to me.

I cannot help thinking that they are very sweet, although I do not know why. They somehow seem so improbable in their black tails and white bow ties, with their instruments tucked under their arms, and that gait, that Iraqi gait. They shuffle chairs about, sit down, clatter back up again.

The audience, made up largely of locals, is hardly disciplined. Mobile phones go off constantly and people wander in and out as they please.

The concert begins. Rather than sit back in silence, the spectators just keep doing whatever they were doing: drinking, eating, rustling candy wrappers, opening drink cans, asking neighbors if they want a sip. I love these people! Undisciplined through and through. And it is not as if the motley assortment of musicians is any different. They all seem to be doing their own thing, taking no notice whatsoever of the poor conductor, who is doing his very best to command some respect. Fantastic! Simply exhilarating. It certainly runs in their blood. They have no self-discipline and cannot follow a single order.

But the best is yet to come. The performance climaxes when the trumpets burst on the scene. The strings have been following the score for better or for worse, but the brass section simply follows its own melody, if melody is the right word. Every wrong note blurted out by the trumpet play-ers makes me wince. The trumpet players certainly do not hold back, but play everything at full volume. No hesitation whatsoever. As if they are keeping perfectly to the score and as if every noise they make is welcomed by the conductor. Poor old Strauss and Beethoven.

And during all this fracas, the audience goes on eating their picnics, speaking loudly, bursting into applause at the craziest of moments, answer-ing mobiles, snapping photos with blinding flashes, even though the con-ductor explicitly asked us not to, but who cares? We are in Iraq! The music itself is not local, but its free interpretation makes it fit in wonderfully. An exact rendition of the Berlin Philharmonic Orchestra would be most out of place here in Iraq. This is one of the best concerts I have ever been to. A huge applause for this philharmonic that decides to treat us to an encore. They are loving it!

"And now it's time to give them full power," I say to a friend as we leave the hall. It will be interesting.

"I heard things are improving over there."

It is my mother on the phone, probably having just watched the news.

BOOM! The windows shake. BOOM! I throw myself to the ground.

"What's happening?" I hear the distant words echo in the handset. "Anna? What's going on? Anna!"

"Mom, I've got to go. I'll call you later, I've got to run." It's just as well things are improving, I think.

Today is a great day. They have just chosen the new Iraqi president, Ghazi Ajil al Yawar. Two Kurdish and Shiite candidates have been nomi-nated as vice presidents. June 1, 2004, what a memorable day! The new interim Iraqi government is being inaugurated—the government that will take sovereignty on June 30, 2004.

It will be a nightmarish day for us, one of the worst for us enclosed in the Green Zone. We are prohibited from leaving. But I cannot help thinking that right now the most dangerous place to be in the whole world is here

Iron trailers masquerading as villas

inside Saddam's palace. One explosion after another keeps us running for the bunker, and the siren does not give us a moment's peace all day long. Thank goodness things are improving. The following days are even worse. Even the palace itself gets hit.

"It gave me such a fright," Mark Clark, the advisor to the Ministry of Sport, says. "The office next to mine got hit. There was nobody in it, but I almost died of a heart attack."

Days of fire, in the true sense of the word.

"I was thrown against the wall," my trailer companion tells me. "I was brushing my teeth, and then all of a sudden I was thrown against the wall," she says, as I am getting ready for bed. My flak jacket is next to my bed, ready. My helmet shares my pillow.

"It landed right behind here," continues Shelley, who's in the American navy. "And you? Where were you?" she asks, worriedly. "I hope you're not still venturing out, are you?"

"So you think you're safer here, waiting for them to get you?" I reply.

Our different opinions amount to nothing. In the end, everyone should do what he thinks best. And I have no desire whatsoever to stay here, totally helpless, throwing myself to the ground with every crash. Of course, the images of the kidnapped Filipinos, Bulgarians, Americans, and Italians do make me think. I would prefer to be hit head on by a rocket than have a knife held at my throat. But the probabilities of this happening are minimal, and you need to keep that in mind too. In the meantime, we wait, with trepidation, for June 30, 2004.

The CPA is being dismantled. Familiar faces are disappearing. There are few who want to be here on the day of the handover of power. Anything could happen. And I am also nervous. I am offered the option of leaving for Ramstein Air Force Base in Germany on Bremer's plane, straight after the handover ceremony. I cannot think of a better send-off.

June 28, 2004. The new cabinet takes the country's sovereignty two days earlier than planned. We are all stunned. So are the people who have been shooting at us for ages; they take a break from their irksome pastime. It has been successful. There is no doubt about it. Bremer leaves Iraq a couple of hours later.

And me? What happens to me?

"No military flights to or from Baghdad for a couple of days. We all have to stay here inside. It's too dangerous to venture out," I am informed at the office that deals with flights.

"But Royal Jordanian is still flying," I retort.

"Yes, but you can't go to the airport. So, seeing as they've decided to keep us all shut up in here, there's nothing you can do but wait. Keep calm and wait patiently for further instructions."

I have been in Iraq long enough not to be alarmed by this. Anyway, my suitcases are ready.

"We can't possibly *not* celebrate this memorable day," Ken says to me. "Well, what are we going to do?" he asks Dave and me.

"Why don't we see what David from PMO has to say?" I suggest.

David is English and organizes services within the health sector of the Program Management Office. He has such a great sense of humor that I cannot imagine better company to spend an evening with.

"But the English are barricaded underground," Ken remarks.

The English contingent do not live with us, but instead have their own separate quarters, located in an underground car park. They certainly know how to do things. It is a real underground village, sheltered from all rockets and missiles. They all have their own little trailer, a hall where you can watch films, and a bar. It is all Ikea furnishings, which make me feel quite at home. The red alarm state of these last couple of days has resulted in them each being ordered to stay in their accommodation between 8 p.m. and 7 a.m. They have to wear their flak jackets constantly, even when they are inside the palace. We taunt them mercilessly.

"Will you invite us to Ocean's Cliffs? Seeing as you can't set foot outdoors, I guess we'll come to you. What do you think?" I tease David.

"It would be my pleasure. I have a couple of bottles of wine in the fridge. I think this is a good occasion to open them."

And so I leave Riverside Villas, my beloved accommodation, in favor of his Ocean's Cliffs. With such names, they never miss a single opportunity to create the illusion of heaven on earth.

The evening goes beyond all expectations. After a couple of glasses of wine at the English pub, we head to our friend's trailer for a good glass of Lebanese wine. This is the only decent wine you can get hold of here. We speak about the war, handover, expectations, religion, terrorism, September 11. We tackle many different topics, just as you should on a monumental day like this.

Piled onto a bed, we are four friends about to leave Iraq, discussing life. Our opinions differ. We clash. It cannot happen any other way when Europe and America decide to speak about war, Iraq, and reconstruction. I represent the old-world European view, Dave and Ken the new-world, American view, and David is the wise peacemaker. Sparks fly and our mouths spit lightning. We pounce on each other's arguments. We call each other cowards, warmongers, cowboys, opportunists, feckless incompetents, and then end up dreaming of new things. All together. We are so different. Yet we complement each other perfectly.

The evening began in the best possible way, but the best is still to come. Giggling like three children up to mischief, Dave, Ken, and I are dripping wet as we enter Saddam's palace at dawn the next morning. People already bustling to their offices stop and look at us in disbelief.

"I've been here for over a year. It's my right to have gone mad" I say. I have been here for thirteen months.

It was Dave's idea. You can tell that he lived in Naples for years.

"Where are you taking us?" Ken asks him. Ken is a trifle worried, quite sleepy, and hoping to go to bed soon.

"Trust me," is Dave's response. "I found this place the other night. One of my Iraqi friends took me. Nobody knows about it," he says as he parks the Suburban in front of a closed gate.

There is barbed wire all around—trouble if you get caught on it. The more you wriggle, the more you get entangled, and the more the spikes dig deeper into your flesh. Dave tries to open the gate but it is locked with an enormous padlock.

"We'll climb over," he says, beginning to shinny up the iron bars.

I am hot on his heels.

"Guys, have you forgotten where we are?" Ken asks, even more apprehensive. "If someone sees three shadows lurking about in the dark they'll shoot us down straight off. Honest folk do not roam about climbing over gates at this time of night."

"Okay then, wait for us here," I hiss.

"Well, if I'm relying on your common sense then I'm way up the creek without a paddle," grumbles the Air Force colonel, always faithful to duty. But he decides to come too. He hops over the gate, we walk a couple of steps, and…

"Wow! I can't believe it." In front of us is an immense swimming pool. Or, rather, three swimming pools. And with its slides and diving boards, wild horses couldn't stop Dave as he rips off his shirt and dives into the water. Closely followed by us. What madness! We leap off the boards shrieking like banshees. We race down the slides. We take photos to capture this pure craziness. There it is, once again, the film.

Finally, we leave by the same way we got in. But we still haven't had enough and we decide to go admire the moon from the famous swords of Saddam's Victory Arch. We take more pictures here, this time posing with the Iraqi guards. They seem to enjoy the spectacle of these three strange, soaking wet characters prancing about in this place that oozes history.

"Think about it. This is where Saddam organized his parades," says Dave. "I reckon we should climb on up there," he continues.

"Yes, and have you seen the tanks over there?" Ken demands. "Oh yes, and the guns too? They'll be itching to have a shot at us."

"Ken's right. Let's not go too far," I intervene. "I would hate to be taken out by friendly fire. I've only got a couple of days left here, so let's behave ourselves."

Dave is obliged to give up his plan of climbing the towers.

"You still haven't told me what you got up to last night," John says when we make our entrance in the dining hall just hours after our night-time escapade.

"Of course, anyone who celebrates two consecutive birthdays here in Baghdad must be a bit bonkers," says Ambassador Gianludovico De Martino.

"Look who's talking," I answer back. "You've surely had many more yourself."

"Yes, but you're on the right track," remarks my friend.

There are few people I feel more comfortable with than him. Especially now after all the computer lessons I have given him. A whole new world has opened up to him, and it fascinates him. Every time he sends e-mail he is so elated you would think he discovered America. I am thrilled to be celebrating my thirty-fourth birthday with him. Also present is Carmelo,

Baghdad International Airport (BIAP), June 2004

Gianludovico's right arm, a keen, lively twenty-eight-year-old who arrived here just recently, along with Ken and a Finn who works for the U.S. Department of State. We opt for the Green Zone Café. This is the most laid-back place Baghdad has to offer.

"You've got to go to Mongolia," the ambassador implores. "It's the most beautiful country I've ever seen. And if you know how to ride horses…"

We are each fantasizing. We speak about the Trans-Siberian Railway, the former Soviet Union, Samarkand, and opening a Green Zone Café chain in Baghdad.

Carmelo sets the scene: Iraqi waiters with Kalashnikovs slung over their shoulders, tablecloths printed with the Stars and Stripes, and dreadful Italian pizza will be the key elements to the bar's success. Thin and crispy pizza. Or if you order deep-dish, it should be piled high with meat and pineapple. Or, if you like, cheese and tomato. Exasperatingly slow table service and—how could we forget?—Lebanese wine served at room temperature. That's a cool 122 degrees Fahrenheit. Ambience will be created with background music of the latest Arabic hits.

I look around me. I suddenly realize that everything that seems so normal for us is actually ludicrous.

"Oh yes, one other thing. The bar should be built at an old, dilapidated gas station," adds Carmelo. He is in great form tonight.

Of course, the Green Zone Café, the hippest place in the whole of Baghdad, is really nothing more than an old gas station, a big red awning, warm wine, and pizza that depends entirely on the chef's humor.

"So do you know when you're leaving, Anna?" Ambassador De Martino asks.

"Tuesday. Inshallah."

"And how are you getting to the airport?"

"Well, there's a huge armor-plated bus that looks like some sort of coffin that does the trip twice a day," I tell him.

"You can't go on that."

"It looks safe to me. It's escorted by Humvees and helicopters."

"No, no. I'll send my boys to take you," De Martino decides.

I smile. I suddenly feel a bit down.

"Tuesday, Tuesday, Tuesday. Let's see now, by Saturday, Annina will be back here," the ambassador muses.

"Just enough time to go home, say hi to the family, wash the contents of your suitcase, and get back here."

I shake my head.

"There's a good contract waiting for you. Sign it. It's a job made for you. We've already spoken about it."

Silence. I shake my head again. He is looking at me with that mischievous, inquiring expression of his.

"You know we all want you back here, don't you?"

As I climb into my Land Cruiser to drive back to Riverside Villas, I am feeling empty. I am about to start the engine. Then I remember that I have not checked underneath for a bomb. I get out. I take the key out of the ignition, get down on my knees and perform a months-old ritual.

"Anyway, it's not as if you'd ever recognize a bomb," I say to myself as I push back up onto my feet. No, I'm tired. I can't keep going like this. It's the right moment to get back to a life of normality.

I think it might be more of an attempt to convince myself—convince myself that I can't wait to leave this place behind, convince myself that I can't wait to wave goodbye to this exhausting life. Yes, it's exhausting, but it's also gratifying, intriguing, and exciting.

"Anna, is something wrong?"

The ambassador has seen me leaning immobile against my jeep and is worried.

"Everything okay?"

Our eyes meet. He understands.

"We'll see each other again, Anna. Soon," he says. "I know it."

"Khalid, hurry up! At this rate we're going to miss the plane."

No use. Khalid looks at me with big childish eyes. He smiles, but neither accelerates his pace nor speaks. He is heading for Milan, where his wife and newborn baby girl, who is in critical condition, are waiting for him after being sent to Italy by Medevac.

"Anna, please give us a hand," Rocco from the Red Cross asks the moment I arrive at Rome Fiumicino Airport. "If you don't take him by his hand and pull him, who knows where he'll end up? And then we'll have to go and look for him all over the world."

I raise my eyes to the sky. The thought of babysitting Khalid does not exactly fill me with joy. But I have a weak spot for Rocco. We worked well together in Baghdad, so I give in.

"Naturally, you make me work right until the last moment," I moan.

"C'mon! Gabri will be waiting at the airport in Milan," he adds.

Another magic name: Gabriella. It was thanks to her telephone call more than a year ago that this whole adventure took off. I cannot wait to give her a hug.

Meanwhile, Khalid is lagging behind. Always farther back. It must all be really quite overwhelming for someone who has never left his country before. But that does not change the fact he has to hurry up. Airplanes do not wait in Iraq. Khalid points at a cigarette.

"No, you can't smoke here. You'll have to wait," I say.

He is about to have a withdrawal crisis. The last time he went so long without a cigarette was probably when he was in his cradle.

"Outside. When we go out, you can smoke." I wish I hadn't told him that.

"NO! You'll blow us all up!" I hear an enraged shout behind me.

We are climbing up to the plane. Khalid has lit a cigarette. I admit that I saw him do it but did not think anything of it.

"Tell him to put it out immediately. Do you want to kill us?" our fellow passenger commands.

Khalid gazes at me, looking completely lost. I gesture that he should put it out. He does not understand, because we are outside.

"We're halfway through refueling and he lights a cigarette. He really does want to blow us up!" the man continues.

Okay, enough with this whole "blowing everybody up" thing. It's a bit over the top. It's not as if blowing something up happens just like that. "Welcome back," I mutter to myself.

Then again, the elegant-looking man is right. I am the one who has been distanced from the civilized world for more than a year; I am the one who has forgotten how things are done. I feel out of place. Uncomfortable. Slowly, my memory of all this is coming back to me. It is true that smoking is not permitted near aircraft. It is true that orders and "No Smoking" signs must be adhered to.

I smile at Khalid. I take him by the arm. Affectionately. People are looking at us. "We all have our pros and cons," I try to explain to this man with the soft, bewildered eyes.

You'll see that perhaps Iraq isn't that bad after all.

Postscript

A few days before the vote took place in Iraq, I was asked during a televised panel discussion what I thought about this historic event. Everybody in the room was astonished at my answer. My opinion, as an advisor with the Ministry of Health, was not only different from most people's; it was the exact opposite of what everyone thought I would say—that the Iraqis would stay indoors, that too many of them would not vote.

That interview was followed by the days of waiting. I felt excitement as I had rarely felt it before. And finally, on the day Iraqis waited in long lines to vote, I felt a great happiness. I wanted to hug them all—all those women who would proudly show their colored fingers after having voted—to show them all my admiration.

And to think that, just one year before, those same people had been unable to choose between a red chair and a black chair while we were rebuilding the ministry. Only by forcing them to choose by themselves, by refusing to decide for them, did I help them. But how exhausting! Sometimes I almost had to threaten them. Choosing for them would have been an egregious mistake, though. This is *their* country. I can lend a hand, but I cannot and will not decide for them.

My understanding of what the Iraqi people are capable of all started with these little decisions, in my case with the chairs. But my understanding deepened when I conducted a little informal survey to sort out something that was bothering me. I remember the frustration of that day, and of writing in my notebook those words I would rather forget: "The Iraqis are all liars!" I had written.

Incorrigible liars—that was my hasty, superficial, arrogant explanation. I was so frustrated by the conflicting answers I would get when I would ask my Iraqi coworkers a question about our work in the ministry that I performed my own informal survey to find out why this was happening.

I intentionally selected a question that could not be answered with a personal opinion. There could not be several answers to a question as objective as "Does it snow in Baghdad in winter?" I did not ask whether it was cold, since each of us has a different perception of cold and hot. But certainly not of snow. Either it snows or it doesn't, or it snows once a year, or more than once.

Well, I never got such a diverse range of answers as when I did that survey. Though I asked each of them the same straightforward question, each gave me a different answer. Some said yes, some no; some said occasionally, others tried to quantify their answer. That was why I had been so annoyed and had come to my thoughtless conclusion. Thank goodness believing a statement of that kind is not in my DNA. I could not feel satisfied with myself if I were to form such a peremptory opinion without a second thought.

So here is the viewpoint I had come to after months of considering and observing. I don't know if I am right or not, but surely I am a step closer to the truth: The Iraqis are so used to saying what they think they are expected to say that they will do all they can to please their questioner. They concentrated more on answering something that would not upset or worry me than on giving me the facts. Those who had heard that I am an enthusiastic skier replied that in Baghdad it snows all winter; others who realized that I am sensitive to cold assured me that the icy white flakes have never been seen in town, and so on.

Now, don't tell me that what we have seen is not a miracle. These people, called upon to cast their ballots, rushed to the polls regardless of the danger that was involved. Because—here is another aspect we often tend to forget—unlike us, they are used to danger. They have a completely different perception of it. We don't go to the polls if it rains or if the weather is too nice and we want to spend the weekend at the beach. We Italians, I mean. That is why we can now vote on Monday morning, if we prefer.

How can we understand that there are people in the world who will risk their lives to be able to express their opinion? We cannot, unless we have lived side by side with them long enough, as I have.

I don't have a crystal ball. I am no guru or soothsayer. The only reason I told the TV interviewer that I was sure the Iraqi people would go to the polls is that I had by then started to understand them, to know them, to anticipate their motivations and actions. Yet my understanding had come all at once, as it often does.

I went back to Baghdad in October 2004. I was not returning just a few days after I left the capital, in July, as Ambassador De Martino had bet I would do. No, I did not slip back into the country as if I hadn't left. It was a return in high feather, an extraordinary welcome, beyond all my expectations. And yet, I should have known well the Iraqis' hospitality, their warmth, their affection for those they decide to trust. This greeting had a different mood, and it didn't take much to see it.

"She's back!" were the only two words that people managed to utter when I showed up at the Ministry of Health. They looked happy, but even more than that, they looked surprised. That was what I could read on their faces.

Tariq and Ismail, my two poet friends, couldn't stop staring at me, and then they spoke those few enlightening words: "If she's back, it means she really believes in this," Tariq said to Ismail." And if she believes, maybe we should believe in it a little more too."

So now, when people ask me what I am doing in Iraq, my answer is: instilling hope.